T0247810

This book is dedicated to my father, Mike, and my mother, Kathy, for putting up with the countless edits and rewrites both in this book and in my life.

I Want to Go Where They Went

Stories from My Life as a Small Animal Vet

Jeff Schmidt D.V.M.

I Want to Go Where They Went

Stories from My Life as a Small Animal Vet

print ISBN: 979-8-35093-263-8

ebook ISBN: 979-8-35093-264-5

Table of Contents

Chapter 1.   Roger, the Yellow Cat   1

Chapter 2.   Ginger Harriman   27

Chapter 3.   Nothing to Lose   52

Chapter 4.   Up on the Roof   73

Chapter 5.   Bury 'Em Deep   92

Chapter 6.   Charlie's Island   114

Chapter 7.   SMASH   130

Chapter 8.   SHRED   152

Chapter 9.   So, You Wanna be a Vet?   169

Chapter 10. Watson   192

Chapter 11. FLAT   241

Chapter 12. Two Kinds of Crazy   268

Acknowledgements   314

List of Illustrations

Roger, the Yellow Cat by Brice Borchers 2

Mr. & Mrs. Evans by B. Borchers 26

Me & Casey by B. Borchers 30

Me & Maray by B. Borchers 40

Dr. Tony strikes again... by Tony Johnson 44

Tool jacket by B. Borchers 60

Puppy basket by B. Borchers 74

Spooky by B. Borchers 89

Buck gets a bath by B. Borchers 113

Charlie by Ann Ranlett 126

Llamas by A. Ranlett 129

Stomach anatomy by B. Borchers 141

Paperclips by B. Borchers 151

Toby by B. Borchers 166

Shredder by B. Borchers 168

Mr. Clarke by B. Borchers 206

Me & Watson by B. Borchers 233

Cheeto by A. Ranlett 242

Me & Cheeto by A. Ranlett 267

Microscope by B. Borchers 271

Me & Sally by B. Borchers 313

List of Photos

Sadie on my shoulder, photographed by Amy Burke — 31

Tony the trickster, photographed by Tony Johnson — 38

Cupid, photographed by Tony Johnson — 70

Dr. Tony Johnson, photographed Tony Johnson — 72

Patches & Freckles, photographed by Jeff Schmidt — 99

Me & September, photographed by Larry Sullivan — 179

Gobi, photographed by Kikuma Yamaguchi — 182

Antony, photographed by Jeff Schmidt — 191

Dr. Frank Lux, photographer unknown — 219

Dick & Maggie, photographer unknown — 240

Dan & Smokey, photographed by Kathy Flack — 281

CHAPTER 1

Roger, the Yellow Cat

Roger, the yellow cat, wasn't really yellow. He was actually a beautiful sable-gray color. He was a big cat weighing in at fourteen pounds. The problem was he used to (and should) weigh twenty pounds. He looked pretty sad and beaten down and so did his owners. They were worried sick about him. He'd been feeling ill for around two weeks and hadn't eaten anything at all for five days. He needed some serious help, or he wasn't going to make it.

I met Roger in my fourth year of veterinary school. I was on the internal medicine rotation of my clinical year at the U.C. Davis School of Veterinary Medicine. The rotation was four weeks long, then I'd go to another two weeks in neurology. I'd spent the previous three years dissecting dogs, cats, cows, horses, and sheep, absorbing the details of the endocrine system and the ins and outs of three thousand drugs that I'd never heard of before. I was now at the time I'd anticipated and dreaded. This was my chance to do something real: to diagnose and treat real living pets. Roger was one of my patients on my first week of the rotation.

Roger, the Yellow Cat

"Roger Evans," I announced loudly to a waiting room full of people who didn't want to be there. The U.C. Davis School of Vet Medicine was a referral-only facility. We received patients when the diagnosis was vague, the treatments weren't working, or specialized equipment was necessary. For many pet owners, we were their last hope. A composed, retirement-age couple stood up and walked over to greet me. Mr. Evans struggled with a cumbersome blue pet carrier. He was dressed in tan corduroy pants and a thick flannel shirt. Mrs. Evans trailed behind him in a heavy parka and a homemade knit beanie. I briefly introduced myself and escorted them into exam room number three.

I'd already looked at Roger's chart, but I wanted to get the story from Mr. and Mrs. Evans directly.

"So, how long has Roger been feeling ill?" I asked.

Mrs. Evans spoke up from her perch on one of the cheap plastic exam room chairs. "He started moping around about four weeks ago. He just wasn't as playful and active and he wasn't finishing all his food," she said. "Normally, he gobbles his food in two seconds, so we got a little worried about this."

"Was he vomiting at all?" I asked.

"Nope," said Mr. Evans. "He was just not acting himself. We took him to his regular vet, and they couldn't find anything wrong. They did some blood tests and thought something may be wrong with his liver."

I closely scrutinized Roger's lab work from two weeks before and his more recent results from one week ago. Roger had elevations in all his liver enzymes. His bilirubin was also elevated (*forty* times higher than normal). Based on the two lab panels, it was evident all the values were getting progressively worse.

"Can you think of anything that would have made him sick?" I asked. "Did he get new food? Did he get in a cat fight? Did you start a new medicine?"

"Nothing that we can think of," replied Mr. Evans. "We've had Roger since he was a little kitten and he's always been a lazy boy. He sleeps twenty hours a day. So, when we noticed he was sleeping a little more, we didn't think it was a big deal. But when he didn't eat all of his food, we knew he was sick. I've never seen him pass up food . . . ever."

"OK," I said. "Let's get him up on the table so I can take a look at him."

Mr. Evans gave the big worn carrier a rough two-handed heave to get it on the metal exam table. Then he opened the carrier door so I could have my first look. Poor Roger was hiding in the back. If he weren't so sick, he would have been terrified. Most cats don't like carriers and they don't like car trips. They don't like strange sounds or smells; they don't like vet clinics and they definitely don't like veterinarians. Maybe he wouldn't consider me completely evil. I was only a vet student at this point. Maybe I didn't smell like a vet just yet.

The big gray cat wasn't going to come out on his own, so I reached inside and gently grabbed him by the scruff of his neck. It felt like a handful of leather that'd been left out in the sun. It wasn't the pliable skin of a living creature. He was so dehydrated that his eyes were sunken in, and he looked miserable. I looked in his mouth and I looked in his eyes. Strings of saliva hung out of his mouth from his nausea. It appeared difficult for him to swallow. I felt his abdomen and listened to his heart and lungs. His temperature was at the low end of normal at 100.5 degrees. He gave no resistance to my prodding. He was so sick that it was a big effort for him to just hold up his head.

As I examined Roger, I felt a growing sense of hope. He was a sick guy, but I started to believe I knew what was wrong with him. His skin was so yellow. Not a faint tinge of yellow. It was highlighter felt-tip pen yellow. The color was especially obvious in the sclera of his eyes, the membranes of his mouth, and his sparsely furred belly. Out of the thousands of obscure cat diseases I'd learned about, Roger happened to have one I recognized. Better yet, I think it could be fixed.

"Mr. and Mrs. Evans," I said, trying to sound calm and doctorly. "I think I may know what's wrong with your kitty, and we may be able to fix him." I wanted to give them some hope, but not false hope.

"I think Roger has hepatic lipidosis. I don't know what caused it in the first place, but when a cat doesn't eat enough, they mainly burn their own fat for energy. Did he used to be chubby?"

"Oh yes," said Mrs. Evans. "I've told my husband a thousand times to stop feeding him, but he gives him treats all the time. He used to weigh twenty pounds. I was afraid he'd pop."

Mr. Evans looked like he wanted to say something to defend himself. He started to open his mouth, glanced at his wife, and closed it again. On the vet-cat-wife hierarchy he clearly calculated he was at the bottom rung. Anything he said in his defense would just make it worse.

I continued, "So the problem is the conversion of fat to energy takes place in the liver. The fatter the cat, the bigger the load on their liver. The liver can only manage so much. I think his liver's clogged up with fat and it's interfering with its function. When this happens, the cat will start to feel sick and nauseous, and they won't want to eat. Of course, when they don't eat, they burn even more fat, and their liver gets even more sick. We'll need to do some more tests to make sure there isn't something more sinister going on, but I think there's a good chance he'll be OK."

Mr. and Mrs. Evans seemed relieved at my explanation.

"Why is his skin yellow like that?" asked Mrs. Evans.

"Well," I said. "When the liver gets all clogged up with fat it impairs the ability of the liver to process bilirubin. Bilirubin is a waste product made by the liver. Normally it's pushed out into the gallbladder and from the gall-bladder into the small intestine. When the liver can't do this, the bilirubin overflows into the bloodstream and permeates all the tissues of the body. It's this bilirubin that stains his skin and eyes and mouth and makes him yellow. When the liver starts working again, it will process the excess bilirubin and he'll gradually go back to his normal color."

I left the room to consult with my resident supervisor, Dr. Gossien. She was an incredibly bright first-year internal medicine resident from the Netherlands. She had short blonde hair and a beautiful Dutch accent. She always dressed like she was heading out on a date rather than going to work as a veterinarian. No matter how messy or smelly our patients were, she always came out looking good (and smelling good as well). She'd graduated from the University of Utrecht, which was one of the best veterinary programs in the world. Luckily for me, she never made me feel too bad when she knew more about something than I did. When she examined Roger, she concurred with my tentative diagnosis. She then conferred with Mr. and Mrs. Evans. They agreed to leave him with us as an in-patient of the small animal teaching hospital so we could get to work on him right away. They were a three-hour drive away so it would be difficult for them to visit Roger regularly. I assured them I would call every evening at six with an update.

That afternoon poor, yellow Roger went through a checklist of tests. Even though I suspected hepatic lipidosis to be the likely diagnosis, the treatment for this condition is long, laborious, and expensive. We needed to make sure we weren't missing some other hidden disease.

CBC, chemistry panel: Roger's kidneys were working well. His blood cell counts were good. His blood sugar was normal which ruled out diabetes. His thyroid hormone value was normal which ruled out hyperthyroidism. The rest of his analytes were normal, except for high liver enzymes. No surprises here. This is what you'd expect in hepatic lipidosis.

Urinalysis: Roger was concentrating his urine well. This showed good kidney function. There were no bacteria or white blood cells present that would indicate an infection. The only abnormality was the excessive amount of bilirubin in his urine. This was spillover from the abnormally high bilirubin in his blood. This pigment made his urine look fluorescent yellow, but this was to be expected.

Catogram: Cats are small enough that their entire body will fit on a single large X-ray plate. In veterinary medicine jargon, this is often called a *Catogram*. Two full body X-rays were done on Roger to look for evidence of tumors, pneumonia, or injury. They were fine.

Abdominal ultrasound: Roger was given a light sedative, and his yellow belly was shaved bald for the procedure. The ultrasound was unremarkable except for an enlarged, bright "echogenic" liver. In hepatic lipidosis, the liver cells get so full of fat that the entire liver swells. There was no evidence of liver cancer, pancreatic cancer, bile duct obstruction, or ascites (free fluid in the abdomen).

Fine Needle Aspiration (FNA): This procedure utilizes a long, tiny needle and syringe to suck cells directly from the liver. The cells are then transferred to a glass slide for examination by a pathologist. The pathologist would stain the slides and examine them under a high-power microscope. The FNA results weren't expected back until the following day.

An I.V. catheter was placed into Roger's left front leg. He was put on an aggressive rate of I.V. fluids to correct his dehydration and compensate for his daily fluid losses. To be cautious, he was placed on twice daily I.V.

antibiotics. Although he had no obvious infection, the concern was that he was so debilitated (and now stressed from his environment) that any infection could be the end of him.

At six that evening, I called Mr. and Mrs. Evans. I was excited to give them an update on their boy and the results of all the tests performed that day. Mrs. Evans picked up on the first ring.

"Hi, Mrs. Evans. This is Jeff Schmidt. I'm the vet student looking after Roger in the hospital. We met earlier today."

"Hi, Dr. Schmidt (I wasn't really a doctor yet, but it sounded good. I went with it). How is my kitty doing? Do you know what's wrong with him yet?"

"Well," I said. "It's looking good so far. The lab work and X-rays and ultrasound don't show any other problems. There was no evidence of *cancer*." Cancer really scares most people, so I always put *extra* emphasis on this.

I continued, "So it looks like he truly has hepatic lipidosis. We have one more test pending, and the results should be back tomorrow morning. If the cells in his liver show just fat and no cancer, we can start treatment for his fatty liver tomorrow. We'll be inserting a feeding tube so we can get some calories into him to reverse this process. Hepatic lipidosis is a pretty common problem. We see it all the time (I'd only seen it one time). It can usually be successfully treated (I hoped to myself)."

"OK. Dr. Schmidt. Whatever it takes to help him get better. We love that cat to death. I don't know what my husband would do without him. Roger sleeps on his chest, you know. We trust you with him."

Roger was like a child to Mr. and Mrs. Evans. They trusted me implicitly. *No pressure here*, I thought. If this cat doesn't make it, these poor people are going to be devastated and I'm going to be responsible.

At seven the next morning, it was time for daily internal medicine rounds. Each student would give a brief presentation on their cases from the previous day. The aim was to concisely summarize each patient by sharing the physical exam findings, the lab results, your diagnosis (or tentative diagnosis), and treatment plan. Each student was supported by a resident (a licensed veterinarian who was in training to be a board-certified specialist) who was ready to bail you out when asked questions you couldn't answer.

These residents worked themselves to death. The rounds were overseen by a chief staff clinician, generally a senior veterinary specialist. Since U.C. Davis was renowned for its veterinary medical program, it attracted veterinarians from all over the world. Some real heavy hitters. My chief clinician was Dr. Harry Felderman. He was considered the best veterinary endocrinologist in the country. He co-authored the premier veterinary textbook in the field. Dr. Felderman was a thin middle-aged man standing around six feet tall. He had short greying hair and rounded glasses that often rested on the tip of his nose. He was often seen with a subdued sarcastic grin. His expression seemed to broadcast that he'd been secretly told a dirty joke and he was barely suppressing a laugh. He was a bottomless well of medical knowledge and I couldn't help but find him intimidating. He was also a quirky goofball. One of those personalities that had you guessing whether he was being serious or not. If I thought he was being serious, he was pulling my leg, and when I thought he was joking, he was being completely sincere. I never felt completely comfortable around him, and I think that was exactly how he liked it. The formal rounds presentation in front of my peers was often the most stressful part of the day. I self-consciously went over the mysterious case of my big yellow cat. *I didn't make too big of a mess of it*, I thought.

In between seeing other pets, I kept checking the computer terminal for the results of Roger's liver cytology. U.C. Davis hosted a clinical pathologist residency program so the lab that processed these results was right downstairs. At 10 a.m., Roger's cytology report popped up. Official report: *Vacuolar hepatopathy consistent with hepatic lipidoses as previously suspected. No evidence of neoplasia.* Roger was in the clear. In a situation like this, time is essential. With each passing moment, Roger was getting sicker, his prognosis was getting poorer, and his recovery longer. Luckily, there was an advanced, sophisticated medical treatment that worked ninety percent of the time. Roger needed food!

The dilemma is that sick cats won't eat much. Nauseous cats really don't want to eat at all. And big cats need a lot of food. And there is no force-feeding a cat. They will spit, gag, vomit, and bite and that's just trying to get them to swallow one damn pill. Roger needed at least three hundred calories a day to fulfill his minimal metabolic needs. Most liquid blend mixtures of cat food come out to about one calorie per milliliter. So, Roger would need to get three hundred milliliters (about half a pint) of food at the minimum. Until he was in a positive caloric balance, his liver wouldn't be able to clear the logjam of fat and he wouldn't get better.

The solution is to place a PEG tube. PEG is an acronym for *percutaneous endoscopic gastrotomy* tube. The tube completely bypasses the cat's mouth. Voila! No spitting, gagging, and biting. And, hopefully, no vomiting.

I called Mr. and Mrs. Evans to let them know about the test results. They wanted to go ahead with his tube placement ASAP.

Dr. Gossien did the procedure at three that afternoon and I functioned as her assistant. (Basically, I stood around and held some stuff for her.) Roger was fully anesthetized and monitored by a board-certified anesthesiologist and Dr. Felderman. First an endoscope was advanced down Roger's esophagus into his stomach. Next his stomach was inflated with air to push it outwards against the body wall. A needle with an attached guidewire was passed through a channel in the scope. The needle then punctured the inside of Roger's stomach and was pushed out through the left side of his body wall. The other end of the guidewire was attached to the stomach tube positioned near Roger's mouth. The endoscope is pulled out and the guidewire is left in place. Then Dr. Gossien firmly pulls on the end of the guidewire coming out his left abdomen. This tugs the feeding tube down his esophagus, into the stomach and out the left side of his body. The portion of the PEG tube that remains in his stomach has a mushroom-shaped flange that presses against the stomach wall. The outside of the stomach wall then heals against the inside of the abdominal wall and forms an airtight seal. The entire procedure took twenty minutes. In twenty-four hours, I could start using the tube to feed him. A thick mushy gruel of food would be injected right into Roger's stomach. He would finally get the nutrition his body needed and be on the road to recovery. If all went well, he could go home in one to two weeks.

I called the Evans at six that evening. First ring again. In my mind's eye I could see Mrs. Evans anxiously hovering right by the phone.

"Hi, Mrs. Evans. This is Jeff Schmidt. I'm calling to give you the update on Roger."

"Oh, Dr. Schmidt, thanks so much for calling us. We've been worried about Roger all day. How's he doing?"

"He's doing fine. The tube placement went well. He's in the ICU right now for monitoring as he wakes up from anesthesia. We have to wait twenty-four hours for the tube pexy site to seal up before we start feeding him. But, tomorrow at this time, we can start the process of making him better."

I explained to her that "pexy" is a medical term meaning fixation. In Roger's case, it meant where the outside wall of the stomach would seal against the inside wall of the abdominal cavity. This would prevent any leakage.

"Oh, Dr. Schmidt, that's great news. Earl and I are so grateful you are taking care of him, and we know he is in good hands. He's the best cat we've ever had. We pray for him every night."

These pet parents were truly kind, generous people and Roger was certainly a deserving cat. I really wanted him to get better, but this extra pressure weighed heavily on me. He had a good chance of improvement, but nothing's one hundred percent. If he doesn't make it, these people are going to be devastated and I'll be responsible. I dreaded letting them down.

The next day Roger was stable in the ICU. He was still on intravenous fluids with added dextrose and potassium chloride. He was still on twice daily I.V. antibiotics. I transferred him to ward number four where all the internal medicine cases were housed. I found a quiet spot for him on the right side of the ward without any neighbors. This allowed me to use the cages next to him to store all his supplies. And he had a lot of supplies. The cage to his left held bags of lactated ringers solution (LRS), I.V. tubing, I.V. flush syringes, and absorbent pads. The cage to his right was stacked with cans of food, feeding syringes, bedding, and cat litter. For the next couple of weeks, he was going to be a high-maintenance cat.

Later that day I found a brush for him so I could groom out his fur. Sick cats don't have the energy or inclination to groom themselves. We generally take it for granted, but a healthy cat will spend hours each day carefully licking themselves to keep clean. Cats are instinctively tidy creatures who don't like to be greasy, dirty, or unkept. It was clear that in his healthier days, Roger was a handsome kitty, but now his hair coat was greasy and matted and speckled with dandruff. Since he was too sick to clean himself, I did it for him. I was as gentle as possible, knowing he hurt all over. Roger visibly enjoyed these grooming sessions, stretching out and closing his eyes as I ran the brush over his back, sides, and head.

The next couple weeks were tough going for Roger. It would take a while before he could stomach the needed three hundred calories a day. You can't expect a cat who hasn't eaten for two weeks to tolerate that much food. This is especially true when they feel so terrible.

My treatment plan for Roger: Thirty milliliters of blended food given by syringe six times a day. Each feeding to be given over a ten-minute period and then the tube was flushed with ten milliliters of water. I would come in at 6 a.m. to give him his morning food. I would scratch him on the chin and talk to him while I gradually injected the warmed slurry with a sixty-milliliter syringe. I repeated the process at 10 a.m., 2 p.m., and 6 p.m. The 10 p.m. and 2 a.m. feedings were administered by the internal medicine night technician.

Roger tolerated the feedings, but barely. It was obvious that he felt nauseous after each one and occasionally would vomit up some of the food. He still felt very ill. He would hardly move all day long and most of the time he was huddled up under a blanket in the back of the cage. He would barely make it two feet to the other side of his cage to urinate in his litter box. He hadn't had a bowel movement since before his treatment.

After three days of this feeding schedule, it was time to up the amount. But increasing it from thirty to thirty-five milliliters per feeding proved a no-go. Poor Roger couldn't tolerate the new volume in his stomach. He would vomit *every* time, which was counterproductive. Not only did he lose the calories, but the act of vomiting left him exhausted. After throwing up, he would lie there, not moving, with his head bowed and strings of saliva hanging from his mouth. He'd be fairly unresponsive. The increased risk of him aspirating food into his lungs had me worried. After a full day of this, I approached Dr. Gossien and Dr. Felderman and gave them an update on Roger's status.

"Well," said Dr. Felderman with a smirk, "I think it's obvious what the problem is . . . every time that cat sees you, you're pumping him full of food that's making him hurl. He sees you as a giant trout that he's being forced to eat. Just the mere thought of you is making him nauseated."

Was he kidding me? Trying to make me feel better? I wasn't sure.

"So, Dr. Trout, how do you think we should manage this situation?" quipped Dr. Felderman.

I hesitated for a moment. I was still trying to process the whole trout analogy.

"I think we've got to lower his food intake back to thirty milliliters every feeding. In addition, we'll start giving him metoclopramide (a.k.a. Reglan) before every single feeding," I said. "If we can't get him to tolerate the full amount of food, he's not going to get better and the bill's going to get huge. Eventually he'll get euthanized."

Metoclopramide is an old drug that isn't used much anymore. It functioned as a mild anti-nausea and pro-motility medication. It came in a pill, an injection, and as a bright orange, sticky, oral suspension. It was found on the shelf of every veterinary clinic. Back then Reglan was considered the cat's meow, but today it's considered fairly useless. It's been replaced with much more potent and effective antiemetic medications.

Between Dr. Gossien, Dr. Feldman, and myself, we developed a new protocol for Roger. In addition to his I.V. fluids and antibiotics, he would get a stomach protectant. An injectable antacid medicine called famotidine twice a day. Twenty minutes before each feeding, he'd get metoclopramide suspension injected directly into his stomach by his feeding tube. His feeding amount was reduced back to thirty milliliters. He would still get fed six times per day.

The new protocol seemed to help. His drooling (a common sign of nausea in cats) went down significantly. He seemed to feel better and be more alert. He went back to enjoying his grooming sessions and moved around his cage with a bit more energy than before. It was encouraging and a relief to see him improve.

I called Roger's parents every evening around six. They were both kind and patient and extremely grateful for every conversation. I was lucky (as was Roger) that these were the people in charge.

Roger's recovery was already longer than expected and certainly more expensive. He'd been with us for eight days and was still a very sick cat. He'd been on the new treatment regimen for two days. Even the most patient and well-to-do pet owners have their limits. If we could get him to accept fifty milliliters of food each feeding without throwing up, he could go home. Then Mr. and Mrs. Evans could continue his treatment on their own. But until that time, he was relying on us to keep him alive. We were still a long way away from three hundred milliliters per day.

"Dr. Trout, how's our yellow cat doing?" Dr. Felderman approached me in the hundred-yard hallway that fronted the seven medical wards. It was this area where most of the business of running a university veterinary hospital actually took place. "Is he still vomiting after we changed his treatment plan?"

"No, sir. He hasn't vomited once since we made those changes. It's been two days now and he's taking his feedings like a champ. I think he's feeling better."

"Good job, Trout. Let's go back to thirty-five milliliters and see what happens."

Dr. Felderman had started calling me "Trout" and "Dr. Trout" on a regular basis. His nickname stuck and he took every opportunity to use it.

"Dr. Trout, why does a deficiency of antidiuretic hormone cause a problem, but an excess of the same hormone doesn't seem to do anything?"

"Because atrial natriuretic factor will counterbalance the effects of too much antidiuretic hormone," I answered.

"Perfect, Trout. That's the answer I was looking for," he'd say.

At some point, Felderman started calling me Trout over the hospital-wide intercom system. This was a source of amusement for all two hundred people working in the teaching hospital. "DOCTOR TROUT. PAGING DOCTOR TROUT . . . please report to ward three," he'd announce with undisguised relish.

This wasn't what I needed, but I'd just bear it. At least this esteemed vet knew who I was. I'd survived two years in the U.S. Army as a tank driver. I was in Germany doing patrols in the snow. I'd been called worse on many occasions. I guess I could weather the *Trout-Storm* for another couple weeks.

As soon as we went back to thirty-five milliliters, Roger started vomiting again. I was frustrated and worried. I thought we had this problem under control. He was still losing weight and was still as yellow as a legal notepad. His body needed more food, but it was clear the extra food made him feel worse. He was drooly and mopey. He'd hide in one spot at the back of his cage all day. I was afraid this setback may be the last straw. If we couldn't come up with a new idea, we were going to have to consider letting him go. I dreaded having that conversation with the Evanses, who seemed to be the most patient cat owners in the world.

I mulled over this problem all day. The entire time I was running up and down the stairs of the teaching hospital, writing up records, making phone calls, and examining new patients, the Roger dilemma occupied my thoughts. At seven o'clock, I went to visit him and brush him out a bit. We needed to talk. I'd seen a little of his personality when he'd been feeling better, and I was getting very attached to this cat. He was a sweet little creature and I hated seeing him feel so bad. He was going through hell. It would be such a shame to quit after all he'd been through. He was still getting fed through his gastrostomy tube. An I.V. solution was running twenty-four hours a day through a pump attached to a metal pole.

"Roger-dodger," I said. "You need to stop vomiting and get better." He stared back at me with his piercing green eyes. I leaned into his cage to get closer to him. I stroked the top of his head and scratched around the bandage on his neck. "Your mom and dad really miss you and they want you to come home. You need more food, buddy, or you're not going to leave this place. What are we going to do to get more food in ya?" And in that moment, desperate and exhausted, I had an idea!

At internal medicine rounds the next morning, I spoke with my bosses.

"Dr. Gossien and Dr. Felderman, I have an idea of what we can do about this Roger situation," I said.

"Spit it out, Trout," said Dr. Felderman. "He's been here for two weeks and I'm sure his owners don't have infinite resources. If he doesn't turn the corner soon, we may have to make some really tough decisions."

"Roger just can't tolerate these boluses of food every four hours. It's too much for his stomach to handle. So, how about changing tactics? We can try giving his food as a constant rate of infusion, so his stomach never really fills up. We'd need a big pump that could hold a sixty-milliliter syringe. It would have to be powerful enough to push his thick slurry of food. Do we have anything like that?"

Dr. Felderman thought about it for a moment. "I think the large animal clinic has an ancient Harvard infusion pump. I've only seen them use it once. They had it out a few years ago to feed a preemie foal through a nasal cannula. Go down to the horse barn and ask them if they know where it is. See if we can borrow it."

With a renewed feeling of hope, I hiked downstairs to the horse medicine clinic. The large animal section is a completely different culture from the pampered "pet" hospital area where I usually worked. In this place I had no idea where anything was kept and didn't know anyone either.

"Excuse me," I said to the first tech I saw. "Do you have an old Harvard infusion pump we can borrow? I have a sick cat upstairs that really needs it." The tech, a busy horse person who clearly thought cats were silly little creatures, was visibly annoyed at the interruption.

"Ask Linda in the neonatal ICU," she said. "I think they have one over there."

"OK. Great. Thanks. Where's the neonatal ICU?"

"Aargh . . . go across the paddock to the red building. It's the fourth door down."

Horse people really like to use the word "paddock." To me it just looked like a big asphalt parking lot.

"Thanks," I said. I wandered down to this new and mysterious location.

"Hello!" I yelled out. "I'm looking for Linda." I normally wouldn't have been this tactless, but I was running out of time and patience.

"She's in the blue coveralls in the back!" someone yelled back at me. I couldn't see who spoke. They were crouched down behind a wooden stall gate.

In the dim lighting, I approached a shadowy figure at the back of the barn. "Excuse me, are you Linda?"

"Yep, can I help you?" she said.

Linda was a tall, athletic woman in high muck boots and heavy coveralls. Her face showed the creases of long days outside in the sun. Her hands were dry, and the skin was cracked around her fingernails. She had long, blond hair pulled back in a ponytail secured with Vet-Wrap, a type of self-sticking, stretchy bandage that's used on everything in vet medicine. It comes in a boggling variety of colors and patterns. A black stethoscope hung around her neck and her pockets were overflowing with an assortment of multicolored pens and markers. She was the chief tech of the equine medicine service and was known as a no-nonsense woman. If I were a horse, I think I'd just do whatever she told me. Despite her reputation for being all business, she proved to be much more pleasant and approachable than the previous person. But she was in the middle of some important horsey thing.

"Hi," I said. "Do you have a big Harvard infusion pump we can borrow? Dr. Felderman sent me down to look. I have a sick cat upstairs that really needs it."

"We have one in the storage room on the back side of the barn. It's a big, brown, ugly thing that weighs about fifty pounds. If you can find it, you can have it. Just OK it with Dr. Akers first so I don't get in trouble for lending it to you."

"Awesome, thanks!" I said and took off to complete my mission.

The storage room was dark with only a single bare bulb hanging from the ceiling to light the dusty, cluttered mess. There were hooks and hangers and hoses hanging from the walls. The floor was littered with large plastic tubs and some exotic-looking torture devices that I'd never seen before. After twenty minutes of sorting through the debris field, I spotted a brown, dusty rectangular box sitting on a bottom shelf in a corner. I moved a couple plastic tubs out of the way so I could approach it and wiped away a thick layer of dust. "Harvard Infusion Device" was scrolled in silver letters on a black metal placard. *Hallelujah!* I found it. I felt like Indiana Jones in the Temple of Doom. I heaved it out to get a better look. The excitement of the discovery made the weight inconsequential, but it still had to be at least forty pounds. Linda hadn't been kidding. This sucker was made before plastic was invented. It looked like it would run on steam instead of electricity. It would fit in nicely with a display at a railroad museum.

I went to where I'd found Linda before. "Hey, I found it," I said. "And you weren't kidding about the weight. That thing is a boat-anchor."

"I told you so. Just make sure Dr. Akers is OK with you taking it. He's in the barn doing a lameness exam."

Dr. Akers was the chief of equine medicine at the U.C. Davis teaching hospital. He was a tall lanky guy in coveralls. He was famous for inventing an intricate harness for airlifting horses out of tough spots. He'd recently been on the local news for a horse rescue in the Sierras. He had ninety-nine problems, and the Harvard pump wasn't one of them. I found him in the horse barn after making some inquiries. He was in the middle of a lameness exam. I interrupted him anyway.

"Dr. Akers. I have a sick hepatic lipidosis cat in the internal medicine ward. I think he's going to need a constant infusion of food for at least a couple of weeks. Can I please borrow that big infusion pump you have in storage?"

"Sure, no problem," he said. "If you can find it. I haven't seen that thing in years. Just bring it back when you're done."

"I found it already," I said. "Thanks."

I went back to the storage room and lifted the pump for my journey back to civilization. I had to carry it across the large animal parking lot and up two flights of stairs. I was dressed in spiffy creased slacks with a dress shirt, tie, and a white lab coat. When I made it back to ward four with the pump, I was a mess. I had sweat dripping off my forehead and soaking through my shirt at my armpits. The pump was covered with years of barn dust that was now smeared all over the front of my shirt. But I felt like I'd done something important. I was going to get this cat healthy even if it took chancing a heart attack in the attempt. I didn't care how much sweat and dirt and shitty nicknames it took.

I hoisted the pump into the empty cage adjacent to Roger. I got a damp rag and wiped it down so its poop-brown color could be seen in all its glory. Upon further inspection, I identified a couple of setbacks. Problem number one: the electrical cord had been damaged in a couple of spots. Someone had respliced it and now it was only two feet long. The nearest electric outlet was twenty feet away. A sobering thought gripped me. I wasn't sure this thing worked at all. I hoped I hadn't dragged this clunker across a paddock and up two flights of stairs for nothing.

I went on another scavenger hunt to find an extension cord. This mission was easier than the first. I found one lying on the floor two wards over. No one was around, so I swiped it. I was getting tired of wading through multiple layers of permission to acquire the stuff I needed. Roger was running out of time. *Better to beg for forgiveness than to ask for permission.* I went back to ward four with the cord hidden under my coat. I plugged the extension into the wall socket and the pump into the extension cord. I clicked the silver metal on/off toggle switch and held my breath. If this damn thing didn't work, I planned to climb up on the roof of the hospital and swan-dive off it. The pump came to life and purred like a kitten.

The pump worked by spinning a thick turn-screw type mechanism. A large syringe could be clamped between two metal locking flanges; the rotating screw pushed the plunger to deliver the contents. It was a solid industrial piece of equipment. It could push a football through a garden hose.

Modern pumps have a clear LED or LCD display. You enter the size of the syringe you're using and the rate per hour and push *enter*. The math involved in calculating volume delivered per time (based on the syringe size in use) is done for you by the built-in algorithm. This led to problem number two: this pump had *none* of that. It was all analog. This clunky dinosaur didn't have any scale or gauge to determine the flow rate. There was a single black knob with four settings. Off. Low. Medium. High.

I hadn't thought of this when I dragged it out of the dusty storage room. I wasn't looking that far ahead. The frustration was making my palms sweat and jaw clench. It seemed like each time I solved one problem, another jumped up in its place. In the meantime, Roger was starving to death. He was getting weaker by the minute. I went to the supply cabinet and filled up a sixty-milliliter syringe with Roger's brown food slurry. I hooked the syringe up to a length of clear tubing and pre-loaded the tubing, so it was full of food. I then placed the end of the tubing in a stainless-steel dish. Mounting the syringe in the pump, I placed the pump pusher against the plunger and turned it to "Low." I set a kitchen timer for one hour and looked at my watch. On an eight-by-eleven inch sheet of paper with a large red Sharpie, I wrote, "Do Not Touch!" and Scotch-taped it to my second-grade science experiment.

An hour later, I returned to assess the results. I sucked up the food slurry in the metal dish and measured it. Over the past hour, the old pump had efficiently delivered twelve milliliters of food. I did the math and realized I'd gotten lucky. This was a reasonable amount. Twelve milliliters an hour for twenty-four hours would deliver 288 milliliters of food, which is 288 calories per day. This was a decent starting rate, and I didn't want to waste any more time. I connected the tubing to the end of Roger's stomach tube, patted him on the head. I made a mental note to check on him every couple hours for the rest of the day.

12 p.m. Roger check: The pump was humming along. It was steadily pushing the food through the syringe. The tubing was still attached to the feeding tube and the feeding tube was attached to the cat. No evidence of vomiting. Yes! Roger had peed in his litter box. Good boy! The urine, as always, was a fluorescent bright yellow. It looked like something that came out of a car radiator. New cat litter. Scratch to the cat's head. So far, so good.

2 p.m. Roger check: The pump was working fine. Tubing all attached. No vomiting at all. Scratch on the rump. So far, so good.

4 p.m. Roger check: Pump working. Tubing attached. No vomiting. The sixty-milliliter syringe was almost empty. I turned off the pump and replaced the syringe with a new pre-filled food syringe. The pump was switched back on. I scratched Roger on the neck (his favorite spot), gave him a new clean cat blanket, and headed back to check on my diabetic dog in the ICU.

6 p.m. Roger check: Pump working. Tubing attached. Enough food in the syringe. Food flowing through the tubing with no leaks. Twenty-four more milliliters of food in Roger's stomach. No sign of vomiting. *Holy crap!*

This might work. I made up a new batch of food slurry with enough to last Roger through the night. This time I mixed up his anti-nausea medication with his food. In this manner, he would get the same daily amount of metoclopramide but at a constant infusion rate. I rewrote his medical orders so his night technician would know what to do. Then I went out to find her in person to make certain she understood the importance of the new treatment plan.

It was 7 p.m. before I broke free from my other patients to call Mr. and Mrs. Evans. The phone was answered on the first ring.

"Hi, Mrs. Evans. This is Jeff Schmidt. I've got some good news today about Roger."

"Hi, Dr. Schmidt, I'm so glad you called. Earl and I were getting worried when we didn't hear from you at six. What's the good news?"

"Well, today we tried something different. I was able to get a pump that would deliver Roger's food at a constant slow infusion. So now he doesn't have to get those large boluses of food. As you know, he had a tough time tolerating those boluses. On every second or third feeding, he would vomit. I couldn't get his feeding volume up to the amount that would maintain him. But, so far today, with the new feeding pump, Roger has received one hundred milliliters of food, and he hasn't vomited once! I'm happy with how he's doing. I'm now much more hopeful that he can pull through."

"Dr. Schmidt, that's great news," she said. "We are so looking forward to him getting better and coming home. We both really miss him. The house seems so empty without him. Thank you so much for all the excellent care. Earl will be so happy when I tell him."

This conversation with Mrs. Evans was the first positive update I'd been able to deliver in almost two weeks. Thank God, I finally could tell her something hopeful. Truth be told, I'd gotten very lucky with this conversation. When I told her that I'd hooked Roger up to a CRI pump and he was doing well, I was fully expecting the logical question, "Why didn't you do that in the first place?" A question I wasn't fully prepared to answer. What would I have said?

Because no one thought of it before.

Because it was buried in a storage shed in a large animal barn and covered with an inch of dirt.

Because I'm an idiot.

Roger didn't vomit at all that entire night.

The next morning at rounds, I presented my resident, chief clinician, and fellow students with an update.

"So, Trout, what's the update on Roger, the yellow cat?" asked Dr. Felderman.

"So far, things seem to be going well," I said. "I found that infusion pump you mentioned. I hooked him up to it yesterday around 11 a.m. and he's been on it since then. He's been getting twelve milliliters an hour for the past twenty-one hours and seems to be tolerating the amount fine. He hasn't thrown up once since the infusion started."

"So, he's getting twelve milliliters an hour?" asked Dr. Felderman. "That's almost three hundred milliliters a day. That's an aggressive starting rate, don't you think?"

"Yes. But that old pump isn't very sophisticated. It only has three settings, low, medium, and high. With a sixty-milliliter syringe of food that's the delivery rate on the low setting."

"Yep," he said. "I do seem to remember that now. I think that's the reason the thing's been in storage, and no one's seen it in a decade. As long as he's not vomiting at that rate, let's keep going. We need to get that cat out of here. His bill is up to four thousand dollars."

"Yeah, I know. So far, luckily, Roger's family has not given any sign that they're giving up."

"That's great. We need to get that cat better. Good job, Dr. Trout."

Roger went another two full days on his infusion of food. He made it a full day without vomiting and 288 milliliters of total food delivered. I happily turned off his I.V. fluids and removed his I.V. catheter. He didn't need it anymore. Over the course of three weeks, he had six different I.V. catheters. Each time the catheter site changed, it left his legs bald and bruised. He looked pretty beat up, but he was no longer vomiting, and his eyes were brighter. He'd now lift his head and focus on noises in the room. He'd look up and respond when I'd come in to change his food, clean his tube sight, and brush him out.

On the third full day of his CRI feeding, it was time to increase his food infusion rate. I'd spent an hour measuring the infusion rate on the "medium" setting. On medium, the pump delivered twenty milliliters per hour. I started running his food on medium for the twelve hours during the daytime when I was monitoring him. At 6 p.m., I'd switch him back to the "low" setting. So, he would get 240 milliliters of food during the day and 144 milliliters of food at night. This was a total of 384 calories per day. This way I'd know right away if he vomited on the higher rate. He didn't.

As part of Roger's daily care, he was weighed every morning. He came into the Veterinary Medical Teaching Hospital with a bodyweight of fourteen pounds. The morning I started using the pump for his food infusion, he was twelve and a half pounds. Despite the food delivery and I.V. fluids, he continued to lose weight. It'd been a frustrating journey. Whenever his food was increased, he'd vomit and feel terrible. But, on the fourth day of his CRI, he was back up to fourteen pounds and . . . he started grooming himself! With Roger feeling good enough to care about his hairstyle, I knew we were on the right track. He started thoroughly licking the fur around his legs where sticky bandage residue remained. Next time I checked, he'd sat up, curled over, and was licking his tummy where he'd been shaved three weeks before. After that I found him meticulously licking the back of his paw and rubbing it over the top of his head.

The next morning, I did my 6 a.m. checkup on Roger. His hair was much improved. He'd obviously been working on it all night. I did a blood panel recheck. His ALT, AST, and ALP liver values were all reduced by half from their previously scary levels. His bilirubin was down to ten. This is still abnormal but compared to his previous value of forty, this was fantastic. I walked directly from the lab to see him and tell him the good news. His pump was whirring. He was focused on cleaning up his paws.

"Good news, Roger. Your liver values are *way* better. If you keep going on like this, you can go home soon. You'll be able to go back to living with your mom and dad."

Roger looked at me with an expression of aloof disdain. He seemed to say "Obviously, Einstein. I'm getting myself all cleaned up for them."

That evening at 6:30, I did one last check on my yellow cat before I left for the day. He was fast asleep curled up on a blanket. His syringe pump was humming. His litter box had been recently cleaned. I woke him up to say good night and scratched his favorite spot on his neck. I noticed with satisfaction he wasn't nearly as yellow as a week before. As I talked to him, he stretched out his neck so I could get a better angle with my scratching. Then, he started purring. I'd never heard him purr before. I didn't really know if he ever purred at all. This was the first time I'd ever seen him feeling good and happy. A big lump rose in my throat, and I felt my face contort. Tears came to my eyes. Roger had worked his way into my heart. I sincerely hoped no one would walk into ward four and witness me crying in a cat cage. I spent a few more minutes with him. I rubbed my cheek on the top of his head. He purred the whole time. By this time in my four-week rotation, I was worn ragged. Weeks of fourteen-hour days and a packed schedule of challenging cases had left me emotionally raw. I left the building, crossed the parking lot, and got into my car for the ten-minute drive home. It was late February and still dark outside. I was happy for the darkness. I'd be embarrassed for anyone to see the fourth-year vet student, a twenty-nine-year-old grown man, with tears streaking down his face.

Two days later Roger started eating on his own. He didn't just eat. He started shoving his entire face in the food and scarfing it down like he hadn't eaten in six weeks. (He *hadn't* eaten in six weeks). He was so intense that his face was smeared with canned food, and he'd then have to spend the next fifteen minutes cleaning it all off. I gradually fed him a little more each day and started turning down the food infusion. He was up to fourteen and a half pounds.

After four weeks on the internal medicine service, I rotated to neurology. Roger was no longer officially my patient, but I checked on him at least twice a day. At this point, he was the longest standing patient in the small animal ward. Everyone there knew him. Now he'd start purring every time he saw me. Whenever I could, I grabbed five minutes here, ten minutes there between my other neurology patients to go pet Roger. His food infusion was turned off over the next couple of days. He was getting all his calories by eating. He looked great. I hadn't realized what a gorgeous cat he was because I'd only seen him when he was sick. No more matted, greasy hair. No more dandruff. He was up to fifteen and a half pounds and was maintaining weight on his own. His feeding tube was removed. It was time for him to get the hell out of there.

The overhead intercom made its obnoxious crackling buzz announcing the start of the actual announcement coming over the outdated speakers. "Dr. Trout. Roger is going home, and his family would like to see you." I knew this was the big day for Roger. The yellow cat was going home. But I didn't know what time it was going to happen. Dr. Felderman was looking out for me. Roger was no longer yellow. Mr. and Mrs. Evans were standing in the hospital lobby and Roger was tucked away in his old blue cat carrier. I hadn't seen Mr. and Mrs. Evans for four weeks. They'd only been able to visit twice during Roger's long hospitalization.

Mrs. Evans gave me a big hug. "Dr. Schmidt, we are so grateful that you saved our cat. We prayed for him every day and we know God sent you to us to save him." Mr. Evans shook my hand. I could tell he was overcome with emotion and unable to talk.

The outpouring of emotion left me a little uncomfortable, but I was so happy that I didn't care. Roger had pushed me to my limits. At several points I really thought he was going to die, and my fears of inadequacy and failure would be confirmed. He'd even bought me a new, unwanted nickname. It was so good to know he had a life in front of him and a family that adored him. I'd cherish this win. Roger was looking proud and happy. He was going home. I opened the cage door and rubbed him on the cheek. He purred.

Mr. Evans picked up the carrier and the elderly couple shuffled off to the elevator that went down to the parking lot. As the doors closed, I tried to keep some composure and choke back the big lump in my throat. I thought to myself, *This is one of the best days of my life.*

Mr. & Mrs. Evans

CHAPTER 2

Ginger Harriman

I could feel the tightening of my skin, the swelling of the flesh, and the burning that indicated the first stages of an infection. I'd experienced it many times before. I fished an amoxicillin pill from my pocket and gulped it down without water. As I did this, I took note of my damaged arms. Even in the dim light I could tell they were a mess.

Carefully, I opened the door from the garage into the laundry room and placed my knapsack on top of the dryer. I then gently padded from the tiled laundry room into the carpeted living room. I was trying to avoid waking my sleeping family. The house was completely quiet. It was pitch-black outside and mostly dark inside. I dragged myself over to the nearest soft spot and eased myself down. That's as far as I could make it. There was a little halo of light coming from the kitchen range hood. More light peeked out from around the master bedroom door on the second floor.

I took an inventory of myself. The front half of my left tennis shoe was soaked in urine thanks to a dog who'd peed on me four hours earlier. My khaki pants were coated with a combination of saliva, blood, and vomit. My plaid short-sleeved shirt was stiff with old sweat and coated with cat fur. I had six more shirts just like it stowed in the closet upstairs. This one might have served out its term. My mouth was dry and gritty, and my breath was terrible.

My grandmother would have said *it could scare a cat off a gut wagon.* My hair was rigid with sweat and grime and was sticking up in some random places. The worst part, though, was my arms, showcasing an interlacing network of scratches. They started at my wrists as shallow grooves and deepened as they approached my elbow. Others went in the reverse direction. Some of the worst scratches ended abruptly where the claw got "stuck" and dug into my flesh. In these areas there was a blob of dried blood clotted over the deepest part of the wound. My right hand had four deep punctures. Two on the back of my hand and two on the palm. Some of the wounds were developing a circle of puffy tissue that surrounded the primary wound. I pushed off each of my shoes with the opposite foot. Man, what a day.

In a few moments I could hear the click-clack of toenails coming from the family room on the other side of the stairs. My buff-colored terrier, Sally, slowly made her way over to me from where she'd been sleeping on her spot in the den. She was still bleary-eyed. Her butt swayed in a sleepy wag as she made her way over and rested her head on my lap. I rubbed her neck as she sniffed me all over. Nothing smells as interesting to a dog as a vet coming home after a long day at work. Her sniffing stopped at my arms, and she began licking my wounds. I appreciated the sentiment, but it hurt a little, so I pushed her away. I'd had enough. I gathered enough energy to push myself up and start the climb upstairs. I'd just finished a thirty-six-hour shift at a twenty-four-hour veterinary hospital. I'd left the house early yesterday morning. I'd only slept for two hours during my shift and caught myself nodding off a few times on my drive home. The effort I took to get up the stairs was rewarded by seeing my wife cozy in bed reading by the light of her bedside lamp. She was engrossed in one of her torrid romance novels with a shirtless barbarian on the cover. She folded over the page and set it on her lap as I entered the room.

"How'd it go?" she said. "Pretty long day, huh?"

"Pretty long *two* days," I said. "I'm beat."

"Riley's been asleep for a couple of hours," she said. Riley is the younger of my two daughters. She is four years old. She was famous for conking out thirty seconds after her head hit the pillow. Once asleep, she wouldn't wake up for anything. There could be a Rolling Stones concert and she would continue to snooze away.

"But Casey's still awake. She asked when you were coming home. I told her you would say goodnight when you got here."

"OK, I'll do that. I'm just going to brush my teeth first. I'm a stinky mess."

"*Casey,*" I say in a mock whisper. "*Are you awake?*"

"Hi, Dad. Yep, I'm awake."

"Good," I said. "I wanted to come tuck you in."

I padded across her bedroom over to her small bed. The room was lit by a single dinosaur night-light in the corner. I'd learned the hard way that walking across a toddler's room in the dark was a hazardous endeavor. At any moment, a Lego brick could become embedded in your instep. I made it over without incident. Her bed was only two feet off the floor, so I knelt next to it. Casey was six years old. She'd had a growth spurt recently and had stretched out a bit. She was at the stage where she was growing out of her chubby little body and looking like a little girl. My firstborn daughter wasn't a baby anymore. I gave Casey a hug and kiss on her cheek. Her face was flushed, and her strawberry-blonde hair was stuck to her face on one side where she'd gotten hot and sweaty. She looked like maybe she had been sleeping.

Me & Casey

"How did things go at work?" she asked. "Did you take care of a lot of animals?"

"Things went pretty well," I said. "I was super busy though and didn't get much sleep. I'm really tired."

"Did you see any puppies?" she asked.

I had to think about this for a moment. My brain was bogged down from lack of sleep. I furrowed my brow trying to remember.

"I don't think I saw any puppies today," I said. "But I did see two little kittens. They were named Oscar and Sadie. They were brother and sister. Oscar was gray and Sadie was a tabby. They were adorable and super friendly. Sadie climbed up my leg and chest, then sat up on my shoulder while I was typing on the computer."

Sadie on my shoulder

As I picked up the edge of her blanket to pull it over her, Casey noticed the ugly wounds on my right arm, touching it with her little hands. With a look of serious contemplation, she asked, "Ginger Harriman?"

"Yes," I said. "You called it."

"I hate that cat."

"I know. But I'm fine. You'd better get some sleep."

Ginger, the cat, was on the feisty side. "Spicy," one might say. Nope, on second thought, I'm being too kind. She was pretty much the meanest damn cat I had ever seen. She hated EVERYONE. She even seemed to hate her owner and biggest advocate, Mr. Harriman. You'd think this wouldn't be a very good survival strategy. "Don't bite the hand that feeds you," and all that. But Ginger never heard this idiom. Even if she did, I'm quite sure her response would have been F-You.

I met Ginger and her dad, Mr. Harriman, twenty-five years ago while working as a staff veterinarian at Largis Veterinary Clinic in California. I'd started working at Largis right out of veterinary school when I successfully applied for a one-year internship. The internship eventually changed into a permanent position. Largis is a town on the outskirts of Sacramento and fifty miles from my house in Davis. It was the biggest veterinary clinic in the region. They were open twenty-four hours for emergencies and daily for routine vet care. The main building, which had recently been remodeled and modernized, was the small animal hospital. Behind this was the large animal hospital with a spacious barn and large animal surgery area. Largis was a wonderful place to work as a young veterinarian. They employed an internal medicine specialist and a board-certified surgeon. It was always busy with a variety of good learning cases. The small animal clinic was staffed with seven licensed veterinarians ranging in age from thirty to sixty. These staff vets were all kind and generous with their time. I considered myself lucky to work in an environment that was so stimulating and supportive.

Largis had an unusual, and often frustrating, method of scheduling appointments. They didn't reserve a specific appointment slot for a particular doctor. Instead, if there were five doctors on duty, they would just schedule five 10 a.m. appointments. They'd just assume it would somehow sort itself out. Most of the time it did. Sometimes it was an absolute disaster. So, when I met Mr. Harriman, it was a random grab of his chart out of the file slot outside exam room two. I opened it up, gave it a quick review, and headed in.

Mr. Harriman was in his forties. He was a good-looking gentleman with short-cropped salt-and-pepper hair and a quiet demeanor. He had the lean, fit body of a runner and always moved in a deliberate, meticulous manner. I never knew what he did for a living, but he seemed meek and shy and quiet and kind. I always pictured him as a kindergarten teacher or running a daycare center.

He calmly explained that he'd brought in his eight-year-old cat, Ginger, for her routine yearly vaccines and a physical exam. Ginger's chart displayed

a red "CAUTION" sticker on the inside of it. This was a warning to the unini-
tiated that you needed to be on your toes. Hands and fingers may be at risk.
Muzzles and quick reflexes were often necessary. Mr. Harriman warned me
that she could get "frisky," showing me the scratch on the back of his hand
from his efforts to get her into her carrier.

I spent a few minutes getting to know Mr. Harriman. He was a pleasant, intelligent, well-spoken guy and I wanted him to feel he could trust
me. During our conversation, a continuous guttural growl emanated from
Ginger's direction. The sound was demonic, but I chose to ignore it. I discovered that Mr. Harriman wasn't married and didn't have kids. Seemingly,
in place of these family commitments, he'd made it his solemn duty to take
excellent care of this cat. I don't know if he swore on a bible, but it was an oath,
nevertheless, that he took quite seriously. He seemed to have the patience of
a saint and he loved this cat to death. In contrast, the noises emerging from
the pink carrier indicated that Ginger wouldn't hesitate to kill us both, and
possibly eat us, at the first opportunity. I wasn't inclined to share his affection.

At some point, it was time to get Ginger out of the carrier for her exam.
Mr. Harriman got up from his seat and took several deliberate paces back
from the exam table. He then looked at me expectantly. This was unusual.
Could Ginger really be that bad? I hesitantly opened the cage door and tipped
the cage forward to encourage this frisky feline to come out. Ginger had
solidly wedged herself to the inside of her carrier. Her legs splayed rigidly
against the walls so she wouldn't slip out. I jostled the cage a bit trying to
shake her loose. No luck. She was dug in like a tick. Huh, this was going to
be a bit more difficult than I thought.

"OK," I said. "She's obviously pretty scared. I don't want to have to reach
in and drag her out, so maybe I'll try just taking off the top of her carrier."

Often, this approach works great. You just leave the cat carrier on the
exam table, removing the "roof," and examine the pet while they remain snug
in their home away from home. When you're done, you just reapply the roof
and send the happy patient on their way. Nowadays most pet carriers have a

clever system of plastic hinged clamps that hold the top to the bottom. You release these eight clamps, and the top is easily removed. Cat carriers in the nineties were not as sophisticated. They were attached with ten to twelve bolts and wingnuts. It was widespread practice for the carriers to be stored in the barn or under a tarp in the backyard. They were often exposed to dirt, moisture, rodents, and spiders. The metal bolts were usually rusted to the nuts and had to be twisted off with pliers. During a thirty-minute appointment, it wasn't uncommon to spend the first twenty minutes in a frustrating attempt to take the carrier apart. For Ginger it only took ten minutes to get the top off. Finally, I could see her clearly. She was an Abyssinian breed and quite beautiful once you got beyond the slit eyes and bared fangs. She was an attractive light red-brown color. In Abyssinians, this color is called "ruddy." Her fur was shiny, and her eyes were bright green. I could tell she was enjoying the experience by the robust growling and hissing noises coming from deep inside her chest.

"OK," I said. "Now that I've got the top off, let's just try to hold her in there with a towel and I'll look her over and give her vaccines."

"OK," said Mr. Harriman. "Good luck with that. I can't help you. Ginger gets very mad."

Jeez, I thought to myself. *This guy is terrified of his own cat. How does this relationship work?*

I went out to the treatment room and recruited an unsuspecting vet tech to help me with Ginger.

"Hey, Amber," I said. "I've got a cranky cat in exam room two. Can you please help me hold her while I do an exam and give her two vaccines?"

"OK, be right there," she replied.

Amber came in holding an old, faded blue beach towel to securely hold Ginger in place. At eight and a half pounds, Ginger wasn't very big, but she was a solid ball of rigid muscle. She was strong and ticked off. Evil hissing sounds continued to emanate from her tiny frame.

With Ginger coiled in the bottom half of the carrier, Amber put the folded beach towel on top of her, applying firm pressure to hold her in place. This method left me a small safety zone. I could just peek around the edges of the towel to examine her. First, I lifted off the front part covering her face. Ginger tensed and hissed, and Amber braced herself for the onslaught. I was able to get a decent look at Ginger's eyes. There were two of them. I got a surprisingly good look at her mouth and teeth as she let out several intimidating hisses with her jaws wide open. Her mouth and tongue looked normal. *Thank goodness.* I really didn't want to stick my fingers in there. I put the front end of the towel back over her head.

Next, I attempted to get a look at the other end of this ball of fury. It was away from her head, so the risk was less, *right*? Amber shifted her hold forward. I slowly lifted the towel so I could see her hind end. Her body weight and body condition looked normal. I didn't try to take her temperature. I didn't want to push my luck that far, but I really needed to get a palpation of her abdomen. I'd feel terrible if I missed some abdominal swelling or a tumor. With the towel pushed up, I placed my hands on either side of her abdomen to get a feel. She was as tight as a bowstring and this move turned out to be a big mistake. With an ear-splitting shriek, Ginger contorted her body onto her left side. She savagely wiggled loose from the towel restraint and brought her hind legs into violent action. She drew both hind feet up to my left elbow and raked her claws all the way to my wrist. It happened so fast that it didn't have time to hurt. Amber swiftly shoved the towel back down and used her body weight to lean on the demon cat. Ginger writhed and screamed like she was being electrocuted.

With my heart pounding in my ears and Amber holding on for dear life, I grabbed the vaccines from the countertop.

"OK, Amber. She's really fired up, but we still gotta get the vaccines in her. If you let me sneak in behind her, I'll give these in her back legs. I'll be super quick."

Amber eased off the back end and added more pressure to the front. Ginger twisted under the towel. I quickly lifted off the towel and jabbed in the two injections. Then I grabbed the carrier lid and poised it in position above her.

"OK," I said. "One. Two. Three. Go!"

Amber yanked her hands out and I slammed down the lid. We hastily replaced the door and tightened down the screws, making sure they were *extra* tight. The towel remained behind. A sacrifice to the god of war. It wasn't worth the blood loss to retrieve it.

Amber and I were panting and disheveled.

I gave Amber a shell shocked thumbs up. "We survived," I quipped. "Good job. You may have saved my life."

Poor Mr. Harriman was visibly traumatized. His emotions vacillated between embarrassment at his cat's temperament, worry over her distress, and concern about the damage she'd done to my arm.

"I'm so sorry she scratched you," he said. "It seems like she's getting worse as she gets older."

What I said: "No problem, Mr. Harriman." I realized I was breathing hard and needed to calm myself down. "Some cats get like that when they are scared. Not your fault. It's part of my job."

What I was thinking: *"Have you considered calling in a priest to perform an exorcism on this cat?"*

Mr. Harriman grabbed the pink cat carrier and headed back to reception. Amber and I escaped out the opposite door into the pharmacy lobby.

"Oh my God," I said. "Thanks for the help. That cat was crazy."

"I'll say," she said. "I hope we don't see her again any time soon."

As we walked back towards the treatment room, my colleague, Dr. Johnson strolled past carrying a little Jack Russel terrier puppy. Dr. Tony Johnson joined us as a staff veterinarian seven months ago. We'd sometimes carpool into work as we both lived in the same town. We'd hit it off right away.

He was an outgoing, friendly, funny guy and everyone loved him immediately. He couldn't resist making a remark.

"What the hell was going on in there?" he said. "It sounded like you were slaughtering a pig."

"Just a really pissed-off cat," I replied.

"You're leaking," he said, looking down at my right arm.

I looked down. Blood was running down my right arm and dripping off the end of my pinky finger. A little puddle was forming on the floor.

"Yeah. She got me pretty good."

"What the hell is that cat's problem?" he said.

"She pretty much hates everyone and wants to kill them."

"What's her name?"

"Ginger Harriman," I replied.

"Remind me to schedule a vacation the next time she needs a vet," smirked Dr. Johnson.

Despite working in a stressful emergency clinic, Dr. Johnson always found a way to have fun. He'd show up to work with his shirt untucked, his hair sticking up, and wearing a lab coat that looked like he slept in it. Nobody cared. He would get away with everything. He'd sweet-talk the receptionists and they'd do anything for him. (I'd be waiting two hours for them to retrieve a fax for me). He had a gleeful flare for practical jokes. He would rearrange your files, so they were no longer in alphabetical order. He'd glue your coffee cup to your coaster. He'd place an open bottle of vodka on your desk when he knew the boss was coming by. Not only was he a professional smart-ass, but he was also an amateur cartoonist. Thanks to him, the hospital cage cards were regularly decorated with caricatures of angry dogs, drooling dogs, and grinning cats. The cartoons began to appear in his medical records, and I'd randomly discover them. They were extremely unprofessional, but pretty damn funny.

Tony the trickster

Unfortunately, I saw Ginger again just three weeks later. I grabbed the chart from the pending appointments slot. When I looked down at the name, my heart sank. I was still healing up from my last go-round with her. I was the Wile E. Coyote to her Road Runner.

"Hi, Mr. Harriman," I said. "Good to see you. What brought ya in with Ginger today?"

"A few days ago, she got out of the house at night," he said. "About two in the morning, I heard a catfight outside and went to my sliding glass door. When I opened it and turned on the porch light, she came running inside. She was panicked. I found a wound near her left armpit, and I'm worried it's become infected."

"Does she act sick?" I asked. "Is she eating and drinking alright?"

"She didn't eat that first day, but I figured she was just stressed. She's been eating OK the past two days. But I'm worried about that wound."

"Alrighty," I said. "Could you please start taking the carrier apart? I'll get someone to help me examine her."

Here we go again. Ginger vs. Jeff for round number two. This time would be different, I reasoned. I knew what I was getting into.

Amber lucked out. It was her day off. Who else could I recruit for the upcoming cat rodeo?

"Maray, could you help me hold a fractious cat in room three?"

"Sure," she said cheerfully. "Be right there."

Her perky, lighthearted mood wouldn't last too long, I thought. "Bring a towel," I said, "or some gloves. This could get ugly."

She appeared a few moments later, armed with heavy leather gloves. They were huge welding gloves and looked ridiculous on her. We kept a couple pairs of these gloves in the clinic specifically for this purpose. She could barely lift her arms and she could only wiggle her fingers a little bit. This was the alternate strategy to the "beach-towel restraint" approach and was her armor of choice. May the force be with her.

"OK, Maray. Mr. Harriman says Ginger has a wound on her armpit from a cat bite. We need to get her on her side to look at it. The gloves are a good idea but be ready. She's a pistol."

Me & Maray

Maray had handled thousands of difficult cats. She knew the rules of the game and had been in this business longer than me. She assumed I was exaggerating the danger. She responded with a condescending look that screamed *amateur*.

Alright, I thought. *I tried to warn you.*

We went into the room like Frodo and Sam entering Mount Doom. I knew this was going to be bad. Perhaps we could save the security footage for rebroadcast on *Shark Week*. Mr. Harriman already had the screws out of the cage top. As before, he'd established himself safely against the far opposite wall.

Maray and I positioned ourselves on opposite sides of the carrier for maximum tactical advantage. "OK," I said. "One. Two. Three. Go!"

I lifted off the top of the carrier and Maray pushed down on Ginger with her triple layered welding gloves. Ginger screamed, hissed, and struggled. She twisted her head and managed to bite Maray's left hand, but thankfully, the glove absorbed the bulk of the damage. While Ginger busied herself mincing up the glove, I was able to look at her wound. "*Whew.*" The wound wasn't that bad. It was a modest two-inch scratch with another shallow scratch right next to it. No surgery required. It just needed a little clean up and some antibiotics.

"Hold on!" I said. "I'll be right back."

I ran back into the treatment room, grabbed some clippers, and frantically drew up a Penicillin injection. I hurried back into the exam room. Maray and Mr. Harriman were still alive. Ginger was still pissed. With Maray holding onto Ginger like a bull rider in a rodeo, I quickly shaved away the fur from the wounded area, disinfected it, and gave Ginger the antibiotic injection. I grabbed the carrier top and readied it for action. Maray and I were poised to slam the lid back on. But she needed to release her grip so she could get her hands out. As soon as Maray's pressure came off, quick as a cobra, Ginger lunged to get out. Imagining a psycho-cat running loose in the exam room, I made a spontaneous decision to grab her by the scruff to push her back in. As I shoved her back, she was able to twist her head one hundred eighty degrees, *Exorcist-style*, and make a meaty bite into my palm. She coiled her hind legs beneath her and raked her feet along my still-healing left arm. Almost simultaneously, she reached out with her front claws and dug them into my right arm. I yanked my arm loose, making the wounds even worse, as Maray slammed down the top. Maray and I stood there panting. I was shaking and sweating. It took a few deep breaths for me to gather myself.

"Man." I said. "I don't think she liked that very much. But that wound should be OK, Mr. Harriman. Just monitor it over the next few days and let me know if it's looking any worse."

"I'm so sorry, Dr. Schmidt. I hope she didn't get you too bad," he said.

"I'll be OK. I just feel bad that everything is so difficult with her."

"She's always been a pretty ill-tempered cat," he said. "But it seems to be escalating."

As Maray and I were leaving the exam room, Dr. Tony was in the hallway reading a patient chart. He eyeballed my bleeding arms and hands and said, "Ginger Harriman?"

"Yep."

"Better you than me."

Cat scratches and bites like this almost always get infected. It can be more than just a nuisance. A cat bite infection not only is painful, but it can make you systemically sick. After cleaning out my wounds with a surgery scrub brush, I snagged a handful of amoxicillin pills from the big bottle in the pharmacy. I'd take these preemptively for a few days so that I wouldn't lose my arms.

I made it home in time for dinner that night. I was sitting at the table with my two young daughters and my wife, Kim. Casey was always curious about my animal doctor life. I was hoping someday she would think about joining the veterinary profession.

"Daddy, what happened to your arms?" she asked.

"I saw a pretty mean cat today," I said. "She's fast and strong. She gets vicious when she gets mad."

"That's a bad cat," she said. "Look what she did to your arms. Why does the owner keep her?"

"I'm not sure," I said. "I don't think she's very nice to him either, but he seems to really love her."

"That's weird. I wouldn't keep her."

"Me neither," I agreed. "I guess he'd miss her."

"Is that the same cat that gave you all those scratches a couple of weeks ago?"

"Yep. That's her all right."

"What's her name?" she asked.

"Ginger Harriman."

"Ginger Herr-y-man. Ginger Herr-ee-man," she repeated. "I don't like that cat."

Over the next three years, I saw Ginger at least ten more times. It was always the same scene. She never mellowed. Poor Mr. Harriman remained dedicated to caretaking her despite her ill temper. She wouldn't allow him to administer any medications. He couldn't trim her claws. He couldn't pick her up. I was continuously amazed that he was able to bring her in at all. I tried sending home a tranquilizer medication he could use to make her visits easier. She wouldn't take them. Not as a liquid, not in a pill, not on his lap and not on a hill. She'd scratch and she'd scream and make a big fuss. She'd lunge and bite and hurt all of us. It got to the point where the best way to handle her was to realize it was a fight, and just try to get it over quickly. Going slow and gentle ended up in the same place but twenty minutes behind schedule. I always got a bite or a scratch during her visits. The best I could do was try to minimize the damage.

The only people who truly enjoyed the visits were Casey and Dr. Johnson. From a safe distance, they found the drama highly entertaining.

At some point, Dr. Johnson got ahold of Ginger Harriman's medical file. The first page was a patient summary with the patient's weight along with ongoing medical issues and a current list of prescription medications. It was supposed to be thorough, meticulous, and professional. Now appearing on Ginger's medical summary was a scary cartoon. The entire bottom half of the page was decorated with this image.

Dr. Tony strikes again...

From then on, when I got home from work and showed any bite, scratch or bruises, no matter how minor, Casey would ask me, "Is that from Ginger?"

Most of the time the answer was "Yep, it was her."

At Casey's eighth birthday party, a group of little girls were sitting at our dining room table. The table was draped with a paper Winnie-the-Pooh-themed birthday tablecloth. Blue and yellow streamers hung down from the chandelier and a balloon was tied to the back of each chair. Kim had decorated our staircase banister with white, pink, and blue crepe paper streamers. The kids were wearing silly-pointed birthday hats rubber-banded to their heads. Casey had just received an enthusiastic round of "Happy Birthday" and blown out the candles on her cake. My job was to scoop out a dollop of vanilla ice cream on each Winnie-the-Pooh paper plate. As I was scooping the ice cream, one of the girls noticed the scratches running down my right arm.

"Why is your hand all scratched up?" she asked in a charming little girl's voice.

"Oh," I said, glancing down at my arm. It did look unsightly. "I'm a veterinarian, so it's my job to take care of dogs and cats all day. Sometimes they scratch me with their claws."

Casey jumped in to add some much-needed drama to my mundane explanation. "It's probably from Ginger Harriman," she quipped. "Dad sees a really mean cat named Ginger Harriman, and she scratches him all the time."

Casey had a fascination with Ginger and seemed to relish telling her friends the gory details.

"Last time *both* his arms were scratched, and she even bit him on the hand, too."

Her friends were somberly impressed by the veterinary war story.

Occasionally Ginger needed more involved medical care. A blood draw, a teeth cleaning, or an X-ray were a few examples. On these occasions, I'd sedate her with an intramuscular injection of ketamine and diazepam. These injections stung, so we'd have to do them quickly to avoid getting hurt. This drug combination would leave her incapacitated for several hours so we could safely perform any medical procedures. I'd make sure that Ginger was kept completely enclosed in her carrier when she recovered from these sedation events. If she woke up too soon and wasn't safely tucked away, I'd have to figure out how to get her back into her carrier without someone going to the ER. After a while, *every* employee at the vet hospital knew about her.

"Dr. Schmidt. Your 10:30 appointment came a bit late, so I graciously saw it for you. I didn't want you to miss your eleven o'clock appointment with Ginger," said Dr. Tony one day.

"Thanks," I said. "That was very considerate of you."

"Dr. Schmidt, Mr. Harriman's been waiting in the lobby with Ginger for forty-five minutes," said Anna, the receptionist.

"Why didn't one of the other vets see her?" I asked.

"Oh, they all agree you should be the one to see her. You have such a way with her."

"Dr. Schmidt, I know you have tomorrow off, so we squeezed in Ginger Harriman as your first appointment when you're back on Thursday," said Leah after putting the phone on hold. "Mr. Harriman says she's been acting mopey for a few days now."

"Don't we have any openings tomorrow for her?" I replied.

"Well, we do. But Dr. Freed (Dr. Freed was the practice owner) thought it would be best if she waited to see you."

"Great. I look forward to it."

Like it or not, I was Ginger's vet. I couldn't pawn her off on anybody. I liked Mr. Harriman, but that cat hated me.

Thursday morning at 7:30, Mr. Harriman was waiting for me. I'd come in early to see Ginger before the rest of my appointments started. It wasn't the best way to start off the day.

"Good morning, Mr. Harriman. Do you think Ginger is acting sick?"

"Yes," he said. "She's not eating all her food and she looks skinnier to me."

"Is she vomiting at all?" I asked.

"No."

"Is she drinking more water or peeing more than normal?"

"Now that you mention it," said Mr. Harriman, "the urine clumps in the litter box seem a lot bigger than before."

I didn't like hearing this. I was worried for her. Ginger was now thirteen years old. I peeked into her carrier. She did appear thinner than the last time I saw her. Her previous lab work was normal, but it was from over a year ago. When older cats produce a lot of urine and lose weight there are three common conditions to blame: kidney failure, diabetes, or hyperthyroidism.

Usually, cats with diabetes or hyperthyroidism eat *more* than normal, but Mr. Harriman thought Ginger was eating *less*. This wasn't good.

I outlined my concerns to Mr. Harriman.

"OK, I think the only way we're going to figure this out is to get a blood sample and a urine sample from her. As you know, we'll only be able to do this if she's completely sedated. I hate to do it, but I don't really see another way."

"Yeah, I understand," he said. "Lets' go ahead with that."

After the customary biting, screaming, and scratching, Ginger was drowsy and limp. I carried her to the treatment room so a tech could assist me in getting a blood and urine sample. I administered some subcutaneous fluids just to help her feel better when she recovered. I returned her to Mr. Harriman forty-five minutes later when her sedation was wearing off. I promised to call him the next day when the results were available.

"Thanks, Dr. Schmidt," he said. "I look forward to your call tomorrow."

The next day the lab printout appeared on my desk. I was a bit nervous to look at it. I really didn't want to deliver any bad news to Mr. Harriman. Ginger's blood urea nitrogen level was seventy-five and her creatinine was 3.6. These values are closely associated with kidney function. Her numbers were three-times higher than normal. Her urine was abnormally dilute which showed her kidneys had lost their ability to concentrate. Her blood sugar was normal (no diabetes), and her thyroid value was normal as well (no hyperthyroidism). Ginger had mid-stage renal failure.

There's no cure for renal failure in cats. Only management steps to slow the process and help them feel better. A low-protein diet will minimize the waste products the kidneys must eliminate. Antacid medication can lower the acidity of the stomach and reduce nausea. Fluids can be administered subcutaneously to "flush out" the kidneys and reduce the buildup of metabolic wastes. Hypertension can be a secondary problem and blood pressure medications can be prescribed to address this. Often, when the kidneys are damaged, their ability to produce erythropoietin is impaired and cats will become progressively anemic. Synthetic erythropoietin can correct this. A *cooperative* cat with a treatment protocol of diet, fluids, and medications, can last a couple years before they succumb to the deterioration of the kidneys. Ginger was the poster cat for *uncooperative*. She wouldn't tolerate any medications by mouth. She wasn't likely to eat any of the special foods. She would certainly *not* allow Mr. Harriman to give her an injection. We were screwed.

I called Mr. Harriman to discuss the lab results.

"I'm sorry. This isn't very good news. Ginger's kidneys will likely get worse over time. This will make her weaker and her appetite will continue to decrease. She may start vomiting as the kidney toxins build up in her system."

"Is she in any pain?" he asked.

"No. I don't think so. It's more just a feeling of being tired and weak."

"Dr. Schmidt, I'm pretty sure she won't let me do any of those treatments you talked about."

"I know. We can try some of the special foods and see if she takes to any of them."

"OK. I guess we can try that."

As expected, Ginger wasn't interested in any of the prescription diets, neither canned nor dry. We tried three different brands. She was just too damn stubborn. But she still enjoyed sleeping in her favorite spot on the rocker in the sunroom and she was still eating a little bit, so Mr. Harriman decided to wait it out. It didn't take long.

Three weeks later, I got paged on the overhead speaker. "Dr. Schmidt, Mr. Harriman is on the phone asking for you."

I took the phone call preparing myself for the worst.

"Dr. Schmidt. Ginger hasn't eaten anything at all in two days. She's very weak. I think it's time."

I arranged to see Ginger after my last appointment of the evening.

Mr. Harriman was visibly deflated as he shuffled into the exam room at 6:15 p.m. He was carrying Ginger in her pink plastic crate. Even from the doorway, it was evident that she was very light. He was supporting the crate with just two fingers.

"I'm sorry Mr. Harriman. I know this is tough. You think it's time to let her go?"

"Yeah," he replied. "She's getting very weak. Earlier today she tried to jump up on the back of the couch. She just fell over. She's been drinking some water, but no food in two days."

"I understand. I'll try to make this as easy as possible for her. Do you want to be with her when I put her to sleep?

"Yes. I think I owe her that much."

Ginger was dehydrated and weak, but she still gave me a hearty hiss when I took the top off her carrier. I wanted to avoid her being stressed when I gave her the intravenous phenobarbital that would end her life, so I first injected her with a sedative to help her relax. In her weakened state, it did its job in just a few minutes. With my tech holding her, I shaved the inside of her back right leg. I gently inserted the twenty-five-gauge needle into her vein and slowly injected her with one milliliter of the thick pink solution. Ginger took a few shallow breaths and then stopped. Mr. Harriman was petting her on the head the whole time. It was a very peaceful death.

Mr. Harriman was bent over Ginger. His elbows rested on the table and his face was inches from hers. I noticed he had a lot more gray in his hair then when we'd first met. He continued to gently stroke her head. After a moment he spoke. "Thank you, Dr. Schmidt. You were the only vet willing to take care of her."

"It was my pleasure Mr. Harriman. She was very lucky to have you."

I never saw him again after that night.

On the drive home, I couldn't help thinking about Mr. Harriman and Ginger. The poor guy had to be feeling pretty blue right now. He'd done the best he could for years to care for that cantankerous cat. A lot of time and money was invested in her. What did he get out of it? From what I could tell,

Ginger never liked anybody. She seemed to barely tolerate Mr. Harriman. Maybe he could occasionally pet her? Did Ginger prevent him from feeling lonely? Or did caring for her give him a sense of purpose? Now that she was gone, maybe, in some way, he was relieved. Loving that cat couldn't have been easy. I don't think I could have done it. I hoped someday he would go out and get a nice big, loving, friendly cat. He certainly deserved it.

What about Ginger? She'd been raised by Mr. Harriman since she was a kitten. She never went hungry. She'd enjoyed a safe and loving home. With all the advantages she had in life, why was she so angry? I found myself wondering if her ill temper created a stress level that contributed to her early demise. Was there something else I could have done to help her? It's a frustrating quandary to have the tools and training to make a difference but not be able to do anything. At every opportunity, Ginger fought our attempts to help her. I felt like I'd let her down. I think I let Mr. Harriman down as well. What could I have done differently?

Then my thoughts wandered to Casey. She didn't know this cat, but *she thought* she did. Over the years, we'd talked about Ginger many different times. Besides telling tales of Ginger to her friends, she regaled her grandparents too. If I didn't say anything, she may never know that I euthanized Ginger. The subject may never come up. But if she did find out, would she feel betrayed that I never told her? Would she be sad that Ginger was gone, even though she only really knew her from my wounds and my stories? Casey loved our family dog and cat. I knew she'd be devastated when someday their time came. As the daughter of a veterinarian, she knew that euthanizing pets was part of my job. But I'm not sure how *much* of this she understood. I decided it would be best to tell her.

When I got home, everyone was already in bed. I went up to Casey's room, cracked open the door, and peeked in my head.

"Casey, are you awake?"

"Yeah, Dad. I'm still awake."

I went over to the side of her bed. She'd graduated to a big girl's bed and no longer needed the night-light.

"How'd it go at work?" she asked. "Did you see any puppies?"

"Yeah. I did see a few puppies today. I saw two little golden retriever puppies that were brother and sister. They were in for their first puppy shots. They were pretty sweet and licked me all over my face. I also saw a ten-week-old pit bull puppy named Stanley. He was all glossy gray. When he wagged his tail, his whole butt shook all over. I like those dogs. He was really cute."

"That's awesome. I wish I could have seen them."

"Casey, there's something I want to tell you."

"What, Dad?"

"You know that cat Ginger that we've talked about a bunch?"

"You mean Ginger Harriman?" she asked.

"Yeah, that's her. She came in to see me today. I had to put her to sleep. She had kidney failure and was feeling sick and weak. She hadn't eaten anything for a couple of days, so Mr. Harriman decided it was time to let her go."

"Good," she said. "I never liked that cat."

CHAPTER 3

Nothing to Lose

Dr. Schmidt, please come to the treatment room immediately!

The announcement cracked alarmingly over the intercom speaker. My heart jumped into my throat.

The scene: Saturday evening around seven at Largis Veterinary Clinic, well past my leaving time. The daytime practice vets (and most of the staff) closed up shop at six and were gone for the day. Dr. Tony Johnson was the Saturday night emergency shift vet. He typically had things well in control. I knew he was in the building. I'd seen him arrive an hour earlier. I was due back to work for the Sunday emergency shift at 8 a.m., so I was anxious to get home.

It'd only been five seconds since the overhead page when Cindy, one of the vet techs, rushed into the office. She was normally a cool customer, so seeing her rattled quickly increased my anxiety. *What was the big panic?*

"Dr. Schmidt, Dr. Johnson wants to see you," she said out of breath. "He wanted me to catch you before you left for the day."

"What's this all about?" I asked Cindy as we both hustled out of the office. She trailed behind me as I made a hurried left turn into the hallway, past the break room and into the lobby. I crossed the green tiled floors of the lobby and braced to shove open the heavy swinging doors to the treatment room.

Cindy was flustered and stumbling over her words. "Animal control just came in. It's Troy. He parked his truck just outside and ran right in. Dr. Johnson's with him now. He was carrying a bloody blanket in his arms. He's got a cat that was shot through with an arrow."

By this time, we were entering the treatment room, and I took in the scene before me. I knew Troy on sight, but I'd never seen him look this intense. He was a big, sturdy red-headed animal control officer and was currently bent over one of the treatment tables with a blanket bundle in his arms. Tony was wearing a white lab coat with the sleeves pushed up to his elbows. He had his penlight in his left hand and was peering under the blanket. With his right-hand, he was administering oxygen to the critter hidden underneath the folds.

"Hi," I said to Troy, and to Tony, "What's going on?"

Tony looked up at me from his bent position at the table. He had a look of astonishment on his face. "Jeff, come look at this. Tell me if you've ever seen this before?"

I'd been working as a small animal veterinarian for four years at this point. I worked five day-shifts and two emergency shifts per week. I'd *seen* a lot. Gross, weird, and sad. A dog that chewed up and swallowed razor blades, a dog with its foot caught in a bear trap, arsenic poisoning, gunshot wounds, marijuana toxicity, and a whole slew of hit-by-car injuries. I didn't think Troy or Tony were tending to anything that could shock me. I was wrong.

I walked over to see the object of concern: an orange tabby cat who was clearly miserable. All I could see was her face, streaked with foamed saliva. She was gasping through an open mouth.

"What do you think of this?" Tony said as he abruptly pulled off the blanket.

"Holy crap!" I exclaimed. "How is this cat still alive?" I was caught off guard. It wasn't my most professional moment.

This was not the arrow injury I was expecting. The long slender arrow penetrated the cat's body LENGTHWISE. It had entered the cat through its left shoulder just lateral to the neck. It exited out the right side of the caudal abdomen. This cat had been shish-kabobbed. The arrow pierced most of the cat's body with six inches sticking out from the right side of the caudal abdomen. Another four inches of the fletched end protruded near the left side of the cat's face. It had passed through the entire chest and abdominal cavity. It was a silver aluminum target arrow with a tapered tip. Whoever shot this cat had been lying close to the ground, or the cat had been in an elevated position, like up on a fence. Evidently it missed any vital organs. Luckily, it wasn't a hunting arrow, or this cat would already be dead.

"Where did you find this cat?" I asked Troy.

"She was out on the side of Stillman Road. One of the residents there saw this strange site. She was actually walking around near the bushes on the side of the road with the arrow sticking out of her like this. She tried to run away but I was able to throw a net over her. She couldn't move too fast, because of the, uhm, uh, arrow sticking out of her."

"This cat was *running around* with this arrow in her?" I asked.

"Yep, she was."

"That's incredible," I said. "No owner?"

"Not that we could find."

I switched on the overhead exam light and leaned in to get a better look. The entrance and exit wounds of the arrow looked clean. There wasn't as much blood as I'd expected. Just a smear around the entry wound and a thin coating of caked blood where it exited her right side. The cat's gum color was a nice healthy pink. It was impossible to tell whether her gasping was from pain, panic, or a mortal wound. But she was still alive, and based on the dried blood, this injury had occurred at least an hour ago.

54

"What do you think we should do with this critter?" asked Dr. Johnson. Without an owner present, we had to make the call about how much care to render for a stray. Our contract with animal control topped out at $300. Something told me this was not a $300 case.

"I guess we've got nothing to lose," I said. "This cat should already be dead. Why don't we get this arrow out of her and see what happens. I doubt she'll survive, but she's obviously a tough little cat."

Troy quickly signed the bottom of a form mounted to an industrial metal clipboard. He tore off the yellow bottom sheet of the carbon copy and handed it to me. The form listed the basic information about where the animal was found and the circumstances. It was the minimum documentation we needed to authorize treatment by the county.

"OK, boys," said Troy, "I'll leave her here with you then. I've got to get over to another call. Here's her paperwork. Good luck. I'm off to the next calamity."

Tony spoke up, "Let's start by placing an I.V. catheter. Then we can give her some fluids and pain meds. After that we can figure out what to do with that arrow."

Cindy was two steps ahead of us. She'd been listening to the conversation to anticipate the next steps. She'd already pulled up a metal instrument stand with all the catheter supplies. I gave the cat a small injection of pain medication and a mild sedative to alleviate some of her panic. As Cindy shaved and prepped the cat's left front leg for the catheter, I gently held her head and petted her in an attempt to calm her. After a few minutes, I could feel her relaxing in my hands letting me know the medications kicked in. Tony ducked into the surgery room to make sure the lights were on, the table warmer was running, the anesthesia machine was hooked up, and the fluid pump was ready.

"OK, Cindy," I said. "She's relaxed now. Let's get the I.V. catheter in her."

Dr. Johnson, we have an emergency waiting for you in room one!

"Let me go see what that's about," said Tony, reacting to the intercom. "I'll be back to help you as soon as I can."

I'd heard just about enough from the intercom for one day, but Dr. Johnson seemed unperturbed.

Cindy efficiently inserted a twenty-two-gauge catheter into the cat's left front leg. I watched as she deftly attached a T-port to the catheter and quickly taped it all in place. Cindy was sometimes a bit quirky and scattered. But tonight, she was the model of focus and efficiency. She knew it was a life-or-death situation and this Arrow Cat needed her full skills and attention.

Dr. Tony popped back into the treatment room to check on our progress. "How's it going?" he asked.

"So far so good." I replied. "We've got her sedated and an I.V. catheter in place. I'll start her on fluids and antibiotics, then we'll take a quick X-ray to see what we're dealing with."

"OK," he said. "This new emergency shouldn't take me too long. It's an allergic reaction to a bee sting. The dog is stable so I should be able to come help you in ten minutes."

"OK," I said, "We'll be in X-ray."

I couldn't predict what organs or major vessels were being impinged by the arrow, so I thought a minimum of jostling would be prudent. I gently lifted the Arrow Cat using a towel to support her. Once in X-ray, Cindy calculated the exposure settings and slid a large X-ray plate into the cassette holder under the table. If this cat survived removal of the arrow, she could still die from the subsequent infection. To mitigate this risk, I drew up an injectable antibiotic called cephalexin. I administered this intravenously over a minute using Cindy's I.V. catheter. Cindy took the first X-ray. It was a lateral view of the whole cat. While she was switching out the exposed X-ray plate for a new one, I drew up another dose of potent pain medication. If this cat was going to die, I didn't want her to die in misery. Cindy snapped the second X-ray by tapping the footswitch under the table. She quickly pulled out the exposed plate and jetted off to the dark room where she would feed the films into the automatic developer. We would have the results in about five minutes.

While I waited, I took the opportunity to perform another assessment of our injured cat. She seemed stable. Her breathing had slowed and became more even. Her eyes had a drug-induced glassy quality, but she would still occasionally blink and turn her head to look around the room. Her heart rate had slowed from 200 beats per minute to 120. She'd further relaxed now that her pain meds had kicked in. Her gum color was still pink. *Amazing*, I thought. *This cat's been completely impaled and she's hanging in there.*

Tony appeared in the doorway of the X-ray room. He'd obviously rushed to get back. His collar was flipped up on one side and he held his stethoscope clutched in his left hand. "How do the X-rays look?"

"Still waiting."

He too instinctively gave Arrow Cat a quick look-see. "She looks pretty decent. Hard to believe."

"I'm amazed too," I said. "But what kind of person would do this?"

"A future serial killer," he said.

Just then the door opened from the dark room and Cindy came out with the two films. She slapped them up on the view box so we could all get a look. On X-rays, metal shows up as bright white. Soft tissues, like muscle, are gray. Air appears black. This cat had a bright white metal spike penetrating at least ten inches of her body. It stood out like a beacon against the black background of her lungs. The arrow looked enormous next to her petite internal organs. It crossed her thorax diagonally from left to right, penetrated her diaphragm, traveled through her abdominal cavity, and exited out her right side.

I studied the X-ray images intently looking for an injury that would spell the end for her. She didn't have any sign of a punctured lung as there was no free air in her chest. She didn't appear to have any blood or intestinal contents floating around in her abdomen. Neither of us identified any broken bones. From what we could tell, the arrow had pushed the vital organs out of the way as it penetrated, rather than puncturing them.

"What do you think?" I asked, wondering if Tony was seeing things the same way.

"Well," said Dr. Johnson with a little smirk, "based on *all* my past experiences of cats getting skewered by arrows, this one doesn't seem too bad. She doesn't appear to be leaking air or blood. But I guess we can't just leave that thing in there."

Sometimes in veterinary medicine, you get cases that are oddly liberating, where the only option is risky but apparent. Where there is basically nothing to lose. This poor cat couldn't live like this, wandering around skewered by an arrow. But we still had the issue of no owner and only $300 to "spend." If she died, despite our best attempts to save her, it would be an understandable and expected outcome. However, if we were able to save her, it would be epic. Between the two of us, we had a combined experience of six years of practicing medicine. Neither of us had encountered this predicament before. With no grown-ups in the building to dissuade us, we forged ahead.

"Agreed," I said. "Let's take her into surgery. We'll see if we can get that thing out without her bleeding to death. We might as well give it a try. We've got nothing to lose."

Tony gave the orange tabby a potent drug cocktail to induce anesthesia. Cindy bundled up the cat in a blankie, being cautious to avoid poking herself with the pointy end of the arrow and rushed the cat into the surgery suite.

I held the cat's mouth wide open and extended the tongue so that Cindy could expertly slide a small endotracheal tube into her trachea. The tube was tied in place to prevent it from slipping and connected to an anesthesia machine. The machine was turned on to deliver a vaporized anesthetic gas.

"I think we should cut off the feathered end of the arrow first and then pull it out through the wound in the abdomen," said Tony. "That's the way they do it in all the old cowboy movies."

Since the proper technique for arrow extraction was not a class they taught in vet school, we had to fall back on our Hollywood medical training.

"Should we pour some gunpowder on it and light it on fire?" I asked.

"I'm fresh out of gunpowder," remarked Tony.

"Okay," I replied. "I'll be John Wayne and you can be Henry Fonda. Why don't you guys prep the entry and exit wounds. I'll go find something to cut off the end of the arrow."

I left Arrow Cat in the capable hands of Tony and Cindy and jogged to the clinic's maintenance shed to search for something suitable for arrow cutting. I wiggled the locking bolt back and forth to get the old, creaky wooden door open. I dug around through a rusty and dusty toolbox. Pliers? Those won't work. Wire cutters? Nope, too small. Hacksaw? Maybe. Bolt cutters? Hmm . . . this might do the trick. I grabbed the bolt cutters and the hacksaw. As a second thought, I slipped a pair of heavy pliers and a metal file into my pocket and ran back to the surgery room. Tony and Cindy were finishing up their work shaving and cleaning the wound sites.

"I think these will work." I said holding up the bolt cutters.

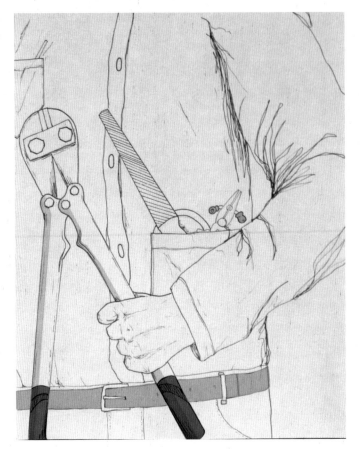

Tool jacket

"Looks good to me," he said. "I'll hold the arrow and you cut it."

Tony stabilized the arrow by grabbing the four-inch portion protruding from the cat's neck. I positioned the bolt cutters two inches from the blood-caked fur. I then gave the handles a solid squeeze. The hollow aluminum arrow was easily cut in two, but it crushed the weak metal in the process. The arrow was too soft. Instead of it cutting through cleanly, it had collapsed before it cut, thus making the ends wider and sharper.

"That's not going to hack it," I said. "We can't go dragging that sharp, jagged piece through the cat. It'll lacerate everything it touches."

"Time for the hacksaw?" said Tony.

60

"I guess so," I said. "That's going to be a bit more work."

Cindy reached in to push the cat's head to one side because now there was even less space for me to work. Tony again held the arrow so I could cut it with the hacksaw, but now he only had a two-inch piece to grasp with his fingertips. It was a brave gesture. His arms bowed outwards to make room for the saw and my arm. I needed some space to maneuver.

"OK," I said. "If I saw off one of your fingers, I'll just have to sew that back on later."

"No problem," he said. "I trust you."

I carefully placed the blade of the saw midway between his fingers. Slowly at first, I began dragging the blade over the arrow shaft. The blade made a nice groove that allowed me to increase the cutting pressure. Tony continued to hold the arrow firmly to protect the cat from the vibrations and minimize organ trauma. It only took a few more seconds to make a nice clean cut through the arrow, removing the jagged end completely. I used a small metal file to smooth out the sharp edges of the aluminum shaft.

"OK," I said. "Is everybody ready?"

I stood towards the back right side of our Arrow Cat. Tony positioned himself near the cat's neck. In one hand, he held a stack of sterile prepped gauze; with the other hand, he held the cat's head out of the way. Cindy leaned in near the cat's mouth, making sure the trach tube, catheter, and anesthesia machine were stabilized and functioning properly.

"Yep. Ready," said Tony.

"OK. Ready," said Cindy.

I placed my left thumb and forefinger on the cat's abdomen around the arrow, making the "OK" sign. With my right hand, I started a firm, steady pull on the arrow. I held my breath. If this arrow was hitting anything vital, she'd be dead in a minute. It took more strength than I expected. Evidently there's a lot of friction between an arrow shaft and twenty inches of cat tissue. As the freshly cut end of the arrow disappeared inside the cat's chest, Dr. Johnson slapped the ointment impregnated gauze over the entry hole. He wanted to form a seal quickly to minimize air getting sucked into the cat's chest. I kept on pulling. I'd removed about ten inches of the arrow, and I needed to regrip. I repositioned the arrow in my right hand, close to the cat's body, and pulled the rest of the arrow out with a wet popping sound. The last few inches came out more easily as the friction lessened. I watched the arrow hole for a half second, half-expecting a gush of blood. There were only a couple of drops. I placed my own betadine gauze over the exit hole and fixed it in place with gauze and stretch tape.

It wasn't till then that I looked at the arrow. It was streaked and smeared with blood, but nothing that looked like bile or feces. A good sign. I looked at Tony. He looked at me. Cindy looked at both of us with a raised eyebrow and a "What's next?" look on her face. We all looked at the cat expectantly. We fully expected a gasp, a cough, or a spasm that would spell the end. Nothing happened. Arrow Cat just kept on breathing. Her heart kept on beating. Results you'd expect from extracting a bad tooth rather than a twenty-inch metal spear.

We stood by and watched the cat for several minutes. Her vitals remained stable. I briefly peeked under the bandage on her abdominal wound. No gush of blood.

"I'm keeping that arrow," said Tony.

There was a sudden shift in the mood. The three of us went from a feeling of impending doom to a renewed sense of hope and pragmatism. We turned off the gas anesthetic and transferred the cat to a recovery cage. Cindy tucked the cat into a warm nest of blankets and hooked up an I.V. fluid pump. Dr. Tony began filling out a medical orders form. She'd get I.V. antibiotics three times a day and pain medication every six hours. Her weight would be checked daily, and her temperature checked four times a day.

Despite my temptation to stick around and see what happened next, I got ready to leave for home. Tony and I could re-hash our adventure another time. I'd learned early on in my career that every minute I stayed created another chance for me to get pulled back in. It was 8:45 in the evening. The last rays of daylight had vanished over two hours ago and I could barely make out the leafless trees outside in the unlit parking lot. I was due back at work the next morning for the twenty-four-hour Sunday emergency shift. There was a narrowing window of time to get home and still get some rest before my long shift tomorrow. I grabbed my belongings and headed out the door.

"Alrighty" I said. "I guess I'm headed home. Good luck with her. I hope she makes it. I'll see you tomorrow at eight."

As I drove home, I speculated on the odds of that cat still being alive in the morning. *Not too good*, I thought. If that arrow penetrated the cat's colon or small intestine, she would die of peritonitis (a bacterial infection of the abdomen). If she developed a blood clot in a major vessel, her circulation would be fatally compromised. If she had a nick or tear in her lungs, she'd develop pneumothorax (air leaking into the space between the lungs and the chest wall and that causes the lungs to collapse).

Under different circumstances, with a full medical facility and an CT machine, imaging of the damage might have preceded removing the arrow. Surgically opening her abdomen prior to pulling out the arrow would have allowed visualization of any damaged organs and provided the opportunity for repair and clean up any bacterial contamination. We hadn't done any of this. We didn't have the facilities, the time, or the budget to handle the case in an ideal manner. These compromises were commonplace in veterinary medicine.

It was a bright, clear day when I pulled into the frosted parking lot of Largis Vet Clinic the next morning. I was anxious to see if our Arrow Cat was still with us. I tried not to get my hopes up too high. It was 7:45 a.m. The large aluminum thermometer outside the large animal barn read twenty-seven degrees. Not for the first time, I pitied the poor souls who worked in these conditions. They were bundled up in thermals under their coveralls. Over their coveralls, most of them added a hoodie sweatshirt. Each breath created a cloud of condensation as they went about their duties. I waved hello as I walked past the barn and headed for the heated sanctuary of the small animal building.

My day's pack was abnormally full due to the need for a change of clothes, toiletries, and some sandwiches for the twenty-four-hour shift ahead of me. I dropped it next to my desk as I fully took in my partner. Tony was sitting at his desk with his head down onto his crossed arms. I thought he was asleep, but he lifted his head and gave me a groggy "Morning" when I scooted out my chair and took a seat. His brown hair was as rumpled as his soiled lab coat, along with a good start to a beard growing on his chin.

"Rough night?" I said.

"Yeah," he said. "I only got about an hour of sleep. I saw eight more emergencies after you left last night."

"Jeez. I'm glad I got out when I could. How's our cat with the arrow?"

"Believe it or not, that cat seems fine. We just gave her fluids, antibiotics, and pain meds. After surgery, she was pretty cold. Temp down to ninety-four degrees, so we put the Bair Hugger on her. She pretty much just slept all night."

A patient warming device that comes in handy occasionally, the Bair Hugger, blows heated air through small perforations in a thin cloth blanket.

"Wow, she's still alive? Amazing," I said. "I didn't want to get my hopes up."

"Yep," he said. "She doesn't consider getting skewered by an arrow too much of a big deal. She's wondering what all the fuss is about."

"Man, that's one tough cat," I said.

It would be my top priority to check on the Arrow Cat first thing, but right now I needed to relieve my partner in crime so he could leave. He looked exhausted.

Tony filled me in on the cases he admitted overnight, their status, and where we stood regarding communication with their human owners. During this morning handoff, I tried not to interrupt too much. He was worn out and needed to go home and sleep. In between slurps of coffee, I did ask a few clarifying questions.

"So what time are they picking up the dachshund with the bad back?" I asked.

"Should be around ten," he said. "I spoke to Dr. Katz at UC Davis and they're planning on doing surgery on him around noon."

This little dog was suffering from a prolapsed disk, which is quite common in dachshunds. He was in a lot of pain and couldn't use his hind legs. He needed surgery to remove the disk and fenestrate his vertebra. This wasn't a procedure we did at Largis.

"OK," I said. "We'll have him ready to go at ten. Is it OK for the mom and puppies over there to go home?"

Tony had done a 2 a.m. C-section on a bulldog with four puppies. They all seemed to be doing well smashed up against mom's belly competing for nipple space and slurping loudly. It reminded me of a litter of newborn pigs.

"I told the owners they could likely go home around noon," he said. "I figured that would give you time to look 'em over."

"Sounds good. What about this little Chihuahua in here? Are we sending him home?" I was referring to a little brown dog piled high with blankets. He was bundled in a cage near my right shoulder. And all I could clearly see was a tail hanging out. Tony told me how this poor little guy had been mauled by his German shepherd housemate and how it took over an hour to stitch him up in eight different places.

"That's Pedro," said Tony. "I told the Bexleys that he'd stay with us at least one more day. That dog is hurting *all* over. I'm also worried about infection. He had some pretty bad wounds. I'm back tomorrow morning so I can take over his care then."

"OK," I said. "Get the hell outta here. See ya tomorrow."

"Ten-four," he said and lumbered out the door headed to his car.

Thus began my next twenty-four hours. I was the only veterinarian on duty serving a community of fifty thousand people on a Sunday. Every emergency shift was stressful and hectic. It was never boring. Sometimes it was exhilarating. I always survived it. Most of my patients did too.

Around four that afternoon, Troy was back with another stray cat, this one with a foxtail in its left eye. He'd picked up the skinny black cat on the side of Swan Falls Road after a bicyclist saw the cat wandering around with its eye slammed shut. They'd called animal control. I was able to remove the foxtail without too much fuss. Its eye would be fine, but it would hurt for at least another few days. Scratches to the cornea are incredibly painful. He crated up the sedated kitty for the ride back to the county animal shelter.

"What happened to that cat that was shot with the arrow?" he asked.

"She's right behind you," I said, pointing at the stainless-steel cage right behind him. "She's hard to recognize without an arrow sticking out of her."

"That made quite a convenient little carry handle," he joked as he opened the cage door to look her over. "Wow," he said. "She's still a bit of a mess, but she's alive. I assumed she was a goner."

"She seems to be doing fine so far. She's just been lying there and sleeping for the past twenty hours. I can't say she's out of the woods yet. I'm still worried we could lose her to an infection."

"That's a damn tough cat," Troy said. "I've never seen anything quite like that before."

Coming from Troy that was a big statement. He'd seen some horrible things.

"Any luck finding her owner?" I asked.

"Nothing so far," he said. "I'll take some pictures of her and ask around the neighborhood where I found her."

"I hope you find the guy who did this and pull out his fingernails." I said, only semi-joking.

"Yeah, I know," he said. "People can do some pretty sick stuff."

Over the next twenty-four hours, Arrow Cat's tale and nickname became known by everyone at the clinic. For the next few days, she continued to gradually get better. Sunday evening, she started lifting her head and looking around. She was a sweet little creature who'd extend her head so you could rub her neck. She was amazingly trusting considering she had no idea where she was or what had happened.

Dr. Tony took over Arrow Cat's care on Monday morning. He'd shaved, his hair was combed, and he had on a fresh lab coat. I hardly recognized him. That afternoon she developed a fever of 103.2. Although this is mild for a cat, it was what we both dreaded. Tony added in a second injectable antibiotic to address her temperature spike and adjusted her treatment instructions. Despite the fever she still seemed to feel OK. She moved about more in her cage, even looking outside the cage to observe the goings-on. Tony changed her bandages, and they looked pretty clean.

On Tuesday morning, she started grooming herself. She began showing interest in food, wolfing down half a can of food that afternoon while I sat with her. My inner eight-year-old self flashed back to an old Wiley Coyote cartoon. Wiley was injured by a shotgun, leaving him full of holes. After all his running around, he was thirsty and drank a whole pitcher of lemonade. The lemonade drained out all the shotgun holes. With an inward grin, I found myself wondering if the canned food would start leaking out of the arrow-holes. She hadn't seen this cartoon and was unconcerned. She proceeded to use her front paws to clean off the particles stuck on her whiskers.

On Wednesday, her fever resolved. She was now eating everything put in front of her and drinking water on her own. We turned off her I.V. fluids.

Thursday morning, Tony and I bumped into one another in the hallway behind the exam rooms. I was going into room one and he was coming out of exam room three.

"Hey, Arrow Cat is doing great," I said. "She probably doesn't need to be here anymore. Dr. Freed wants to know what we're going to do with her."

He rubbed his chin and said, "Well, I talked to Troy yesterday. They still haven't found her owner. They also haven't located the bastard who shot her."

"That sucks," I said. "I guess we'll just have to send her back to the animal shelter and see if they can find her a new home. We can't keep her here much longer. She's doing great and I guarantee you her bill is well north of $300."

"I was telling Ashley about that cat," Tony said referencing his wife, a horse surgeon. "She's a sucker for orange cats and was super impressed by her resiliency. She said I should take her home and keep her. "

"Really? That would be great! You'd sure have a good story to tell. What about the dogs?"

Tony had a big goofy Labrador mix and a bigger, goofier German shepherd mix. I wasn't sure if they would tolerate a fuzzy orange cat in their house.

"We had to put our old cat Ruby to sleep last year," he said. "The dogs got along fine with Ruby, so I think it'll be OK."

"That's awesome. When are you going to take her?"

"Maybe tonight after work. I'll call Troy to make sure that's OK."

"I think he'll love it," I said.

Sure enough, that evening Tony tucked Arrow Cat into a beat-up borrowed clinic cat carrier and headed home. They had a long drive back to his house in Davis. I felt grateful knowing she was going to a good family instead of the animal shelter path of hits and misses. She'd had a horrible trauma and deserved a break. I was a little worried about how she'd get along with two large dogs. But with two licensed vets as pet owners, this deserving kitty was in good hands.

That Saturday, our shifts overlapped once again. Tony leaving, my arriving.

"Hey," I said. "How's the new cat situation working out? She hasn't managed to poke herself with any sharp objects?"

"She's doing great," he said. "She moved right in like she owned the place. The very first night, she walked over to the sofa and jumped up to take a nap. Then later, she went over to eat some leftover food from one of the dog dishes."

"Uh-oh. I bet the dogs didn't like that."

"They're staying well out of her way," he said. "I think they're scared shitless of her. A couple of times they went over to sniff her, and she stared them down and hissed. They backed away and got the hell out of there. She's only been with us for two days and she's already queen of the whole house. Those poor dumb dogs don't know what hit 'em."

"I guess when you've survived being impaled by an arrow, you're not inclined to put up with any crap."

"Evidently not."

Two weeks later, Tony and I had a rare occurrence: a day off work on the same day. We lived in the same town, and both of us enjoyed doing some amateur woodworking. Between the two of us, we had enough tools to build some rudimentary items. I owned a router, and he owned a table saw. He had a drill press, and I had a belt sander. You get the idea. We kept a healthy supply of Band-Aids on hand. It was also a thinly disguised excuse to drink some beer and complain about work. Today I was helping him build some new shelves in his garage. It was noon, and we were both standing in a pile of sawdust. The garage door was open and so was the door to the side yard. Tony's dogs were lying on the garage floor, enjoying the show. There's a lot of entertainment value in two veterinarians pretending they know how to operate power tools. In the middle of the activity, Tony's new cat wandered in the side door from the backyard.

"There she is now," said Tony. "She likes to hang out by the pool and hunt grasshoppers. I guess she's decided to come in to supervise the situation."

Both the dogs saw their new queen coming. They got up and moved to the opposite side of the garage.

I hadn't seen Arrow Cat since the day Tony took her home from the vet clinic. Now I could see her in her full glory: her fur was glossy orange with a few random creamy patches on her sides and face. The shaved parts on her chest and abdomen were filling in with a new growth of white fuzz. And her face was fuller than I remember with a haughty smirk of superiority that matched the confident swagger she displayed walking into the garage. She was getting a bit of a belly droop, but I kept this observation to myself. I know they were feeding her as much as she wanted out of sympathy for her awful trauma.

"Wow," I said. "She looks terrific. You can't tell that anything happened to her. And, the dogs sure get out of her way."

"Yeah," he said. "She pretty much rules the place. She's turned out to be a great cat. Ashley and I just love her."

"By the way, did you ever come up with a name for her? What do you call her?"

With a smirk he replied, "Cupid."

Cupid

Afterward by Dr. Tony Johnson:

I met Cupid on the worst day of her life, full of life-death drama. But her last day was one of peace, the kind every pet parent hopes for.

She was brought in by Animal Control like a pig on a spit, a twenty-inch arrow pierced through the length of her body. After Jeff and I removed the arrow and spayed her, she lived a happy life for another sixteen years. She moved several times with my family. She spent time as an indoor cat, an outdoor cat, lived in a log cabin, and lived a life of suburban comfort. She saw three children born and grow up, and a host of other pets come and go in our household.

As an ER vet in Portland, Oregon, I saved and adopted another cat who was a victim of human cruelty. This poor cat was set on fire by some miscreant (who was caught and brought to justice). My wife and I named him Crispy, and he became Cupid's best buddy. They'd often be found curled up together, head to tail, in a cardboard box, or on the patio in the sun.

Later in life, many moves later, Cupid's favorite spot was in an old, beat-up easy chair in our basement. The chair came with the house. It was missing patches of fabric and stuffing and was a constant eyesore. It looked like a frat boy's hair after a three-day bender. We didn't have the heart to toss the chair because Cupid loved it so much. Often, I found her sleeping on it, curled in a ball, fully blissed out. I liked to think she was dreaming of firing arrows back at whomever shot her.

As she entered her late teens, Cupid made the basement her kingdom and joined us less and less often upstairs. One day, my brother-in-law was visiting. It was his first time in this house, and I was showing him around. We got to the basement, and I pointed out the chair and its ginger-colored occupant.

"And that's Cupie, sleeping in her favorite chair," I said. "C'mon, Cupie, say hi to Uncle Ben."

I reached down to ruffle her fur and expected to hear her usual throaty "mrrrowww," but my hand touched unmoving muscle and bone. She'd died peacefully in her sleep, curled up in her favorite chair. In my thirty years of veterinary medicine, I've found, unfortunately, this to be exceedingly rare. Cupid left this world in the way most pet owners pray for, and I'm so grateful.

RIP, Cupid.

Dr. Tony Johnson

CHAPTER 4

Up on the Roof

I was in the midst of a puppy production line, and I was only half-way through.

"But, Dr. Schmidt, they've just *got* to be one hundred percent *all* rottweiler," insisted Mrs. Lewin. "I was there *in person* when Queeny mated with Thor."

The roly-poly puppies were climbing all over one another inside a towel-lined laundry basket that sat at Mrs. Lewin's feet. There were nine of the hamster-sized balls of fur presented for my inspection. We were in exam room number three at Largis Vet Clinic. Glass vaccine vials and plastic syringes were scattered over the stainless-steel exam table. Queeny, the mother of the litter, was eyeing me suspiciously, visibly worried about her pups. I was hoping she didn't decide to take a chunk out of my leg.

There were two pups on the table. One I was examining and vaccinating, with the other "on deck," in the hands of my vet tech Sarah. She was struggling to weigh the squirming pup and get its temperature before passing it over to me. I had an hour to examine nine puppies and I was only done with four. I glanced at my watch; it was already 9:30. I did a quick calculation. About seven minutes per puppy. That didn't give me a lot of time for small talk. I was already behind schedule but needed to properly address her questions.

"I understand Mrs. Lewin, but what I'm trying to say is that just because you saw her breed with a purebred rottweiler doesn't necessarily mean that's the *only* dog she mated with. She was in heat for what . . . three to four days. Did you keep her inside the house with you that entire time?"

Puppy basket

"Well, no," she admitted. "Queeny sleeps outside, but the yard is *completely* fenced in. She has a big dog igloo out there to keep warm. So, you're saying other boy dogs might have snuck in there?"

"Yes, I'm afraid so. It's certainly possible," I said. I felt a little embarrassed giving a *birds and bees* talk to this fully grown woman, but here I was. I gently placed puppy number four back in the box with the others. It burrowed in with the others and disappeared into the pile of pups. Sarah passed over the next tiny brown and black puppy. She had a subtle smirk on her face as she was clearly enjoying my discomfort.

"When dogs are in heat, they are not very picky about their choice of partner. If she was outside most of the time, and there were any intact male dogs in the neighborhood, it's almost a certainty that she had more than one partner. Male dogs go *bonkers* when there's a female in heat. They'll dig under fences and chew through gates. I've seen them really hurt themselves attempting to get to a female."

Mrs. Lewin was a small woman and she seemed even smaller now as she sat huddled at the corner of the church pew that Largis used for exam room benches. She wore black pants and a beige blouse with a frumpy brown and red plaid shawl wrapped around her shoulders. A brown beanie and round black-framed glasses highlighted her expression: mouth agape, horrified at this newfound fact. She obviously didn't want to be known as the owner of the neighborhood's sluttiest dog. Plus, she'd been counting on the money for months: a purebred litter of rottweiler pups would cash in for some serious dough. She was definitely not liking where this conversation was headed.

"But both Queeny and Thor are fully papered by the American Kennel Club Dr. Schmidt," she said, hoping this fact would change reproductive biology.

"Yeah. And they're both fine specimens," I said. "But some of these puppies just don't really look like purebred rottweilers. So, unless your fence is one hundred percent horny dog–proof, you probably have a mixed litter of pups." As I said this, I looked down at the puppy in my arms. It had a white blaze down the middle of its face and blue eyes. *Siberian husky, maybe*?

"What are you saying exactly?" she said. My news was throwing a stick into the spokes of her whole plan.

"Well," I said. "In theory, if a female dog has a litter of five puppies, and she mated with five different males, each puppy could have a different father."

"Nooooo," said Mrs. Lewin in disbelief. "You're saying some of these puppies might be Thor's and some could belong to the Beagle next door?"

"Yes, and the husky down the street and the border collie up the road," I said.

"Well, how can we figure out which are which?" she asked.

"You really can't, I'm afraid. (Noting that this conversation predated doggie DNA testing.) You'll just have to wait for them to grow up a bit more and see which ones look like rotties and which don't."

"But I've already accepted deposits for five of the puppies. I was going to sell them for fifteen hundred apiece. Now what am I going to do?"

"I'm sorry Mrs. Lewin. That's a tough one. I think the only thing you can do is be honest with the buyers and tell them you can't guarantee they are one hundred percent purebred dogs. They all look like healthy puppies. I'm sure they will all turn out to be great dogs. Maybe they'll still be willing to pay full price for the ones that appear to be all rottweiler. But I'm pretty sure they won't be able to get them A.K.C. certified."

"Jesus, Mary, and Joseph," she exclaimed. "This is a disaster."

"Yeah, I'm sorry," I said.

When we finished vaccinating all the puppies, I stepped back and thought, *this is a good-looking group.* I kind of enjoyed the puppy variety pack. Each one would be a little surprise. We left the exam room and closed the door behind us. Sarah had a devilish sense of humor and couldn't resist her opportunity to twist the knife a little. "That was a really good sex talk you gave in there, Dr. Schmidt," she said with a grin. "Maybe you'll be invited as a guest lecturer at the local high school."

"God help me," I said. "I think I aged three years during that conversation."

As Sarah and I walked towards the treatment room, Dr. Tony Johnson burst out the door coming the other way. I'd never seen him this panicked. His hair was disheveled and one of his shirt buttons was undone. There was a yellow stain on the left side of his white lab coat. *Urine?*

"Have you guys seen a calico cat come this way?" he asked. He was out of breath.

"No," I replied. "We just came out of room three. We've been in there for the past hour. Why? What's going on?"

"Oh my God," said Tony. "We were trying to take X-rays on a cat with an injured leg. Cindy and I were holding her down to get a lateral view when she went ballistic. She bit Cindy on the arm and peed all over the front of my lab coat. She managed to break loose and jumped on top of one of the cabinets. I grabbed a step ladder and climbed up there to get her. But, when I went to grab her, she jumped down and hid under the X-ray machine. Cindy got a broom and was using the handle to shoo her out. I almost had her when Dr. Zappan opened the door, and she darted out. Now we don't know where in the hell she's at. Half the clinic is looking for her. Keep your eyes peeled."

"Uh, OK. We will," I said.

Renegade cats are the bane of a vet's existence. Unfortunately, cats getting loose in vet clinics is not uncommon. Cats are strong, fast, and flexible little predators. When they get startled, they can panic. Even a calm kitty will sometimes freak out if a dog suddenly lunges or there's a loud noise. Some of the worst injuries I've had were from cats that panicked in the middle of an exam. Once a cat gets loose, the game is afoot. They can scamper high into the rafters or squish into tiny spaces. On one occasion, a frightened cat got away from me and found a three-by-three-inch opening between the cabinet and the floor. It took me twenty minutes with a crowbar to deconstruct the cabinet to get her out. The cat's owner was not amused.

Sarah and I continued back to the treatment room. When we got there, the place was in a tizzy. Veterinarians and techs scurried about looking for the renegade cat. Cindy had a penlight and was on her belly looking under the cabinets. Dr. Zappan was up on a step ladder looking on top of the metal cages. I saw Jason, one of the vet assistants, upend the laundry basket in case she dove in there.

"Jeff," said Dr. Zappan. "Watch out. There's a loose cat running around here somewhere."

"Yeah, I heard," I said. "Dr. Johnson was telling me. What's this cat's name?"

"I think it's Spooky," said Dr. Zappan as he peeked his head over the rim of the cages.

"Spooky? Really?" I said. "That's apropos. Did anyone see where she went?"

"She darted out past me when I opened the X-ray door. After that no one saw where she went. She's hiding around here somewhere. Keep your eyes peeled."

This was the second time in less than a minute that I'd been told to keep my eyes peeled. Now I *was* getting paranoid. My gaze wandered around the large treatment area. It was about the size of the showroom at an auto dealership. The ceilings were ten feet high. It was strewn with medical equipment. There were a *bazillion* places where a scared cat could hide. I entered the room cautiously. At any moment, I expected a crazed cat to launch from a shelf and land on my head.

It didn't look like they needed any new seekers for their game of hide-and-seek. That job was well covered. So, I went over to one of the second-tier cages and peeked inside. Charlie Brown, an all-white cat was in there contentedly grooming himself. He was nonplussed with all the activity going on outside his cage. That was a good sign. He'd come in the day before, dehydrated with a high fever. He was suffering from an infected bite wound. He was already looking a lot better and could probably go home later that day.

"Have you guys tried calling olly olly oxen free?" I asked sarcastically. It was easy for me to be a smart ass. It wasn't my cat that was missing. Looking back, I shouldn't have said it. *It didn't help.*

I exited the side door of the treatment room and headed across the reception area towards the doctor's office. Tony was coming towards me again from a completely different direction. He must have circled the entire clinic. He'd buttoned up his shirt and had on a fresh lab coat.

"Did they find her yet?" he asked, wide-eyed.

"Nope, I don't think so."

"Crap. If we can't find that cat, I'm dead."

I was only at my desk for five minutes before Sarah found me again. She was my tech for the morning, and it was her job to keep me moving.

"Your next appointment is ready," she said. "It's a cat named Sophie. She's got a sore leg. I think it's just a badly ingrown toenail."

"OK, be right there," I said. "Did they find Spooky yet?"

"I don't think so," said Sarah. "Poor Dr. Johnson. He's really stressed out."

A few minutes later, I finished writing up the chart for the nine basket puppies and headed back towards the chain of exam rooms. As I walked through the treatment room, I noticed that the search had expanded into the surgery area. People were banging open cabinets, and the surgery prep and the laundry area were being turned upside down. I wanted to join in and help but I still had a full appointment schedule. It would only make matters worse if we had a lobby full of angry clients.

At 12:30, I finished the last of my morning appointments. I walked into the break room and headed to the fridge. Dr. Johnson was sitting on an old yellow garage-sale sofa pushed into the corner of the room. His hands covered his forehead, and his elbows were on his knees.

"Still no luck?" I asked.

"No," he said. "We've been looking all over the place. I don't know how in the hell we could have lost her *inside* the clinic. It's a friggin' disaster."

"Does Dr. Freed know about this, yet?" I asked.

"Yeah, he does. Dr. Freed said he's positive we'll find her."

"What about Spooky's owners? Do they know she's missing?"

"No. Not yet," said Tony. "They weren't planning on picking her up until six. So, we still have some time to find her before they show up. I'm just praying she pops out somewhere before then."

"I'm going to get something to eat real quick," I said. "Then I'll go look around for her. Has anyone looked in the upstairs offices yet?"

"I don't think so," said Tony with a sigh of resignation. "I don't think she could get up there. She'd have to go all the way down the hallway with no one seeing her. And the doors up there are almost always shut."

"Yeah, it's not likely. But stranger things have happened. I'll go look around up there just in case."

"Thanks," he said. "I'm just taking a quick break to have a nervous breakdown. I'll head out soon to look again."

"Try not to worry too much," I said. "We'll find her."

But we didn't. All through the lunch break, employees searched the clinic from top to bottom. The receptionists especially adored Dr. Johnson and were dismayed to see him so upset. Most of them gave up their breaks so they could search for Spooky off-the-clock. My hunt in the upstairs office was fruitless. At 2 p.m. I had to begin my afternoon appointments. I'd run out of time and was also running out of ideas. Largis employees were now beginning to look in the parking lot. The large animal crew was notified, and they were scouring the large animal barn. No one saw Spooky get outside, but it was possible, and we were getting desperate.

My 4:30 appointment for Murphy the Irish setter was a no-show. This gave me an unexpected thirty minutes to make some overdue phone calls. Dr. Freed was sitting at his desk next to mine. He'd just come back from a ranch call for fifteen lamas. He wore grimy blue coveralls and calf-high rubber boots with his customary SPAM cap on top of his head. He was filling out fifteen lab forms for fifteen individual fecal samples sitting in plastic containers on his desk.

"They haven't found that cat yet?" I asked. I knew the answer, so I'm not sure why I asked. I'm sure Dr. Freed was not pleased about the course of the day's events. It did not reflect well on him. It was his clinic, so everything that happened there was his ultimate responsibility.

Dr. Freed looked up from the paperwork on his desk. His grim expression made me wince. "No, they haven't. We're running out of places to look. She's probably still in the building somewhere, just in a really good hiding spot. We're wasting a lot of manpower hunting for that damn cat. We may just have to put out some food overnight and wait until she gets hungry."

Just then Tony joined us in the office. He looked terrible.

"We still haven't found Spooky," he said. "The owners will be here in an hour to get her. They don't know she's missing yet. How do you think I should handle this, Dr. Freed?"

"Just call them right now and get it over with," he said. "Be honest and let them know we've turned the whole place upside down looking for her."

"OK, I'll do that. Here goes nothing."

I didn't envy Tony for that phone call. If you work the counter at Dairy Queen and lose an order for a chili cheese dog, that's embarrassing. Losing someone's cherished pet was a catastrophe. This was one of those times where being a veterinarian really sucked. I'd been in some bad spots before and knew how awful it felt, but I'd never quite been in this predicament. I didn't start my own calls in favor of soaking up this spectacle. Roadside traffic accidents had less drama than the scene unfolding before me.

Tony's desk was right behind mine. He picked up the phone handset like it weighed fifty pounds. He dialed each digit meticulously and waited for someone to pick up.

"Hello. Mr. Ramsey? Uhhh . . . hello. This is Dr. Johnson from Largis Vet Clinic. I'm afraid I've got some bad news for you. We lost your cat. Yes . . . yeah . . . you heard me right. She's lost. I'm very sorry. She got loose when we were taking her X-rays. She ran under the X-ray table. Just as we were getting her out from under there, someone opened the door, and she ran out into the treatment room. No one saw where she went from there. The entire staff has been looking for her for the past five hours. I don't know . . . I feel terrible. Uhm . . . yes . . . he's here. Just a minute."

Dr. Johnson put the call on hold and held the receiver up to his chest. "Dr. Freed. I'm sorry. Mr. Ramsey is asking to talk to you."

Dr. Freed's head drooped down so his chin was touching his chest and he let out a big sigh.

"Is that Randall Ramsey?" he asked.

"Yeah," said Tony. "Randall and Donna are Spooky's owners."

"Yeah. I've known them for a long time," said Dr. Freed. "I used to take care of his horses. Our kids went to school together. OK, I'll manage it from here."

Dr. Freed was only on the phone for a minute. I didn't hear any yelling or screaming, so I figured that was a good sign. There were a lot of *I'm sorrys*, and *we'll keep looking*, before it was over.

When he hung up, he looked over at Tony, who'd been staring at him the whole time.

"Well, I guess that went OK," he said. "He was still shocked. And he's still got to tell his wife about this. That's not going to be fun. Donna wears the pants in the family, and I'll probably still get a royal ass chewing from her. I can't forget the time some poor sucker backed over her flower bed. I doubt they'll sue us, though. They're not those kinds of folks."

"I'm sorry I put ya in that situation, Dr. Freed," said Tony. "I guess maybe I could have handled that better."

"Yeah, maybe," said Dr. Freed. He paused for a few moments and glanced out the window to the right of his desk. With a thoughtful expression, he turned back to face us. He removed the SPAM cap from his head and ran his fingers through his hair. With the cap off, random rebel clumps of grey hair sprung up from his head. It would have been comical except for the stern look on his face. "Let me tell you a little story . . ."

There're these two neighbors. Let's call them Dick and Tom. They've known each other for years. They help each other out on yard projects and fence mending and such. At one point, Dick and his wife, Wanda, are planning to go on vacation to Hawaii. It's their thirtieth anniversary and the trip has been in the works for a while. The problem is that they've got this older cat, Trixie. She's seventeen and has some kidney issues. She's still pretty frisky but they're afraid the stress of spending twelve days in a kennel will be too much for her. Dick explains the situation to Tom, and Tom (being a very generous guy) agrees to take care of Trixie while they're out of town.

So, Dick and Wanda pack up their shorts and suntan lotion and head for the airport. They leave the house stocked with cat food and give Tom instructions on how to take care of Trixie. As they pull out of the driveway, Tom's there to wave goodbye and assure them he'll take good care of Trixie.

For the first couple of days, everything went fine. Dick and his wife are in Hawaii drinking Mai Tais and getting a suntan. Trixie seems OK and is eating her food. On the evening of the third day, Tom notices she hadn't finished all her food from breakfast. When he goes back the next morning to check on her, he finds her stone-cold dead in the middle of the living room floor. This isn't good. It's 8 a.m. in California, so 6 a.m. in Hawaii. Poor Tom feels terrible, but he makes the dreaded call and gets connected to Dick and Wanda's hotel room. The phone call wakes them up.

"Hello, hello. Dick. This is your neighbor, Tom."

"Yeah. Hello, Tom," Dick says groggily. He's still trying to remember where he is.

"Dick. I'm very sorry to tell you this, but your cat Trixie is *dead*," says Tom.

Dick sits bolt upright in bed. Suddenly he is wide awake. His eyes pop open. His heart's pounding in his chest and he scares the bejesus out of his wife when he screams, "*Holy shit*! Oh my God. Trixie is dead? Oh, no. What happened?"

It takes Dick and Wanda a few hours to calm down. Eventually they realize nothing can be done for poor Trixie. They decide they might as well stay in Hawaii and make the best of what's left of their vacation.

When they get back home, Tom is in the driveway waiting for them. He feels terrible and apologizes profusely. While Wanda unpacks the car, Dick pulls Tom aside to speak with him.

"Look, Tom," he says. "It's not your fault Trixie died. She was old and was not going to make it much longer anyway. But I sure wish you would have broken the news differently. You almost gave me and the missus a heart attack. Let me give you some advice."

Dick continued, "Tom, when you must tell people really, really bad news, it's best to break it to them gradually and slowly. So, you found Trixie dead and you knew we weren't going to be home for another week. You could have just called and said something like you noticed she's not eating all her food. This would give us time to get used to the idea that things weren't going well. Then maybe the next day, you could call and say you're having a tough time finding her. We would be worried, but at least we could adjust our expectations. Then you could give me a call and say you did manage to find her, but she was up on the roof, and you couldn't get her down. Maybe, on the third or fourth call, you could tell me that she passed away. At least then it wouldn't be such a shock."

"Yeah, I get it," said Tom. "I should have handled that better. I've never been very good at this kind of stuff. I'm sorry I was so abrupt."

"That's OK, buddy," said Dick as he clapped him on the shoulder. "I appreciate all your help."

Ten years go by. Dick and Tom live in neighborly harmony. It was coming up on Dick and Wanda's fortieth wedding anniversary. This time they decide they'd like to celebrate in the Bahamas. One problem though. Two weeks before the trip, Wanda's mother moves in with them. She's in her eighties and can't fully care for herself.

Dick goes over to Tom's house to lament the problem. "Tom, Wanda and I have been planning this vacation to the Bahamas for a year, but now her mother's moved in with us. She's fairly healthy, but she can't drive and gets tired easily. She just needs some help with groceries and laundry and such."

Well, Tom got the hint and stepped right up to the plate. "Hey, neighbor. I don't mind helping out with your mother-in-law for a week while you're gone. Why don't you two lovebirds go enjoy yourselves and I'll do the shopping and laundry for her? What's her name?"

"Thanks a lot for the offer," says Tom. "Her name is Gladys. Let me check with Wanda and see what she thinks."

Dick's not sure if Wanda will agree to this plan. But they've already put down a substantial deposit on the trip. And Gladys did seem spritely for her age. They both agree to have Tom take care of her while they enjoy their vacation.

Dick and Wanda pack up their swimming suits and sunhats and head for the airport. They leave detailed instructions for Tom on how to take care of Gladys. As they pull out of the driveway, Tom's there to wave goodbye.

For the first few days, everything was great. Dick and Wanda are in the Bahamas drinking Piña Coladas. Gladys is eating her oatmeal and watching *The Price is Right*. On the morning of the fourth day, the phone rings in Dick and Wanda's hotel room. Dick sleepily answers the phone.

"Hi, Dick? This is your neighbor, Tom. Uhm . . . Gladys is up on the roof."

Dr. Freed finished the story, leaned forward in his chair, and sat looking at us with his elbows perched on his knees. His glasses were smeared with fingerprints and his unruly hat-hair was competing with his Albert Einstein eyebrows for bragging rights today. Tony and I sat there in an uncomfortable silence. *Was that it . . . the end of the story?* I looked over at Tony to read his expression. The events of the day had clearly sapped him. His hands were deep in the pockets of his lab coat, and he leaned back in his office chair as if he didn't have the energy to hold himself up. I didn't understand. . . . Was the joke supposed to make Tony feel better? I'm pretty sure it didn't work.

Tony finally broke the silence. "So, I guess I should have delivered the bad news to Mr. Ramsey a little more delicately, huh?" said Tony.

"Yeah, a little," said Dr. Freed.

No one could find Spooky. One day turned into two days. Two turned into four. The clinic staff was emotionally exhausted from looking. By this time, we assumed that she somehow got outside and ran off. Another week went by. Tony felt personally responsible for the lost cat. He was normally gregarious and full of life. Now he was just going through the motions of the day. Dr. Freed updated the Ramseys every day on the search. He kept expecting a court summons notice or an inquiry letter from the state veterinary board. *How could a cat escape the X-ray room and completely disappear?* It was confounding.

By day thirteen-PS (Post-Spooky), there was a general feeling of hopelessness about her: if she hadn't been found by now, she wasn't going to be found. Everyone needed to come to grips with this fact. It was time to get back to the day-to-day job of caring for all the other animals that needed our help.

I was in exam room five with my 9 a.m., Mr. Harkland and his dog Sparky. Mr. Harkland was a gregarious older gentleman. He always had a grin at the corner of his mouth that gave the impression he had a secret. I always enjoyed his visits. Sparky was a fluffy black-and-white dog weighing fifty pounds. He had a long nose and brown eyes. He looked like a cross between a border collie and a chow chow. He was fairly quiet and reserved, but although he bore his vet visits with stoicism, his eyes kept darting furtively to the door. It was obvious he just wanted to get the hell outta there.

"So, Mr. Harkland, it sounds like you're worried about Sparky. What's going on?"

"He just doesn't seem to feel that great," replied Mr. Harkland. "He moves kinda slow and isn't eating as well as normal. He seems like he might be urinating more as well."

"What makes you think he's urinating more? Is he peeing in the house?"

"No, no. He's not going in the house but when we're out on our walks he sometimes just stops mid-stride and pees right there in the middle of the sidewalk. He never used to do that. Do you think he could have diabetes?"

"Yeah, I guess that's possible," I said. "Diabetes will make a dog more tired, and it certainly makes them pee more. It would be a good idea to get a blood sample and a urine sample to send to the lab. That may help us out with the diagnosis."

"Oh, I've already got a urine sample," he said. "In fact, I've been getting a fresh sample every day for the past three days and saving it in the fridge. I'm pretty sure it's diabetes because when I taste the urine, it seems pretty sweet to me."

I tried to keep a neutral "I'm a doctor and nothing surprises me" look on my face, but I'm not sure Mr. Harkland bought it. I looked down at Sparky, partially just to disguise my astonishment. Sparky was looking directly back at me. His expression seemed to say, *See what I have to deal with*? I looked back at Mr. Harkland, not quite sure how to proceed. Finally, I asked, "You've been *tasting* his urine?"

"Yeah," he said. "I read somewhere that with diabetes they lose a lot of sugar in their urine. So, I started tasting it to check. It seems to me like the urine is sweeter each day."

"Wow. Well, you're a very dedicated dog owner. That sure sounds like diabetes. Why don't you give me those urine samples? I'll take Sparky to the back and find a tech to help me get a blood sample."

Mr. Harkland reached into the breast pocket of his flannel shirt and handed over the three urine samples, precariously stored in small Ziplock bags. He passed over the end of Sparky's leash and we headed out of the exam room and back towards the treatment area. When Sparky and I arrived, we were greeted with a cacophony of noise. There was an anxious bloodhound baying from its kennel. A Siberian Husky was waking up from anesthesia and yipping in dysphoria. Two techs were trying to wrangle an angry cat for a blood sample. It was chaos. There must have been six different things all happening at once. It was much too chaotic for poor Sparky. He was already on edge and the frenetic noise and activity were making him panicky.

"Hey, Debbie. Can you please help me get some bloodwork on this dog?" I shouted over the din. "I'm taking him into the X-ray room to get some peace and quiet."

Debbie nodded and gave me a thumbs-up from across the room to acknowledge that she heard me. I guided Sparky into the X-ray room and shut the door. Immediately the volume was reduced to a mild background noise. What a relief.

A minute later the door opened, and Debbie joined me.

"So, what are we doing, getting blood?" she asked.

"Yep," I said. "This is Sparky, Mr. Harkland's dog. He thinks the dog may be diabetic."

"What makes him think that?" she asked as she busied herself gathering up a needle, syringe, and two blood collection tubes.

"He's been drinking the dog's urine for the past three days. He thinks the urine tastes sugary."

Debbie stopped in her tracks. "What the heck? You're kidding me, right? He's not really drinking the urine, is he?"

"Well, more like sipping it, I guess." I was enjoying seeing the same shock on her face that I'd just experienced myself a few minutes ago.

"Wow," she said. "Just when you think you've heard it all . . . OK. You hold him and I'll get the blood sample."

I was hunched over behind Sparky, holding him between my legs to keep him still. Debbie was knelt on the floor directly in front of him carefully drawing a blood sample when I distinctly heard some creaking noises from the ceiling over my head. I wanted to look up, but I'd risk losing my grip and having to start over. Debbie heard it too. I could see her eyes briefly shift upward by the distraction. It sounded like one of the suspended acoustic ceiling tiles was cracking. She couldn't move either. Just a . . . few . . . more . . . seconds. Whew! All done. We were able to draw eight milliliters of blood from Sparky's left jugular vein. I used my fingers to hold pressure over the puncture and Debbie deftly transferred the blood into the collection tubes. I stood up and arched my back to stretch. Sparky gave a little shake of relief. Then we all heard a loud crack. Directly overhead, a ceiling tile had split into several pieces and opened downwards. I stood frozen in astonishment as a calico cat paratrooped down from the ceiling. She yowled in fear as she dropped six feet down to the X-ray table. She landed safely, legs splayed in a pile of dust and broken ceiling tiles. A fine white particle mist hung in the air. The four of us, myself, Debbie, Sparky, and the cat that fell from the sky, stood there stunned for a moment, trying to figure out what had just happened.

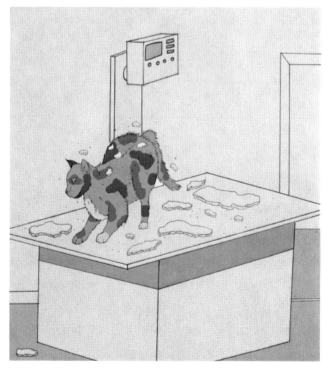

Spooky

"Jesus Christ!" exclaimed Debbie.

Sparky ran to the corner of the room to get as far away as possible from the alien cat invasion.

I stood there stunned, staring at the cat. *What the hell just happened?* Then it dawned on me. This was the cat the entire clinic had been looking for the past two weeks. In an adrenaline-charged moment, I lunged forward and grabbed her by the scruff of the neck. Again, she howled in fear. But I was damn sure NOT going to let this cat get loose again. Spooky struggled a little, but not as much as expected. She was weakened from not eating for two weeks. With one hand gripping her scruff and the other wrapped around her body, I ran out of the X-ray room and threw her in one of the metal cat cages. I slammed the latch down with a clatter. Then I checked the latch a second time. Spooky wasn't getting away this time.

After securing the rebel cat, my first thought was to call Tony. He'd been worried sick for the past two weeks. I knew it was wearing on him. He wasn't working that day, so I dialed his home number. My heart was still pounding in my ears.

"Hey, Tony, this is Jeff from work," I said, trying to sound calm.

"Hey, Jeff, what's up?" he said with a yawn. It sounded like I might have woken him up.

"I found your cat," I said.

"You found Spooky?" he said excitedly. He sure wasn't groggy now. "Where in the hell was she?"

"I was in the X-ray room drawing blood from a dog and she fell through from the ceiling," I told him. "Evidently, she was walking around on top of the ceiling tile when it gave way. I guess she's been up there the whole time. I don't know how in the world she got up there in the first place."

"The top of our storage cabinets are only inches from the ceiling," he said. "That's where she went initially when we first lost her. If she got up there, she could push one of those tiles up and get inside the ceiling."

"Yeah, I guess that makes sense," I said. "So, she really *was* inside the clinic the whole time. Poor thing. She must have been starving up there. Maybe there were some juicy mice or something for her to eat."

"How does she look?" he asked.

"Not too bad," I replied. "Maybe a bit skinny, but I've never seen her before so I can't compare."

"Do you want to call the Ramseys?" I asked. "If you give me a sec, I can get you their phone number."

"Yes, please," he said. "That goddamn cat took years off my life. At least I can have the satisfaction of letting them know she's OK. Does Dr. Freed know yet?"

"No. I called you first. I'll call him right after I get you that number."

"Oh, my goodness, Jeff. Thanks a million. What a flipping relief. I owe you a case of beer, my friend."

"I didn't do much," I said. "She practically fell into my lap."

I got the phone number for the Ramseys and passed it on to Tony. Then I called Dr. Freed to fill him in.

"See, I told you all along we'd find that cat," he said.

"Yeah, you were right. And she really was *up on the roof.*"

Author's note: It turned out that Sparky didn't have diabetes. He had a bladder infection. This would cause him to feel bad and urinate more frequently. He was successfully treated with a course of antibiotics. I'm not sure why it would make his urine taste sweet, and I never had the guts to try it.

CHAPTER 5

Bury 'Em Deep

Buck didn't look so good. He walked in the front door of the clinic under his own power, but just barely. His head was down, and he moved with excruciating slowness. Drool leaked from the corners of his mouth. He was dirty and smelly. The sixty-five-pound Australian shepherd was my one o'clock appointment, and I was immediately taken aback by his appearance.

I watched the dog as his owner, Mr. Hadley, coaxed him into the exam room. He made it about five feet past the door and plopped down with an audible grunt. He was breathing OK. Why was he moving so slow? Was he in pain? Was he drugged? I did a quick assessment of his heart and lungs. He sounded fine. I had to lift his head off the floor to look into his eyes and mouth. His gum color was normal, so his circulatory system was functional. His eyes were clear, no evidence of jaundice.

Mr. Hadley was a local rancher, a small, slender man wearing a long-sleeved Western shirt, jeans, cowboy boots, and a big belt buckle. He also sported a big tan cowboy hat. He looked like the type of chap who would be perfectly comfortable riding a horse all day or mending fences in the pasture till the cows came home. I'd met him a few times in the past for routine vet care. He was soft spoken, respectful, and didn't usually mince words. I liked the guy. He had a first name, of course, but I didn't know it. He seemed like the type of man you should address as mister.

"Hi, Mr. Hadley. How's it going?" I reached out to shake his hand. He returned the handshake with the rough calloused hands of a guy who works hard for a living.

"Hello, Dr. Schmidt," he said in a gravelly voice. "I'm doing OK, I guess. But there's sumthin wrong with my dog."

"He looks pretty dopey to me. Any idea what's going on?"

"I'm not sure," he said. "I was a little concerned about him last night. He just seemed extra tired. But today he's worse. He ate his food this morning, but he had to lie down next to his bowl to do it. That's definitely not like him. I had to lift him up into the truck to come over here."

"Does he seem in pain to you?"

"Nope, not really. Just like he's really tired or drunk."

"Have you seen any vomiting or diarrhea?"

"Nope," replied Mr. Hadley.

"Remind me again. How old is he?"

"He's only around four years old. He's one of the best sheep-herding dogs I've ever had."

What the heck would make this young, normally vigorous dog act so dopey? I started building a mental checklist of rule-outs.

"Do you have any type of drugs, chemicals, poisons that he might have gotten into?" I asked.

"Well, I do keep a few boxes of rat poison in the back corners of the barn, but I built plywood boxes to contain them so the dogs and cats can't get to 'em."

Alarm bells went off in my head. Rodenticide toxicity was a frequent problem at this practice. A lot of the locals used warfarin or related products to control the mice and rat population on their properties. The poison was mixed in with a tasty bait that was very appetizing for dogs. They would go to extreme measures to get to it once they got a whiff of it. These types of poisons interfere with the blood's ability to clot. Within two to three days of ingesting the poison, rodents would bleed to death internally, mainly into their lungs. The same thing would happen to a dog. The good news was that it was usually easy to treat. The antidote was vitamin K. If you caught the poisoning early enough, you'd give a hefty injection of the yellowish vitamin solution that would reverse the process. Then you'd send the patient home with thirty to sixty days of vitamin K pills. It was one of those treatments that made the vet look like a real hero, so I was quietly hoping this was the answer to Buck's woes.

I explained all of this to Mr. Hadley. "Even though you took some precautions with the rat bait, some dogs really love the stuff. They'll do almost anything to get to it. We see quite a few cases here. Let's just test for that first before we do anything else."

"Sure," he said. "Can we do it right now?"

"You bet. I'll be right back."

Mr. Hadley took a seat on the wooden church pew that served as an exam room bench. He stretched his legs out in front of him, obviously prepping himself for a long wait.

I left the exam room and scoured the hallway for a helper. "Cindy, can you come help me in room three?" I said when I spotted her at the end of the hallway. "I have a dog in there that may have eaten rat poison. I just want to do a quick ACT on him."

"Sure. I'll be right there," Cindy replied cheerfully.

I ducked into the treatment area and pulled out the drawer where we kept our blood tubes. The activated clotting tubes (ACT) weren't used very often and were stored in the very back of the drawer. I pulled the purple- and red-topped tubes forward so I could reach the plastic baggy with the ACT tubes. They are transparent plastic tubes with a gray rubber stopper. Each held a loose gray powder at the bottom of the tube holding diatomaceous earth: a powder that caused normal blood to clot in less than two minutes. I grabbed a tube and syringe and headed back to the exam room. Cindy met me there. As she held Buck with her left arm around his neck, her right hand gripped down on his foreleg to raise up the cephalic vein on the top of his leg. She tucked her chin down firmly on the top of his head to help hold him still. I poked his vein and drew out two milliliters of blood. While she held off the vein, I injected the blood into the ACT tube. Once the blood was in the tube, I rocked it back and forth a couple of times and carefully stuck the tube in the left side of my mouth. I then looked at the second hand of my watch to mark the start time for the test.

Cindy looked over at me, wrinkled her nose, and made a "gross" face. She didn't approve of my "keeping the tube warm" method. It was a clean piece of plastic, and it didn't bother me, but some people found this practice distasteful. My colleague Dr. Zappan had taught me this little trick, and it was a good one. I did it not only to keep the tube warm, which was necessary to run the test properly, but to allow a hands-free way to keep the tube handy while doing other things. In this circumstance, it gave me time to write some quick notes into Buck's chart.

I checked my watch. At thirty seconds I took the tube out of my mouth and rocked it a few more times. The blood was still liquid. No clotting yet. I stuck it back in my mouth and went back to writing. With Buck's needle puncture safely clotted, Cindy released her hold on his leg and excused herself to go help the other vets. I checked my watch again: sixty seconds. I took out the tube and held it up to the light. The entire two milliliters had formed one solid blood clot. I was now certain Buck did *not* have warfarin poisoning. But then what the devil was wrong with him?

Mr. Hadley had been calmly watching the process from his uncomfortable perch on the hard wooden bench. His eyes had widened, and he tilted his hat back when he observed me putting the blood tube in my mouth. He and Cindy were on the same wavelength on this one.

"His blood clotting is normal, Mr. Hadley," I reported. "That's a good thing. It looks like your bait boxes did the trick. But it still doesn't tell me what's wrong with him. What about marijuana? I've seen dogs act like this after they get into pot brownies and things like that."

Mr. Hadley gave me a disapproving look. His expression clearly conveyed that I'd just accused him of being a drugged-out hippie. *Oops.* My mistake. I wasn't scoring any *brownie* points with Mr. Hadley.

"There's nothing like that at my place," he said with conviction.

"What about exposure to antifreeze? Are there any vehicles on your property with leaking radiators? Sometimes dogs will act drunk when they first get into antifreeze. It's important to find this out early because it can cause kidney failure if not treated right away."

"Hmm, I do have a couple old trucks on my property and an ancient back loader tractor. But I'm pretty sure they're not leaking anything. I try to keep those vehicles in good working order."

I tended to believe him. Mr. Hadley seemed like the type of guy who kept his property and equipment in tip-top shape.

"But maybe you should test him for that, anyways, just in case," he said. "I can't one hundred percent guarantee he didn't get into any. He does roam around the entire property . . . and I'd hate for him to die of kidney failure. When I was a kid, I remember one of my cats got into antifreeze. It was terrible."

"Yeah. I agree. Better safe than sorry. If we miss it, it could be too late for him. So even if it's unlikely, it would still be prudent to check. I'd need to draw some more blood from him, and the test takes about another thirty minutes. Are you OK with that?"

Mr. Hadley looked at his watch. "I'm due back at the ranch in twenty minutes. I'm meeting a guy about digging a new well. Could you just keep Buck for me and give me a call when you get the results?"

"Sure. I can do that. No problem. I'll call your cell number in an hour, and we'll go from there."

"Sounds good to me. Thanks, Dr. Schmidt."

"You're welcome," I said. "Oh, by the way. When you get back home, look around the property and see if you find anything out of place, anything he might have gotten into."

Mr. Hadley gave me a nod, grabbed the door handle, and left to meet the well digger.

I grabbed the end of Buck's leash and gave it a tug to get him moving. *Nothing*. He just looked up at me like he wanted to sleep right there on the floor for the rest of the day. I gave him a more vigorous tug. *Nothing doing.* Finally, I put both my hands around his chest and hoisted him to his feet. Once he was up, he reluctantly and sluggishly moved off towards the treatment room.

It must have taken me five whole minutes to go the ten yards to the treatment area. Buck would take one step every few seconds. I was about to give up and just carry him, but he eventually stepped up the pace a little and we made it there.

The treatment room was busy that day. Techs and assistants scurried about in a flurry of activity. There was a dog getting a dental cleaning and you could clearly make out the mosquito buzzing sound of the ultrasonic scaler. Another dog was on the surgery prep table being readied for a neuter.

I spotted Debbie Mayfield, our chief vet tech at Largis Animal Clinic. She wore a pair of reading glasses held around her neck with a sparkly chain. On this day, she was wearing a peach-colored scrub top and matching scrub bottoms. Debbie ran a tight ship. There was no beating around the bush and no political correctness in her repertoire. If she needed something done, she just told you to do it. If you weren't moving fast enough or efficient enough, she would tell you that as well. She wasn't mean or spiteful, but she was direct, got stuff done, and had no patience for dillydallying. She was a small woman with short dark brown hair.

Debbie was exactly the person I needed to run the ethylene glycol test. Here's why. At this time (the nineties), the in-house test for ethylene glycol (antifreeze) was a monster. Most tests for in-clinic use are designed to be simple and foolproof, meant for harried veterinary staff being pulled in three different directions at once. So, most tests involved adding a few drops of blood, a few drops of a reagent, and setting a timer for ten minutes.

Not the ethylene glycol test. It was a sixteen-step test that took a full and concentrated thirty minutes. The individual performing the test had to dedicate the entire thirty minutes *solely* to running the test. The instructions were printed on a flimsy fold-out packet in eight-point font. If there was an error in the amount of reagent, the timing, or the order of the steps, then the test was invalid and had to be started all over again. On multiple occasions, I'd seen this test messed up. I was guilty of this myself on at least one occasion, and I avoided running it like the plague. Debbie knew this more than anyone. She was usually the one called upon when the test wasn't run properly and had to be repeated. She hated doing this test too. It was thirty minutes of her day that she was never getting back, so she preferred to just do the test herself correctly the first time. *Fine with me.*

"Debbie, I need to run an ethylene glycol test on this dog."

She gave me a scowl.

"Come to think of it, we should just run a whole CBC and chem panel," I said. "That way you only need to draw the blood once more. Now that I think about it, we're going to need the full work-up whether or not the antifreeze test is positive."

"OK," she said. "Just leave him with me and get back to seeing your appointments."

She was all business today. She was like that every day. "Ten-four," I said and gave her a mock-salute. I turned around, went back into the exam room lobby, and grabbed another chart from the wall. I hoped my next case would be more straightforward than Buck. This was already looking to be a tough afternoon.

Forty minutes later, I emerged from my appointment. It proved to be a fun one: two cattle dog puppies—Patches and Freckles—for their last series of vaccines. These siblings were furry little comedians and had been brightening my day since their first appointment eight weeks before.

Patches & Freckles

Debbie was waiting for me with the test results for Buck. "The ethylene glycol test was negative," she said as I entered the treatment room. "And here's the CBC and chem panel results." She handed me two sheets of paper loaded with numbers and graphs.

"Thanks for running that test for me," I said. "I know that thing is a pain in the butt."

"No problem. At least I only had to run it once," she said with a wry grin.

I was relieved that Buck wasn't sick from ethylene glycol. It's a terrible poison. The most common exposure is by car radiators leaking antifreeze. The yellow-green liquid will drip onto driveways or garage floors. It's sweet tasting, so many dogs and cats like the flavor and lap it up. Initially the toxin mimics alcohol and the affected pet will act drunk. But as it metabolizes, calcium oxalate crystals form in the kidneys, causing catastrophic damage to the tissue and sudden kidney failure. The process is painful and miserable. I'm still amazed to this day that this product is not more regulated. It's one of the most toxic substances I know, yet you can buy it at any auto parts store. There are no restrictions, and it only takes about a tablespoon of the stuff to kill a large dog.

I looked at the page with the complete blood cell count (CBC). It looked pretty good. Buck's red blood cell concentration was slightly higher than normal. This is often due to dehydration and isn't serious. I next checked the chemistry values. The kidney values were perfect. This was further evidence that ethylene glycol was *not* the culprit. The albumin level was mildly elevated, again indicating some dehydration. The ALT liver enzyme was up by ten percent, but all the other liver values were normal. Again, not a big concern.

These test results were all good news for Buck, but not super helpful to me. He didn't eat rat poison. He didn't drink antifreeze. His organs were working fine. So, what was wrong with him? I went over to his cage and stooped down to check on him. He looked the same. He was lying completely still, in a semi-comatose state. I rubbed his head, and he opened his blue eyes for a moment, looked up at me, and then closed them again. "Hey buddy. What did you get into? It would be a lot easier if you'd just tell me." He wasn't talking. He sure looked like he was drugged up on something.

I went over to the wall-mounted phone at the treatment desk and dialed the number for Mr. Hadley. I tapped my foot impatiently against the tile floor waiting for him to pick up. He answered on the third ring.

"Hello?" he said.

"Hi, Mr. Hadley. It's Dr. Schmidt from Largis Veterinary Clinic. I'm calling to give you an update on Buck."

"Hi, Dr. Schmidt. How's my boy doing?"

"He's pretty much the same. He still just acts drunk. His test for antifreeze came back negative. So that's good. We also ran a full blood cell count and chemistry panel on him, and it looks mostly normal. So, his organs are working fine. Did you find anything around the house that would indicate what he got into?

"I haven't had time to look since I got home, but I'll get on that shortly."

"OK," I said. "Please let me know right away if you find anything suspicious. In the meantime, I'm still just not sure what's wrong with him. I'd recommend we keep him in the hospital until we know what's going on. He does seem a bit dehydrated and he's in no shape to eat or drink anything on his own. We'll just put him on I.V. fluid support and watch him closely for any changes in his status. I really want to make sure he's breathing regularly. If his state of consciousness deteriorates further, he could stop breathing."

"Keeping him there is fine with me, Dr. Schmidt. I'd feel better if he was with you folks so you can watch him. He's a great herding dog and I'd hate to lose him. And I can't watch him all night."

When I was done speaking to Mr. Hadley, I once again approached Debbie.

"Debbie, Mr. Hadley OK'd keeping Buck in the hospital. Let's start him on I.V. fluids at one hundred milliliters per hour. Also, I want to keep him right up front in the treatment area. That dog seems really drugged and I'm worried he might stop breathing. We'll need to watch him closely."

"OK," she said. "Leslie's just finishing taking some X-rays. I'll have her do it as soon as she's finished there."

"Thanks," I said. "I've got to get back to my appointments."

It was now nearing 6 p.m. I'd been talking with clients and treating their pets for the past ten hours. This was just the beginning of the workday for Dr. Tom Zappan. He'd see outpatient appointments from 6 to 8 p.m., then any emergency cases that came in during the night. Tom was a fantastic veterinarian and a great human being. He was about ten years older than me and had been a wonderful mentor since my first day at Largis. He had a straightforward and practical approach to medicine, which I found particularly helpful. Tom was also the *fastest* vet I knew. During a normal day of appointments, he would see twice as many as me. Despite his speed, he had an amazing ability to make each of his clients feel personally cared for. I never once heard a complaint that he didn't spend enough time with them.

Tom always wore a blue short-sleeved doctor's coat. He had a full beard and mustache that was just starting to go gray. He was also beginning to go a bit bald on top. He was the only veterinarian I ever met who could consistently pull a foxtail out of a dog's nose with the dog *completely* awake. He would first drip some lidocaine up their nostrils. He'd wait for a minute then firmly hold the dog's nose and insert a plastic tapered otoscope cone. Once he spotted the yellow spiky frond of a foxtail, he would slide the four-inch metal shaft of an alligator forceps through the cone, grab the foxtail, and yank it out. It would take him about five seconds to complete this procedure. The dog would startle and jerk back, but too late, by then the job was done. I'd tried to copy this technique a few times and I was just too clumsy and slow. I always ended up sedating the dogs before I could get the foxtail out.

I saw him come in through the rear entrance of the doctor's office. "Hey, Tom. I have a case I need you to monitor for me tonight."

"No problem, but I've already got an appointment waiting. Just tell me about it before you go home for the night."

"OK. Talk to you later."

It was 7:30 before I could pin him down for an update on Buck. In the meantime, Tom had seen four routine vaccination appointments and two emergencies. One emergency was a dog with a foxtail up his nose (his personal specialty). The other was a dog with a four-inch laceration on his shoulder from a run-in with barbed wire. Tom shaved and prepped the wound and then stapled it closed in less than ten minutes. He was a whirlwind of activity. Like always, he got more stuff done in two hours then most vets did in four or five.

"Tom, I'm about ready to head home. Can I update you on this dog that's staying the night?"

"Yep. Whatcha got?" he asked.

"This four-year-old Aussie came in around one. He was really sluggish and looked drugged. This dog lives on a ranch and roams freely on the property, but the owner can't think of anything he could have gotten into. His ACT was normal. He was negative for antifreeze and his lab work was unremarkable. He's just on I.V. fluids at the moment. I don't know what's going on with him. He's almost comatose, and if this progresses, I'm worried he might stop breathing."

"Wow. A real nebulopathy," said Tom. He used a common vet med term that combines the word *nebulous* with the suffix *pathy* meaning disease. "Is he from around here?

"Yeah. The ranch is on Barton Road. He's owned by Mr. Hadley."

"Oh yeah, I know Jim Hadley," said Tom. "He's a squared away guy. I can't see much slipping past him."

"He's looking around his property right now to see if he can find anything suspicious. But nothing so far."

"OK," said Tom. "I'm happy to keep an eye on him. Cheryl's my tech tonight. I'll make sure she tells me right away if she's worried about his breathing."

"Thanks, Tom. I'm back in the morning. Have a good night."

It was 7:30 the next morning when I pulled into the dirt parking area behind the vet clinic. I was anxious to talk to Tom and see how Buck was doing. I found him seated at his desk rapidly scribbling some notes into a patient chart. I'm not sure why he bothered with this. Tom had the worst handwriting that I'd ever seen. One of the reasons I wanted to talk with him directly is that I knew I'd be unable to decipher his entries into Buck's chart.

"Hey, Tom. Good morning," I said.

"Morning," said Tom. His hair was sticking up a bit. He was bedraggled and not nearly as perky as the last time I saw him.

"Busy night?" I asked.

"Yeah. I had a bloat that came in at 3 a.m. It was a huge Great Dane. It took me two hours to get his stomach decompressed and back into its normal position, but overall, the surgery went well. I'm just finishing up the record right now. In fact, he should be able to go home today. Do you mind taking him over for me?"

"Sure, I can do that. What's the update on Buck?"

"That's Jim Hadley's' dog, right?" he said.

"Yep. The lethargic Aussie."

"He just slept all night," said Tom. "A couple of times his breathing really slowed down, but Cheryl just shook him awake. We never had to intubate him or anything. I didn't really have to do much with him."

"Any ideas what could be going on with him?" I asked. "I'm not really sure what else to do."

"Not really. Just supportive care unless you can get more information."

"It's hard to give Mr. Hadley a prognosis without knowing what in the heck is wrong with his dog," I said.

"Just tell him not to buy the big bag of dog food," said Tom with a shake of his head.

Tom wasn't usually this jaded or sarcastic. He was obviously worn out.

"Yeah. Thanks. That helps a lot."

I grabbed my stethoscope and doctor's coat to get ready to start the day. My coat was heavy. As a newer vet, I tended to carry way too much stuff with me. I tried to prepare for any contingency and minimize any back-and-forth trips between treatment and the exam rooms. Reflex hammer. Check. Bandage Scissors. Check. Calculator, hemostats, suture removal scissors, Sharpie pen, ballpoint pen, penlight, small plastic ruler, highlighter, staple remover, name badge. Check, check, check, check, check. I might actually be better off with Batman's utility belt.

I walked into the treatment room and knelt down to look at my patient. Buck looked like he hadn't moved in the twelve hours since I'd last seen him. I glanced at his vitals chart hanging from his cage. His temperature was taken twice during the night: 100.5 and 101.0. A bit on the low side for a dog, but not a major concern. His respiratory rate was recorded hourly. It ranged between six to twelve breaths per minute. This was fairly low, but not dangerous. His heart rate varied between thirty and forty beats per minute. This is normal for a dog in a deep sleep. His chart noted that he had urinated twice but did not have a bowel movement. I lifted his lip and checked his gum color. He had some black spotted gums that were common for this breed, but the pink parts were still pink. I lifted one eyelid to observe the color of his sclera. It was a nice bright white, which is normal. I shifted his torso over a bit so I could listen to his heart. It was thumping along at a nice, but slow, thirty-six beats per minute.

During this entire exam, Buck didn't move. At one point, he opened his eyes a few millimeters to look around the room, then wearily closed them again. I banged the metal handle of my reflex hammer on the cage wall to make a racket. He responded to this by opening his eyes a little and slightly turning his head towards the sound. He then immediately went right back to sleep. *Man, he sure is dopey. What could be wrong with him?*

"Good morning, Mr. Hadley," I said over the phone hanging from the treatment room wall. "I called to update you on Buck."

"Morning, Dr. Schmidt," he said. "How's he doing? Did he make it through the night OK?"

"Yes. He made it through the night. They kept a close eye on him. His vital signs are slow, but stable. But he's still dead to the world. Not really any better than yesterday and maybe even a little bit worse. He can barely lift his head."

"Huh," said the grizzled rancher. "Do you think he'll be able to pull through this?"

"I honestly can't say. I still don't really understand what's wrong with him. I don't see any evidence that he's had any trauma. He doesn't show any obvious signs of neurological damage. But he's practically in a coma. Do you have any neighbors who would wish him harm?"

"My closest neighbors are half a mile away," he replied. "And the neighbors I do have, really seem to like Buck. He's a friendly dog. I can't see any of them poisoning him on purpose."

"Maybe you can go talk to them," I said. "Just to see if they saw or heard something that would help us."

"Yeah, OK, Dr. Schmidt. I'll give that a try and let you know if I figure anything out."

I was standing in the hospital lobby several hours later when things really got messy. A green wave of noxious odor wafted across the room from the direction of the treatment area. Everybody in the vicinity grimaced as the foul odor permeated the place. I was going over some medication instructions with a longtime client.

"Peugh," I said with a wrinkled nose to my 11 a.m. client, Mrs. Rafferty. "I'm sorry for the bad smell. Someone in the back must have really let loose."

A stylish, petite, middle-aged woman, Mrs. Rafferty was holding a blue pet carrier in her left hand when the smell found us both. Inside the carrier was a beautifully coiffed white toy poodle named Miss Charlotte who was suffering from a bladder infection. It was in the middle of our discussion about how often she needed to give the amoxicillin drops, that the odor found us. I felt bad that Mrs. Rafferty was getting assaulted by the putrid odor emanating from the treatment area. As a vet I'd become somewhat accustomed to such odors, but even so, this was particularly bad.

"That's OK, Dr. Schmidt. But I'm getting out of here now. I'll just call you if I have any questions," she said as she turned towards the doorway and the promise of some fresh air.

"*Escape while you can,*" I said with a dramatic flair. "I can always talk to you on the phone later."

As I walked back to the treatment area, the smell got worse. *Yuck!* I thought. *I may need a gas mask.* I pushed my way through the swinging door and was greeted by quite a site. Two vet techs and two assistants were swarming around like bees whose hive was being attacked by a bear. They were all wearing rubber gloves. There were towels on the floor, a tray filled with green disinfectant and sponge, a mop and bucket.

"What's going on here?" I asked.

Cindy lifted her head and gave me an accusing look. "That's *your* dog, Buck. A minute ago, he had a diarrhea explosion that went out of his cage and all over the floor."

I noticed Buck was now in a different cage on the other side of the room. They must have moved him to facilitate the toxic spill clean-up.

"Ugggh, I'm sorry," I said. Although I wasn't precisely sure how Buck's digestive problems were *my* fault.

I grabbed the mop and started mopping up under the cage previously occupied by Buck. Swishing around the mop seemed to stir up the odor. I almost gagged.

It's safe to say that I was the most despised employee of Largis Veterinary Clinic that day. Buck had two more diarrhea eruptions and each time a swarm of cleaning ants had to address the problem before the people in the building were asphyxiated. Since Buck was my patient, I was held personally responsible for the swirling cloud of rotten odor slowly killing off all the employees. The smell was truly tremendous even for my accustomed nose, and I did feel a proper amount of guilt for the problems he created.

It was four o'clock in the afternoon when the overhead speaker system came to life with an abrupt crackle. "Dr. Schmidt, Mr. Hadley is on line one for you," came the announcement. "He's calling to check on his dog Buck."

Debbie was standing next to me as the announcement stopped. "Can we please send that stinkpot home?" she begged.

"Sorry," I said. "That dog can still barely move. I don't think it's safe for him to go home yet."

I went to the doctor's office, sat at my desk, picked up the handset, and pushed the blinking button for line number one.

"Hello, Mr. Hadley. It's Dr. Schmidt."

"Hi, Doc. Do you remember earlier today when you said I should go have a chat with my neighbors?"

"Yep. I remember. Did you find out something?"

"Well, first I went to see my neighbor Tom on the east side of my property. He has a collection of classic cars he's always working on. I tracked him down in his garage and told him about Buck's condition. He said that he hasn't seen Buck around for at least a week and he couldn't think of any poisons on his property that could cause a problem."

"OK, go on." I felt like Mr. Hadley was drawing this out on purpose just to torture me. I had an appointment waiting, other phone calls to make, and records to write up. This wasn't a damn Agatha Christie mystery novel. *Just cut to the reveal and tell me what you found out*, I thought to myself.

Mr. Hadley continued. "After that I drove over to Mrs. MacLean's property. Her husband Ron passed away about a year ago and she's a widow now. She lives down the road on the west side of my property. She's a great lady and makes a mean chocolate chip cookie."

"Did she have any information about Buck?" I prompted him.

"She says that last week she had a sheep that died on her property. She buried the carcass behind her barn just on the other side of my fence line. When she went out there this morning to add to the compost pile, she saw that something had dug up the sheep and eaten some of the carcass. She says it might have been Buck. She'd seen him sniffing around that area a couple of times."

I wasn't sure I was following his line of thought. *What was Mr. Hadley trying to tell me here?*

"So, you think Buck might have dug up the sheep carcass and eaten it?" I asked. "Has he done this before?"

"He sure has. I shot a skunk on my land last summer and buried it. I found that damn dog walking around with the stinky dead skunk in his mouth the next day. A few months ago, I found a dead cat by the road in front of my house. I think it'd been hit by a car or sumthin. I buried it in the ground ten yards from the road. Later that day, I could see Buck from my kitchen window trying to dig up the cat. I buried that cat deep though and covered him up with rocks. He wasn't going to be able to get to the cat."

"Did Mrs. MacLean have any idea why the sheep died?" I asked. Fears of anthrax circled in the back of my mind.

"She said the sheep was getting really old and could barely walk. She had Doc Morgan come out and put her to sleep."

A sliver of understanding was beginning to form in my head. "So that old sheep didn't just keel over dead. The vet euthanized her?"

"Yep. You know, Doc Morgan from over at your place."

I did know Dr. Morgan. He was one of the original founders of Largis Veterinary Clinic. He ran the large animal part of the business, so I didn't have much interaction with him. But we were friendly with each other, chatting from time to time.

"OK, Mr. Hadley. Good detective work there. That was very helpful. I should let you know that Buck's condition is about the same. He's still mostly comatose, but stable. He did start having some terrible, smelly diarrhea this afternoon but is otherwise doing OK."

"I guess that's about what you'd expect if he ate a few pounds of rotten sheep carcass," he said.

Mr. Hadley had a good point there.

I hung up the phone and headed for the back door of the Largis doctor's office. Just on the other side of the back door was the large animal barn. I found Dr. Morgan and his tech in one of the stalls *floating* a horse's teeth.

This always seemed to me to be a barbaric practice. The horse was immobilized with a "twitch" around its upper lip. While the tech held the twitch, Dr. Morgan would reach into the horse's mouth with a brutal looking metal file and grind down the pointy areas of its teeth. The sound of metal grinding on bone was like fingernails on a chalkboard.

Dr. Morgan had a grimace of concentration on his face. He didn't see me come in.

"Hey, Dr. Morgan. Can I ask you a question now?"

"Sure. Go ahead."

"Do you remember a client named Barbara MacLean?" I asked.

"Yep," he said while rotating the file into a new position. "I was just at her place past week to euthanize one of her sheep."

"Yeah, about that. What was wrong with the sheep?"

"She was just getting old. She could barely get around. Mrs. MacLean wanted her put down before she ended up collapsed in her yard."

"So, you euthanized her with pentabarb?" I asked, referring to a class of drugs that cause respiratory depression, suppression of the central nervous system, and hypothermia.

"Yep," he said between grunts of effort. "I think I gave her about twenty ccs of Beuthanasia solution. Why do you ask?"

"I have her neighbor's dog hospitalized next door in a coma. Evidently, he dug up that sheep and ate some of it."

"Yeah. That would do it." he said. "Barb didn't want me to take the body away for her. She said she'd rather handle it herself and save the hundred dollars. I told her you have to bury 'em deep."

As I walked back to the small animal clinic, I mulled over my conversation with Dr. Morgan. I was certainly lucky that the vet that euthanized Mrs. MacLean's sheep was available for an immediate interview. He was able to supply a missing piece of the puzzle. The mysterious case of the drugged doggie was starting to make sense. Dr. Morgan had euthanized a decrepit sheep belonging to Mrs. MacLean. He'd put the animal down with Beuthanasia a.k.a. pentobarbital, a potent barbiturate drug used for euthanizing animals. Mrs. MacLean had done a lackluster job of burying the sheep. A few days later, Buck had embarked upon his morbid scavenger hunt, digging up the sheep and eating parts of its rotting carcass. Eating sheep tissue infused with pentobarbital could certainly cause the symptoms I was witnessing. I was feeling like a modern-day Sherlock Holmes!

So, here's a math problem for ya . . .

Q: A sheep weighing two hundred pounds is euthanized with twenty milliliters of Beuthanasia solution. The Beuthanasia solution contains 390 mg/ml of pentobarbital. Three days later, a hungry dog comes along and proceeds to dig up the sheep and eat some of it. The dog weighs sixty-five lbs. If the dog eats three pounds of rotten sheep meat then how many milligrams of pentobarbital did the dog consume? If the LD 50 (dose that causes death in fifty percent of the animals) for pentobarbital is eighty-five mg/kg, then will this dog die? If he doesn't die, how long will it take for the drug to wear off?

A: I have absolutely no friggin' idea.

As I walked back into the clinic, the loathsome smell was like a slap in the face. I didn't realize just how revolting it was, until I'd inhaled some fresh air from outside. Debbie, the head tech, was leaning over a stack of patient charts in the treatment room. When she saw me, she said, "Is there any chance of getting that stinking dog out of here? He's making the entire clinic smell like a sewer."

"I'm afraid not." I proceeded to tell her the story about Buck eating the decomposing sheep carcass.

"Oh my God!" she said. "Dogs are so gross. So, he gorged himself on *buried, rotten* sheep meat and now that's what's coming out the other end?"

"Yep. I think that about covers it," I said.

"So how long do you think we'll have to keep him here?"

"Until the pentobarb has a chance to wear off and he wakes up. Probably at least another couple of days."

It was four days. On the third day, Buck began to lift his head and look around the room. He didn't have any idea of where he was, or how he got there. Thankfully, day three also marked a reduction of his diarrhea. For three full days, Buck oozed a continuous flow of loathsome lava. It was an all-out olfactory assault. Normally employees take lunch breaks, smoke breaks, and bathroom breaks. For the duration of Buck's stay, there were only *fresh air* breaks. Since I was Buck's vet and Buck couldn't defend himself, I took the brunt of the complaints.

"Wow, Dr. Schmidt, what a wonderful new smell you've created."

"How many eggs does it take to make a stink bomb? Quite a phew!"

"Dr. Schmidt, that new deodorant you're using isn't working out very well."

"Why does Piglet smell like farts? Because he plays with Pooh!"

After days of this abuse, no one was more relieved than I when Buck stood up under his own power. He walked outside, sniffed around, and lifted his leg on an old apple tree. He'd been in the vet clinic for four and a half days. He'd gone through stacks and stacks of towels as well as fifty gallons of mop water—and he'd just about worn out our washing machine. On the fourth day, he sat up in his cage and looked at me as if to say, *I'm hungry. You got anything to eat around this place?*

We removed Buck's I.V. catheter and gave him two cups of dog kibble. He ate it all in six seconds. Later, two vet assistants hoisted him up into a tub and gave him a thorough bathing. He needed it. Four days of lying in a smelly heap had left him a revolting, sticky, disheveled mess. The fur around his mouth was stiff with dried saliva. The fur on the back of his legs was saturated with diarrhea. His neck was caked with rotten sheep parts.

He emerged from his bath looking like a show puppy. He was ecstatic with his fresh look (and smell) and pranced around the treatment room.

He thought he was the belle of the ball and couldn't understand why no one wanted to cuddle with him. He barked, yipped, and darted around trying to get some play action. It was good to finally see his real personality. Mr. Hadley showed up an hour later to take him home. Man, what a relief to see him go!

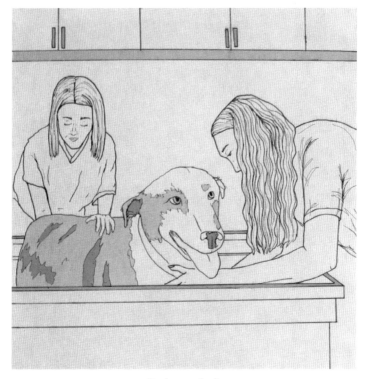

Buck gets a bath

CHAPTER 6

Charlie's Island

"**H**ey, Cheryl. Are you almost ready to go?" I shouted from the doorway to the laundry room of Largis Veterinary Hospital.

Cheryl had agreed to accompany me on an lunch hour road trip. I had a house call euthanasia scheduled at 11:30 and needed to be back in the office for a 1 p.m. appointment. Whenever possible, I always liked to have a tech accompany me on house calls. An extra set of trained hands was invaluable, and Cheryl was definitely my preferred helper for this job. Not only was she experienced and proficient, but she'd grown up in the town of Largis and knew all the backroads. I, on the other hand, drove in from fifty miles away to work at this prestigious clinic. I knew how to navigate my way to work and that was about it. I'd gotten lost trying to find the Burger King down the street. It was now eleven, so I didn't have much time to waste. We needed to get moving. Cheryl was getting the house call box and making sure it had all the supplies we needed for this trip.

Cheryl appeared from the back corner of the laundry room with a stack of clean towels cradled on her left arm and holding the house call box by the handle in her right hand. "Almost ready. Just a sec. I still need to get the Beuthasol bottle outta the controlled drug drawer."

Beuthasol is a trade name for a concentrated form of pentobarbital. This barbiturate anesthetic comes in a dark glass bottle with a pink label.

The injectable liquid is a bright pink color, and the solution is administered intravenously for the humane euthanasia of animals. For that reason, it's considered a highly controlled and dangerous substance (obviously) and locked up at all times. Cheryl walked past me and handed me the stack of towels on her way to the treatment area. I followed behind her as she found the key, unlocked the drawer, and added the bottle to our tackle box of house call supplies.

"OK. Let's go," she said.

A few minutes earlier, back in the doctor's office, I'd prepped for the trip by shoving my wallet in my back pocket, putting my stethoscope around my neck, and grabbing keys to the Suburban from Dr. Freed's desk. There were only a couple vets at Largis Vet Clinic willing to make house calls and we preferred *not* to use our personal cars. Sometimes we were transporting sick, stinky (or dead) animals back to the clinic and they could leave a huge mess. Dr. Freed had long ago volunteered his big blue 1980 four-door Chevy Suburban as the sacrificial vehicle for this task. It was perfect for the job. Already dilapidated and smelly, adding a little more "character" to the old goat didn't make any difference.

As we toted our gear towards the faded blue behemoth, I asked, "You're sure you know how to get to this place?" This was in the pre-GPS era and my sense of direction was terrible. Without her guidance, I'd never arrive on time.

"Yeah. I know how to get there," said Cheryl. "I used to board my horses near there. We'll find it OK."

Although the occasion was sad, part of me was happy just for an excuse to get outside the clinic. I loved being a small animal veterinarian, but I spent long days closed up indoors. Getting outside was a welcome mini field trip for me. And it was a beautiful sunny spring day. It had just rained the night before and the trees and grass still sparkled with the residual moisture.

After spending a few seconds trying to identify the correct key, and another moment trying to finagle it into the lock, I was able to open the airplane hangar of a door that served as the truck's tailgate. Cheryl tossed in the red house call box and a handful of large garbage bags. I added my stack of towels to the pile as well as my maroon doctor's coat weighed down with tools of the trade. I slammed the hatch shut and headed over to the driver's side door. I had to grab the handle mounted to the door frame to hoist myself into this monstrosity, while Cheryl boosted herself up into the passenger seat. I'd driven this metal dinosaur once or twice before, but it had been a while. It took me a moment to adjust the seat (Dr. Freed was bigger than me) and figure out how to release the parking brake. I turned the key, started the engine, and we rumbled off on our melancholy adventure.

"Turn right when we hit the street," instructed Cheryl. "We'll take Sierra Road for a couple of miles before we get to English Colony."

"Alrighty. Here we go," I said as I turned off the gravel driveway onto the blacktop.

Driving the Suburban was quite an experience. You didn't steer it so much as coax it. More like a boat. As we lumbered down the roadway, it would gradually start to drift towards the median. I'd correct by giving the wheel a slight nudge to the right. Then it would sway back in the other direction and threaten to go off the side of the road and into the ditch. I'd give the wheel another nudge in the opposite direction. Now, if you really wanted to turn onto a road *perpendicular* to the one you were on, you first had to slow *way* down, then spin the wheel in complete circles in the direction you wanted to eventually go. Once the turn was complete, it was important to spin the wheel in the opposite direction with the same number of rotations as it took to get you there in the first place. I drove a tank in the United States Army for two years. That fifty-five-ton tank had more responsive steering than this cumbersome Chevy.

The clinic was located on the outskirts of town so wasn't long until we were immersed in the countryside. It was a beautiful day for a drive. The houses became sparser and were separated with rolling hills populated by horses and small herds of sheep. I made the turn onto English Colony Road as instructed. It was late March, and the dogwood trees were in full blossom.

Old oak trees, rich in greenery, completely covered the road with their canopy in many areas. Speckled sunlight made it through and formed a shifting dappled pattern on the blacktop. The air smelled particularly fresh after last night's rain. Again, I thought how glad I was just to be outside. It made it hard to remember that we were heading to someone's house to put their dog to sleep. But this fact did weigh on me and tempered my mood.

We passed by a big, white two-story house on our right side. To the left of the house was an expansive horse corral and behind that an enormous red barn. The entire property lay in the shade of ancient oak trees.

"That's the house where my best friend Susy used to live," Cheryl exclaimed. "We were in F.F.A. together. Her parents decided to move away to L.A. halfway through her junior year of high school. I was so bummed out."

"Wow," I said. "That place looks gorgeous. They must have had some money."

"Yeah, they did," replied Cheryl. "Her dad was a computer engineer at Intel. They owned about six horses and ten motorcycles. I went over to their house in the summer and rode horses and motorcycles all day."

I conjured a mental picture of a fifteen-year-old Cheryl. A red-haired, freckle-faced teen sporting cut-off denim jeans and flying over dirt jumps at forty miles an hour. Knowing her *devil-be-damned* approach, helmets were optional. I hoped her parents had good health insurance.

"Make a left up here on Butler," said Cheryl, bringing me out of my reverie.

I slowed down so I could look for the sign. It was coming up in thirty yards. Time to start turning the wheel left so that the truck might eventually move in that direction by the time we got there. Luckily, no one was coming the other way. I could take my time guiding the HMS Suburban onto this new waterway without any risk of collision.

"I used to live right over there," commented Cheryl pointing to a nice little green house on our left. "Oh, and there's the hill where my brother broke his leg. He tried to skateboard down the whole thing without stopping. He must have been going thirty miles an hour when he crashed into the fence right near the bottom."

I looked over at the hill she was talking about. It was about two hundred yards of smooth blacktop descending at a forty-degree angle. Her brother must've been *nuts*. I was beginning to appreciate a family resemblance. "He's lucky all he broke was his leg. He could've been killed."

Cheryl, sitting next to me, nodded her head in agreement. "We should be coming up on Allen Lane. I think we're getting close."

I made the turn onto Allen Lane, a rough one-lane blacktop road in disrepair. Even as I crept along at twenty miles per hour, the Suburban creaked and lurched as it bumped over the missing chunks of asphalt. The houses here looked more run down, but the countryside was fantastic. This entire area looked like a scene from *Gone with the Wind*. Huge shady oak trees hung over the road from both directions. The beauty of spring had found this dusty part of the world, too.

"Look for number 4-3-4-3," she said. "The address should be on the mailbox. It'll be on the right side."

We inched along looking for mailbox number 4343. We found it about two hundred yards from the last turn. You couldn't see the house at all from the street. The entire property was fronted by an enormous oleander hedge, the dark green bushes in bad need of a haircut. As we turned down the gravel driveway, the overgrown branches made a terrible screech as they scraped against both sides of the truck. The driveway opened into a circular turnabout in front of a faded yellow ranch-style house surrounded on all sides by a lush verdant lawn. I pulled up right in front of the house. The truck came to a stop with a crunch of gravel. I turned off the ignition, put on the parking brake, and hopped off the deck and down to the ground.

I glance at the clipboard in my right hand. Clipped to it was the client information sheet reminding me that the house we'd just arrived at belonged to Bob and Darlene Whittaker, and their dog's name was Charlie, a fifteen-year-old mixed breed shepherd. Poor Charlie. Fifteen is old for a large breed dog, but that didn't necessarily make it any easier to see him go—for me or his family.

The Whittakers came out onto their porch the minute we pulled up. Mr. Whittaker was a big, tall, lean guy. He was likely in his seventies and had all white hair. His wife was half his size and a little plump. I could easily imagine Mrs. Whittaker with a red-checked apron baking a batch of cookies for her grandkids. Cheryl and I grabbed our gear from the back of the Suburban and walked up to meet them on the porch.

"Hi, Mr. and Mrs. Whittaker." I stepped forward and shook hands with both of them. "I'm Dr. Schmidt and this is my vet tech Cheryl. I'm sorry to meet you under such sad circumstances."

"Thank you, Dr. Schmidt," said Mr. Whittaker. "It's nice to meet you both. We really appreciate you coming out to the house. We've been dreading this day for a long time. Charlie's had a tough time getting around for a couple of years now and recently it's gotten much worse."

Mrs. Whittaker held open the front door and gestured us through. From their living room, I could clearly see the backyard through the wide sliding glass doors at the back of the house. They had a huge expanse of rolling green lawn surrounded by oak trees with a bucolic green pond off to the left.

On the mantle over their brick fireplace hung a wood-framed plaque with a quote from Will Rogers: *If there are no dogs in Heaven, then when I die I want to go where they went.*

Huh, I thought to myself. *That's eerily appropriate for today's visit.*

Mrs. Whittaker noticed me reading the plaque. "Charlie's now the fifth dog we've had to let go. It never gets easier. He's just about the kindest, gentlest dog I've ever known. We are really going to miss him around here."

"Yeah, I certainly can understand that," I said. "I've had to put a few of my own pets to sleep and it never gets any easier."

"I imagine this must be really hard for the two of you as well," she said. "As animal lovers, this has to be the most difficult part of your job."

"It can be hard," said Cheryl. "But I guess you do get a little bit used to it over time. And I'm glad we can offer this service. It's the circle of life, I'm afraid."

"Well," said Mr. Whittaker. "I guess we should just get to it. Charlie's in the backyard. He just loves it out there."

Mrs. Whittaker slid open one of the glass doors and we walked out onto their back deck. It was about five feet off the ground and had a series of steps leading down to the grass.

"Whenever the weather is nice, Charlie likes to spend all day out here," said Mr. Whittaker looking out towards the pond. "Lately we've had to help him up and down the steps so he wouldn't fall. But I thought, when it came time to put him to sleep, that this was the place."

While Mr. Whittaker was talking, I was looking around the sweeping property. There was a lot of talk about poor old Charlie, but I didn't see him anywhere. I guess we were going to get to this part eventually.

"Well, you sure have some beautiful scenery out here," I complimented them. "I can see why he'd love it." As I made these comments, I meandered down the steps, figuring I'd be tripping over Charlie any minute now.

"We especially love this spot in the spring," said Mrs. Whittaker. "Everything is so lush and green, and the pond fills up after the rains."

Cheryl finally cut to the point. "So *where* is Charlie?" she asked. I'm glad she said something that kept us on task. I was relishing the time away from the office and the sunshine on my face. If it were just up to me, I may have stood around enjoying the scenery for the rest of the day.

"Oh, he's over there in his favorite spot," said Mrs. Whittaker as she gestured vaguely off to the left.

Cheryl and I both took several steps in the general direction she was pointing. I didn't see a dog. I glanced over at Cheryl. Perhaps she was better than me at this game of *Find Fido.* She looked back at me with a puzzled expression. Nope, she didn't see him either.

I mirrored Cheryl's look of bewilderment. Trying not to appear too dense, I said. "Uh, I'm not really seeing him. Where is he again?"

"Oh, look at that patch of land over there," said Mrs. Whittaker. "Do ya see that little almond tree sticking up? Well right below it you can *just* see a lump of brown and white. That's Charlie lying under the tree."

I looked again in the direction she'd indicated. I saw a medium-sized pond surrounded by old oak trees. Other than that, there was just a lot of nice green grass. *What in the hell is she talking about? A little almond tree?* I glanced over again at Cheryl. She was clearly just as lost.

I scanned again the dark green grass, the majestic oak trees, and the shimmering pond. More meticulous this time. Instead of the nature lover out on a Sunday stroll, I took on the role of the hunter trying to spot a wounded antelope on the Savannah. Off in the distance I did see a sad spindly little tree that might be an almond. *Ohhhhhh, noooo. . . .* The tree was on a small patch of ground and the patch of ground was surrounded by twenty yards of murky green water. Reflected morning sunlight danced off the surface. Charlie's favorite spot was a small island. Cheryl figured this out about the same time as me. I saw her eyes go wide.

I opened my mouth to say something to Mrs. Whittaker. Then I closed it again. A Pachinko machine of clacking metal balls was bouncing around in my head. I turned my head, glanced over at Cheryl, and turned back again to address Mrs. Whittaker. I wanted to express to her the impracticality of the situation. I opened my mouth again. For the second time, I closed it without saying a thing.

Finally, after an uncomfortable pause, what I uttered was, "Uh . . . how do you get out there? Is there a path or something?"

"You just have to wade out, I'm afraid," said Mr. Whittaker. "In the summer that's not a pond at all, just a low spot in the grass. But it does fill up a bit after it rains. Don't worry, though. It's not as bad as it looks. It only goes up to your ankles."

"How the heck did *he* get out there?" I asked.

"He just dragged himself the whole way," said Mr. Whittaker. "He's been going out there his whole life. He's a stubborn old goat."

"Is there any way you can get him back over to this side?" asked Cheryl, not looking forward to the swim across. *She was hoping they had a rowboat or something.*

"Well, he weighs almost one hundred pounds," said Mrs. Whittaker. "I've got bad knees and Bob had back surgery a few years ago. I don't think we could carry him. Besides, that is his favorite spot and I think that's where he'd want to go.

I looked over at Cheryl and shook my head. It was clear that the Whittakers were asking us to trudge through twenty yards of pond water to reach Charlie. Slogging over to their mini island would be a wet, muddy journey we were not prepared for. I'm sure they didn't share this detail with the receptionist when they called to schedule the appointment.

So, we're scheduling a house call to put one of your dogs to sleep, Mrs. Whittaker? Where is he located exactly? Oh, he's on an island in the middle of your pond? Great! In that case, we'll send out Dr. Schmidt. He'll be out there shortly. He specializes in aquatic euthanasias.

This whole scenario gave me a pause. The situation was certainly not covered in the veterinary house-call handbook. Neither Cheryl nor I were looking forward to braving the pond and wading our way over to Charlie's Island. It was a ludicrous thing to ask. On the other hand, this sweet old couple was trying to give their beloved pet the best exit they could. This wasn't the time to debate logistics with these folks. Making the decision to put a pet to sleep is a terribly difficult thing to do. By the time people make the dreaded call, most of them have already waited too long. The Whittakers stood with red, puffy eyes and runny noses. Mrs. Whittaker would occasionally dab her eyes with her handkerchief. They were at the peak of their emotional fragility. I didn't want to make this terrible day any worse for them.

Cheryl looked at me, shrugged her shoulders, and gave me an *Oh, what the hell,* look. This was it then. As bewildering as this situation had become, neither of us wanted to let these people down. We were definitely *not* leaving a crippled old dog stranded on an island.

I need to be back at the office in less than an hour, I thought to myself. The decision crystallized in my mind. If we were getting this done it was all up to me. "OK. I guess we'd better get going then."

Cheryl and I hoisted up our gear and started walking towards the pond, its edge about twenty yards away. Halfway there, I noticed that Cheryl and I were by ourselves. I stopped and turned back towards the Whittakers.

"Are you two coming out with us?" I asked.

"No, I don't think so," said Mrs. Whittaker. "Bob and I have already said our goodbyes."

Huh. I'd just assumed they were coming along with us to be with Charlie at the end. It was going to just be me and Cheryl and Charlie, I guess.

I turned back around and continued along, but when Cheryl and I reached the edge of the pond, I pulled up short. I suddenly had a disturbing thought. I turned to the Whittakers again and asked, "Do you want us to bring Charlie back here with us when we're done?"

"Oh no, you don't need to do that, Dr. Schmidt," said Mr. Whittaker. "I'm going to just bury him right there in his favorite spot. I'll go out later and take care of that."

Thank goodness for that. Slopping back and forth through the cold, swampy pond was bad enough. Dragging the one-hundred-pound dog back with me would be a challenge for which I truly wasn't prepared.

Cheryl and I paused at the pond's edge. The water did *not* look inviting. It was murky, and we couldn't see the bottom. It might be four inches or four feet. Neither of us was looking forward to getting wet and muddy. Plus, I'd chosen a nice pair of khaki dress pants, dress socks, and leather loafers for the day, not anticipating a beach landing. Cheryl was wearing scrubs and plastic clogs.

"All right," I said. "I'll go first, and you can just follow me. That way if I get stuck in quicksand or something, only one of us will die."

Cheryl gave me a grin. She seemed to be rooting for the quicksand in this scenario.

One foot at a time, I started slogging through the pond. The chilly water squished into my shoes, saturated my socks, and quickly wicked up my pants. Once I got going, the damage was done. So, I decided I might as well just cross as efficiently as possible. I was only three yards into the pond, and it was already quite apparent that Mr. Whittaker was a big fat liar. The water was *way* over my ankles. I wondered if he noticed the accidental deception from his viewpoint on the shore. He would certainly find out for himself when he came back later. I kept going, careful with my foot placement as I really did not want to fall in the chilly water. I could hear Cheryl sloshing and swearing ten feet behind me.

At about eight yards into the pond, the water was up just past my knees. One of my shoes started to slip off into the sucking mud, but I caught it midway and was able to shove my foot in deeper. I was about at my breaking point. I truly wanted to help this dog, but I wasn't prepared for a full swim. If it got any deeper I was turning around and heading back. We could try again tomorrow with assistance from the coast guard. But it didn't get deeper. In fact, each step forward became a bit shallower. With seven yards to go, I could finally see that there truly was a dog on the island. A brown and white shaggy mound of fur was looking at me curiously as I trudged toward him.

As I reached the shore, I took stock of my surroundings. Charlie's island was only about ten feet wide and ten feet long. There were a few scrubby bushes, some tufts of grass, and the scrawny, juvenile almond tree. Poor Charlie really did look old. He was lying down under that small tree, looking at me quizzically. His head was huge, and his shoulders were massive, but the rest of his body tapered off to some spindly hips and toothpick hind legs. I'm sure he was once a magnificent muscular creature, but time had worn him down and made him weak. I'm amazed he was able to make the trek I had just survived. He could have drowned along the way.

A few moments after my arrival, Cheryl stepped up beside me. She was carrying one of her mud-logged clogs in her left hand. Her left arm was wet and muddy up past the elbow where she'd had to reach down to rescue it from the swamp.

"Well, that was *really* fun," she said as she banged her clog on a rock. "I guess I was overdue for a bath." She slipped her clog back over her dripping brown left sock.

"Yeah, that was definitely more than I bargained for," I agreed. "And we still have to make it back. I'm not real excited about that."

Charlie quietly regarded both of us. We were both complete strangers to him—invaders on his island—but he lifted his head and greeted us with a weary wag anyway. We walked over to him and joined him on the damp, muddy ground of his final resting place. Cheryl sat down by his right shoulder, and I sat down by his front paws. His left ear was folded. It appeared like a stalk of grass that had lost its battle against a strong wind. He was grizzled, old, and weak. He looked like he'd been laying there for a long time. I looked into his eyes. They were incredibly soulful, intelligent, deep brown eyes. I could see that he was tired and ready to leave this earth. And this was the place that he'd decided to do it.

Charlie

I patted the old shepherd on the head and talked to him a bit. His fur was coarse and still damp from his own venture across the water. "You're a good old boy, Charlie. I'm sorry you're feeling so tired. Cheryl and I are going to help you out."

Cheryl stroked his neck and back. "You're a very handsome dog, Charlie. I bet once you were the best looking dog in the whole neighborhood."

Charlie looked up at her and wagged.

There was something familiar and endearing about this dog. I felt like I was being reacquainted with an old friend. I looked into his eyes again and I realized something important. Charlie *did* know who we were. And, he knew *why* we were there.

While Cheryl stroked and petted him, I opened the house call box and removed a pair of rechargeable clippers. I approached his leg slowly so as not to scare him. But he wasn't scared. He trusted us. We were the people who were there to help him. I shaved a small spot on his left front leg. Next, I took a twenty-milliliter syringe from the box and loaded it with a needle. I tipped the bottle of beuthanol and drew up ten milliliters of the pink solution. The medication is very thick. Usually I dilute it 50:50 with saline. This lowers the viscosity and makes it much easier to inject. But we weren't at the clinic, and we didn't bring any saline with us. I looked around. I was *surrounded* by water. There was no real need to use *sterile* saline in this situation. Charlie wouldn't care. I could see the Whittakers thirty yards away watching us. With my back to them, I pretended to fish around for something in the box while I aspirated ten milliliters of pond water to dilute the beuthanol. Charlie was serene. He was looking at Cheryl and seemed to be enjoying the attention. His eyelids closed to a half-mast position of contentment as Cheryl began scratching him on top of his head. I went back over to sit by him again.

"Charlie, you're a sweet old guy," I said to him. "I'm going to make this very easy for you. Cheryl will pet you and talk to you the whole time. You don't have to worry about a thing."

Cheryl gently reached around Charlie's big head with her left arm. With her right hand she grasped his right leg just below the elbow. I rubbed him on the nose and then inserted the needle in his vein. He never flinched. He seemed grateful for the kindness. As I pushed the plunger to administer the injection, Charlie turned his head and started licking Cheryl on her left cheek. That was the last thing he ever did. Within five seconds of starting the lethal injection, Charlie went limp and let out a big sigh. He was gone.

Cheryl and I looked at each other. She gently lowered his head to the ground. The air was quiet. We had each done this hundreds of times. But this time seemed different. We were wet and muddy and covered in Charlie's fur. There was every reason to get to our feet and get the hell out of there. But we both felt compelled to pause. There was a space on that island that held Charlie's soul and that space was now empty. I could feel it.

I let out a big sigh. "OK. Let's cross the Delaware and get back to the truck."

We packed up our stuff and started the sloppy twenty-yard hike back to the Whittakers' yard. When we got back, the couple was standing shoulder-to-shoulder at the edge of the pond. They were staring out over the water at the lump of fur that used to be Charlie. He was still lying on his own private island. They both appeared weak and shaken. I started to say something to them and then stopped myself. There was nothing to say. As I walked past Mr. Whittaker, I gave him a warm pat on the shoulder. Cheryl went over to Mrs. Whittaker and gave her a brief hug. We walked back to the car by going *around* the house. It didn't seem right to traipse through their living room in our dripping muddy clothes. I unlocked the car, and we tossed in our gear. There were some thrift store towels in the back, and we used these to wipe off the worst of the mud. I climbed in the driver's seat and revived the engine of the old Chevy. Cheryl joined me a few seconds later and slammed the door shut. I put the transmission in drive, and we slowly rolled out to the street. The crunch of the driveway gravel was the only sound.

"Left here," said Cheryl.

On the way back to the clinic, we didn't talk much, both lost in our own thoughts. Both deeply affected by what we had just experienced. This had to be the strangest job in the world. People paid me to come to their house and kill their loved ones. Was this a good thing to do? If I didn't put Charlie to sleep, who would have done it? If we didn't give him a peaceful death on that island, he may have lain there for days. He would eventually, painfully, succumb to dehydration and cold.

By this point in my career, I knew hundreds of veterinarians. Very few would have done what I just did. It took too much time. You didn't make much money. It was too sad. And, on this occasion, my pants were soaked, and my left shoe was filled with mud. But I didn't see it this way. It was a huge responsibility and an important part of my job. Maybe this was the *most* important part of my job. The best gift a pet owner can give their pet is a painless death surrounded by the people they love, in a place they love.

The winding return drive seemed to take longer than before, and the beauty of the day was tarnished by the sadness I knew the Whittakers were experiencing. We arrived at 1 p.m. I'd be a little late for my first afternoon appointment, but that seemed unimportant now. As I guided the Suburban into an empty parking spot, two llamas stared at us from the other side of the fence. Their deep brown eyes regarded us from behind generous lashes as they contentedly munched on some grass. They were enjoying the warm sunshine on the back of their long necks. We paused for a moment, both of us relieved to be back. I was pleased that I'd traversed the countryside in the Chevy without getting lost or taking out a mailbox. My shoes and pants were stained brown and dripping on the floorboards. For the rest of the day, I'd have to answer the question about what happened to my clothes. This was the longest I'd ever known Cheryl to be quiet.

She finally broke the silence. "When the time comes, I wouldn't mind having *my own* island."

Llamas

CHAPTER 7

SMASH

My eyes popped open as a surge of adrenalin pumped through my body. I could hear my heart pounding in my ears. Where *was* I? It was dark except for a crack of light pushing from under the door. It took a moment for my sleep-fogged brain to catch up with my heart rate. Then I recognized the sound that woke me up. There were footsteps coming up the thinly carpeted plywood stairs. Cheryl, the on-duty emergency tech, was tromping up the stairs to my little sleeping loft. I checked my watch. I could just make out the luminous hands that stood out from my wrist. It was 1:50 a.m. I was at Largis Animal Clinic early, early, on a Thursday morning.

The sound of footsteps abruptly stopped and was immediately followed by a pounding on the door.

"Dr. Schmidt, I have an emergency for you," she shouted to make sure I could hear her through the door.

"OK. I'll be right down," I replied groggily.

I hated being woken up this way. I always jolted awake with pangs of anxiety and a tightness in my chest. I spent two nights a week in this small closet-like room. The single bed was covered with a rumpled faded orange bedspread from the fifties. On the right side of the room was a blank white wall with a single small shelf. The opposite wall wasn't really a wall. It was the back side of stacked industrial metal storage shelving. The stack of shelves divided the sleeping loft from the larger records room on the other side. I've been on this work-schedule for three years. Four twelve-hour days and two twelve-hour nights a week. You'd think I'd be getting used to these early morning emergency calls. You'd be wrong. It still felt like a bucket of ice water was being dumped on my head.

"OK," said Cheryl. "It's a nice big dog in room number one. He looks fine to me. The chart is by the door."

"All right. Just give me a minute. I'll be right down, Cheryl."

This was my third emergency case of the night thus far. At 10:30 I'd treated a beagle named Buster. He had a mild fever and a cough. His condition was not life threatening, so I sent him home with antibiotics and a cough suppressant. At midnight, a young couple brought in a tabby cat named Rex. Rex had a large tear in his left ear. The top third of the ear was hanging from a small piece of skin. There wasn't much point in trying to save this dangling piece of tissue, so I snipped off the rest and cauterized the edges. The missing ear tip would give him some character. Rex was sent home on a three-day course of antibiotics. The Wednesday-Thursday overnight shift was usually a quiet one so I could usually get some sleep. Because I'd start my day shift duties at eight the next morning I'd do whatever I could to get some rest. I lived fifty miles away, so I always slept overnight at the hospital for my "on-call" duty. Some of the other emergency vets lived a lot closer. They were allowed to go home on their emergency shifts if they could make it back to the clinic within fifteen minutes.

I fumbled around for the light switch so I wouldn't fall down the stairs, and then squinted painfully when the bright fluorescent lights flashed to life. I took the steep stairs carefully. A lesson I'd learned from a previous emergency shift when I'd almost killed myself rushing down them in the middle of the night. I got to the bottom of the stairs where the carpet changed to a green ceramic tile. A dim fifteen-yard hallway loomed up before it approached the bright row of exam rooms. The left upper half of the hallway was the hospital pharmacy. The shapes of a thousand medication bottles waited patiently to be dispensed into amber prescription vials. My footsteps seemed loud in the eerily silent clinic, and I had to resist the temptation to tiptoe down the hallway.

There was a manilla folder resting in a clear plastic wall holder outside of exam room number one. I picked it up to get a preview of events.

This late-night patient was a male mixed-breed dog named Ruger. New to the clinic, there was no previous history to review. The only details to absorb were Cheryl's guesstimate of his breed—German shepherd-rottweiler mix—and recorded weight—eight-six pounds, as well as the presenting complaint of "ate bad stuff." At 2 a.m. we didn't waste any time with fancy descriptions. The pet owner's name was Kyle Ada. From the client information sheet, it looked like he lived just a couple of miles away.

"Good morning," I said as I slid open the pocket door and walked in the room. "Are you Kyle?" I was pretending to be alert to compensate for the fact that I felt like Rip Van Winkle.

"Yes," he said. "That's me. And this is my dog, Ruger."

Ruger was sitting down tightly next to Kyle's left knee. He had light brown eyes and a black-and-brown-patched face. He seemed tense and looked at me cautiously. He would glance at me then quickly turn his gaze back to Kyle. Kyle reached over and roughly rubbed him on the neck. This touch calmed him, and he wagged his tail despite his nervousness. He seemed like a nice enough dog. He just wasn't sure why he'd been dragged into this strange building when he should have been home in bed.

"Nice to meet you, Kyle. I'm Dr. Schmidt." We shook hands and I gave Ruger a pat on the head.

Kyle was wearing pleated grey slacks and a white dress shirt with pink pin stripes. The shirt was untucked, and it looked like he'd recently been wearing a tie. He was a nice-looking guy with short, cropped chestnut brown hair. I would estimate his age as mid-thirties. He wasn't any happier to be here than Ruger and his expression was one of annoyance and worry.

"Cheryl said that he ate something weird that's got you worried," I said. "What did he eat?"

"I think he ate a whole box of razor blades," Kyle replied.

"Really? Razor blades?"

"Yep."

I looked over at Ruger. He didn't look like a dog that just ate a whole box of razor blades. He looked more like a dog that was ready for a snack and maybe a little nap as he continued to eye me sheepishly. I certainly didn't see any blood coming from his mouth.

"Do you mean like the type you use to shave?" I asked, thinking my addled brain wasn't understanding him correctly.

"No, like the kind you used to cut stuff up. I just got home about an hour ago from a wedding reception. I left Ruger in the garage while I was gone. He likes sleeping in there. He has a nice big dog bed in the corner. When I got out of my car, I saw that there was a cardboard box torn open. There were some blades strewn all over the corner of the garage. Some of the razors were broken up into fragments. I think he chewed them up and ate some of them."

"Why was there a box of razor blades in your garage?" I asked. I was still not sure I understood this situation. I definitely needed some coffee.

"They're replacement blades for my box-cutter," he said. "It comes in real handy when you're cutting up linoleum and carpet."

"Oh. OK. You mean those trapezoid-shaped blades that go in utility knives? I think I understand. Why the hell would he eat those?" At two in the morning my brain-to-mouth filter wasn't working properly.

"I have no idea. He's eaten some weird stuff before, but never anything like this."

I heard what Kyle was saying, but it just didn't make sense to me. I was still a bit skeptical. I'd seen dogs eat some bizarre items. From stuffed toys and tennis balls to underwear, dirty baby diapers, sticks, ear plugs, marbles and so on. But dogs aren't generally attracted to oily, cold, sharp pieces of metal. It wouldn't taste good. Maybe there was some mistake?

"Is he acting OK?" I asked.

"Yeah, he seems fine," Kyle said.

"Have you seen any bleeding from his mouth?"

"No. I was afraid he'd cut up his lips and tongue pretty bad. I'm fairly sure he chewed them. But I haven't seen any blood."

"Hmmm . . . OK. Let me look at him."

I approached Ruger and got down on one knee to see him better. He wasn't sure why he was getting all this attention at 2 a.m. This was way past his bedtime. I felt as confused as he looked. I petted him a little on the head and behind the ears. He looked up at my face and seemed to relax a bit. He wagged his tail and shifted his head into position for more petting.

I figured the first place to look was in his mouth. If Ruger really chewed and swallowed a whole box of razor blades, I would expect a lot of blood. I pried his drooly mouth open and got a good look around with a penlight held in my teeth. Nothing there but smelly dog-breath and some calculus on his teeth. No cuts or blood. This was curious. I shifted his furry head to the left and pulled back his gums to look at his molars. Normal. I shifted his head to the right and looked at the other side. Normal . . . *wait*. Maybe I did see something. On further inspection, where his gums met his upper canine tooth, there was a small glint of metal. I teased it out with my fingernail. A small silver triangle of metal fell into my hand. Where the fragment fell out, a tiny drop of blood formed.

"Well," I said holding up my finding. "I can tell he chewed at least one of them. This piece of metal was stuck in his gum. What makes you think he *ate* the whole box?"

Mr. Ada sighed and dipped his chin down to his chest. He looked tired and frustrated at my endless idiotic questions.

"It was a FULL box," he said. "If he didn't eat them then where did they go? I only found enough pieces to make four or five blades."

I couldn't argue with his logic.

"How many are in a box?" I asked.

"Sixty blades per box," he said.

"So, you think he ate *fifty-five* razor blades?"

"That's what I'm guessing."

Holy crap, I thought to myself. I was finally awake enough to register the facts. *This was nuts. Why would a dog eat fifty sharp metal razor blades? The missing blades must be scattered around the garage floor or something. Is this some type of prank? No dog is stupid enough to chew up and swallow fifty sharp pieces of metal.*

"Well, we should take some X-rays and see what's in there. If he really ate all that metal, it could be serious."

"That's why I'm here," Mr. Ada replied, his impatience still on show.

"OK, then. Let me borrow Ruger for fifteen minutes so I can get those X-rays and I'll get back to you." I tugged the end of Ruger's leash, and he cooperatively followed me out the door.

"CHERYL!" I called as I escorted Ruger into the treatment room. I shouted in these situations because it was a big hospital, and she could be anywhere. She was uniquely industrious and could often be found cleaning, mopping, restocking, and labeling stuff all night in remote corners of the clinic. One day I would find her on the roof with a hot bucket of tar.

"I'm in here," she said from the X-ray room. "What took you so long?" She knew we were going to take radiographs the whole time and had the machine all set up. Her brain was working at ninety-five percent, while mine was hovering at about thirty.

"Mr. Ada thinks this goofy dog ate a whole box of X-ACTO blades," I reported. "You ever see anything like that?"

I knew Cheryl had seen some wild stuff during her many years in the vet business. Her savvy and experience had saved my bacon on several occasions. Cheryl lifted her gaze upward, pursed her lips and brought her hand up to rub her chin. She assumed a deeply thoughtful expression. "Nope, but I did see a dog that ate a stapler once."

I donned the heavy lead protective apron and helped Cheryl hoist Ruger onto the table. He continued to be a cooperative dog, which, at this early hour, was incredibly helpful. I didn't really have the patience for dog wrestling. Due to his large size, we took four X-rays. I needed his entire chest and abdomen visible in case there were any pieces of metal stuck in his esophagus.

We lowered him to the floor, and I parked him in one of the stainless-steel treatment cages. Cheryl ducked into the dark room to develop the X-rays. I hustled to the break room to make some instant coffee. I had about ten minutes to caffeinate before the films would be developed. I drank the whole cup of bitter brew and went back through the lobby to meet Cheryl in the X-ray room. I could still taste the acrid coffee at the back of my mouth. My timing was perfect. She was just opening the door to the dark room and mounting the films on the bank of lit view boxes.

"Oh my Lordy," Cheryl exclaimed in her best southern accent.

The X-rays showed that Ruger had *hundreds* of metal fragments in his stomach. Some were merely slivers. Some were larger, jagged pieces. Some appeared to be whole blades just snapped into two halves. My skepticism abruptly melted. I stood there in disbelief. Mr. Ada was one hundred percent correct. This dopey dog had chewed and swallowed the whole damn box! I'm not sure how it's possible to chew up a box full of razors and not shred your mouth to bits, but evidently Ruger knew. If they were ever hiring a sword-swallower at the local carnival, I'd happily write him a glowing letter of recommendation. Why would a dog left alone in the garage with a cozy nap spot decide to crunch through a box of sharp metal? I looked at the films more closely. There were no razor pieces in his esophagus. From what I could tell, none of the fragments had yet left the stomach and made it into the intestines.

"He must have been pretty hungry," remarked Cheryl.

"Maybe they were those special beef jerky–flavored razors," I said.

"OK. Get the surgery room set up. I'll go talk to Mr. Ada." I grabbed the X-ray films off the view box and headed back to exam room number one.

"Alrighty, Kyle," I said as I entered the dim room. His head jerked up from where it had been resting on his shoulder. He wiped a little drool from the corner of his mouth. He appeared to have been napping. Made sense. He'd been partying the night before and it was now 2:30 in the morning.

"What did you find?" he asked as I mounted the X-ray films onto the viewer for him to see.

"Well, I figured you might be crazy for thinking your dog chewed up and swallowed a box of razors. But it turns out you're not crazy. Your dog is."

"All these bright white objects on the X-ray are the metal fragments he ate. Some of the pieces are pretty damn big. I don't know how he swallowed these without getting badly cut. The good news is that none of the pieces are stuck in his esophagus, and none are in the intestines. He just has a big wad of jagged metal pieces sitting in his stomach. We'll have to perform surgery to get these pieces out. Some of the small pieces might pass without problems, but these bigger pieces could perforate his intestines."

"Fine with me, Dr. Schmidt. I figured that's where this was going to end up. Can you do it right away?"

"Yes. I can get him into surgery in the next half an hour."

"Sounds good," he said. "I've gotta get home and get some rest."

"Do you want me to call you right when I'm done with surgery?" I asked. "Or just later in the morning?"

"You can just call me later, like nine or ten," he said. "Unless there's a problem."

"No problem," I said. "Get some rest and I'll take care of Ruger for you."

"CHERYL!" I yelled again as I went back into the treatment room. *Where did she disappear to this time?* I couldn't see her, but I knew she was lurking within earshot somewhere. "Ruger's dad said to go ahead with surgery, so let's get him ready."

"I'm on it," she said. "I'll be ready to move him in a minute."

I followed her voice to find her hunched awkwardly in the opening of Ruger's large treatment cage. Ruger already had an I.V. catheter in his left front leg and Cheryl was finishing shaving his abdomen for surgery. Her brain was now working at ninety-eight percent while mine had ratcheted all the way up to fifty.

As she finished her shave job, I gave Ruger an intravenous injection of 50:50 ketamine and Valium to make him sleepy, then we hoisted him up onto the treatment table. While I steadied him in place, Cheryl covered his snout with a plastic breathing mask. With her left hand, she reached over to a small silver knob and turned on the oxygen flow. Next, she reached for the palm-sized dial that adjusted the anesthetic gas and turned it all the way up. It only took a minute for Ruger to be completely under anesthesia. He went limp and his breathing slowed to ten breaths per minute. I pried open his mouth and pulled out his tongue to open his airway. This cleared the way for Cheryl to slide an endotracheal tube down his throat. I did some fine-tuning on his belly shave, vacuumed up the stray fur, and we carried him into the surgery suite.

We placed him belly up onto the table, securing his legs to the table with some small blue ties. The stainless-steel surgery table was divided longitudinally into two adjustable halves. This was ideal for Ruger. Because he was big and floppy, we adjusted the table into a "V" shape to secure him in place. While I left the room to scrub for surgery, Cheryl readied Ruger with a sterile prep on his now-bald tummy.

Three minutes later, wearing a blue sterile gown, mask, cap, and latex gloves, I pushed open the double doors of the surgery room with my right foot. I then positioned myself to the right of Ruger's body. "OK," I said. "Let's get to work."

Performing a gastrotomy on a dog isn't that complicated. But for a big dog like Ruger, it is more difficult. After making the initial incision to get through his abdominal wall, I had to reach into his abdomen up to my elbows to reach his stomach. I gently tugged up on his stomach to get it into a position I could reach, then I tacked it in place with four large "stay" sutures. These sutures attached the wall of the stomach to the skin outside the abdomen, keeping it from slipping back inside his abdomen while I was working. The wall of a dog's stomach is thicker than you would think, and it's made of several layers. It's about the thickness of a rubber bicycle inner tube and probably a lot tougher—especially helpful when you decide to eat razor blades.

Using a pair of bulky metal retractors, I held the abdominal wall open so that the muscles wouldn't pinch closed on my hands. This instrument was called a Balfour retractor. It consists of two curved metal arms attached to a bar with a ratcheting mechanism. One arm was placed on either side of the abdominal wall and the arms were stretched apart to hold the abdominal muscles open. The ratchet held the arms in place. One arm of the retractor could be pushed farther out to create a larger opening or moved in as needed to fit the size of the dog. This device allowed me to operate without a surgical assistant to hold things open for me. It was only me and Cheryl in the building, and I needed her to monitor anesthesia as well as open instruments and suture.

Cheryl hovered near Ruger's head. Her gaze darted back and forth between the anesthesia machine and the instrument panel showing his vitals. Periodically she'd lift his lip to check his gum color and make sure his endotracheal tube was staying in place.

"How's it going in there?" she asked. "Have you cut yourself on a razor, yet?"

I had to force myself to concentrate. Operating and talking at the same time with no sleep was a skill I was still working on.

"Nope. So far so good. I'm just getting ready to open his stomach now. You can turn on the suction."

Once the abdomen was held open and the stomach was tacked in place, I packed the area with four absorbent laparotomy sponges. These sponges were about the size of a dish towel and made from a highly absorbent lacey material. Each sponge had a built-in blue-handled loop of cloth to facilitate removal at the end of the procedure. The loop was imbedded with a material that made them detectable on X-ray. If a sponge was accidentally left in the patient after the surgery, you could find it by taking a post-op X-ray. I'd only seen it become necessary once during vet school. It was a potentially life-threatening mistake and to be avoided at all costs.

I looked for a spot on the stomach body with a minimum of large blood vessels and carefully made a three-inch incision. Using thumb forceps, I tented the inner layer of the stomach (the mucosa) and made a stab incision through this layer to enter the lumen of the stomach. As soon as the hole was made, I inserted a blunt-tipped suction catheter to evacuate the fluid in the stomach. This minimized the amount of stomach juices that could spill over into the abdominal cavity. A pint of sickly greenish fluid was slurped up into the suction catheter, through the tubing, down towards the floor, and collected into a glass canister. I swished the tip of the catheter around the stomach to get every nook and cranny inside the floppy organ.

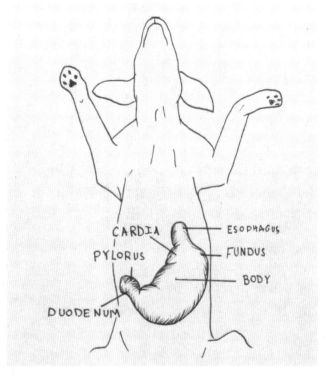

Stomach anatomy

The sound coming from the pump changed from a slurping to a whooshing noise. I was now only getting air. I withdrew the catheter and inserted my gloved right hand into the stomach. I held the wall up and outward with my left hand to facilitate the exploration of the inside with my right hand. The sensation was like sticking my hand into a bucket of wet, crunchy gravel. Metal shards of all shapes and sizes slipped around my right hand and stuck to the back of my glove. Handful by handful, I pulled out clumps of chewed-up razor. I methodically transferred the fragments into a steel bowl Cheryl had opened from its sterile packaging. With each handful I had to release the stomach with my left hand so that I could use it to push the pieces off my right hand and into the bowl. When I released the stomach, it would partially retract back into the dog's abdominal cavity. However, the stay sutures were doing their job and kept the stomach within my reach. The Balfour retractor kept its hold and continued to keep the abdominal wall open.

The stomach of a dog is a very elastic and amorphous organ. It's the shape of an upside-down pear. The esophagus enters the stomach near the diaphragm, and from here, it expands out into the fundus and body of the stomach. The body of the stomach crosses a dog's abdomen then narrows down to where it enters the first part of the intestinal tract. This area is called the pylorus. The interior lining of the stomach is made up of hundreds of floppy folds of tissue called rugae. These rugae aid in the blending and digestion of food, but also allow for an accordion-like stretching of the stomach when a large meal is consumed.

Scoop after scoop after scoop, I methodically cleaned out Ruger's stomach. Once the bulk of fragments was reduced, I had to feel around with my right hand to find individual pieces of metal.

"Jesus," Cheryl remarked as she emptied the bowl for the second time. "How did he eat all that? *Why* did he eat all that? It doesn't make sense."

I could only see about two inches of the stomach interior, so I had to feel my way around to get out all the pieces. This was a slow and tedious process. Each time I thought I had retrieved all the fragments, I would insert my right hand for a *last* feel and come up with one or two more pieces. My hand was too large to reach all the way into the pyloric region. I could only insert my index finger up to the pyloric sphincter. When I did feel a piece of metal here, I had to gently tease it out with the tip of my finger.

Finally, I was done. I had run my right hand into every crevice of Ruger's stomach and could not see or feel any more fragments. I was tired of this tedious game. I looked at the clock on the surgery suite wall. It was 4:30 in the morning. I'd been in surgery for ninety minutes. I rinsed out Ruger's abdomen with sterile saline and slurped up the excess fluid with the suction catheter. I sutured his stomach in three layers and removed the stay sutures. I collapsed the Balfour retractors, removed them, and started the twenty-min-ute process of suturing his abdomen back together.

As I finished the last few skin sutures, I turned to look at Cheryl. She looked like I felt. Disheveled and tired. "OK, Cheryl. Let's get ready to take a couple of X-rays and make sure I got all the pieces out."

Cheryl left me alone to finish the abdominal closure while she read-ied another anesthesia machine in the X-ray room. Five minutes later, we gurnied the big unconscious dog back to take more images. We took both a lateral and a ventral-dorsal X-ray to image the entire cranial abdominal region. Cheryl disappeared for a couple of minutes to feed the films into the automatic developer. It would take another ten minutes for the two films to fully develop into a viewable image.

I once again took advantage of this lull in the action to sprint to the restroom. My bladder was ready to burst at this point. I quickly relieved myself and splashed some cold water on my face. I purposefully avoided looking in the mirror. I didn't want to know how I looked. I pulled the door open and walked back to monitor Ruger. The X-ray films were still cooking, so Cheryl took this opportunity to get her own bathroom break. She returned two minutes later but the developer machine was still humming away. No X-rays yet.

"I'm going to get a quick cup of coffee," I said. "Want one?"

"Nah. I'll monitor Ruger and let you know when the X-rays are ready."

"Thanks," I said as I rushed off to the break room and microwaved a cup of water for another round of Folger's Instant. I needed something to keep me awake and I'd given up on any more sleep for the night. I had to be back and ready for morning appointments in another three and a half hours. I was mid-sip on my cup of Folger's when Cheryl poked her head in the doorway.

"You're gonna have to see this. I think he's still got some pieces left in there."

Oh shit, I thought. This was NOT what I wanted to hear. Maybe the pieces she was seeing were little slivers and we could just leave them alone and let them pass on their own.

I walked into the darkened X-ray room. Ruger was still lying on his left side in the middle of the X-ray table. His anesthesia machine whirred and hissed as he took reassuring steady breaths. I turned to look up at the two X-ray films mounted on the viewer. The pieces were NOT tiny little slivers. They were three jagged bright metal pieces that were three quarters of an inch in size. The bright metal shone like a beacon against the gray and black of his internal organs. As I stared at the images, my heart sank. Part of me wanted to ignore these few inconvenient pieces, but I couldn't. They could cut him and kill him. *How in the hell had I missed these?* I'd felt my way through every inch of his stomach to ensure I wouldn't leave any pieces in there. I had no choice but to open him up again and find the errant fragments. In addition to the large pieces, there were also four to five small shards. I wasn't too worried about those.

"Ugghhh, Cheryl," I said. "We'll have to go back in there and find those big pieces. I'm sorry. I don't know how I could have missed them."

"That's what I thought, too," she said. "Oh well, the night is young. Back to surgery?"

"Yes. Let's get this over with," I sighed.

Cheryl and I both wearily wheeled Ruger back to the surgery room. While she positioned him on the table and did another sterile prep, I left to re-scrub and re-gown. I wasn't in a good mood. I tried to appear resolute and confident for Cheryl's benefit, but I was tired and discouraged. *How had I missed those big pieces? What would happen if I couldn't find them again?* I was full of frustration and fear of failure. I didn't want to let Ruger and Mr. Ada down. They were both trusting me to do a good job.

I quickly undid all my careful suturing of Ruger's abdominal wall. It was demoralizing to undo all the work from just thirty minutes before. What a waste. I repeated my previous preparation by replacing the Balfour retractor and the four stomach stay sutures. I readied the suction and removed all my stomach sutures so I could start the stomach exploration. Once Ruger's stomach was emptied of fluid, I paused and took a deep, calming breath. It was now 4:50 in the morning and I was tired and frustrated. But I needed to be alert, patient, and deliberate. This was my job. Cheryl was depending on me. Ruger was depending on me. Mr. Ada depended on me. I forced myself to perform a mental reset and focus on the problem in front of me.

Once again, I held the outside edge of the incision with my left hand and inserted my right hand back in his stomach. I was determined to be careful and deliberate. I couldn't leave any life-threatening sharp pieces behind this time. With exaggerated slowness, I pushed my right hand up into the dark recesses of Ruger's fundus. Using my fingers, I probed 180 degrees to the left, then 180 degrees to the right. I felt something firm and unyielding pushing against the back of my right ring finger. Keeping my hand pressed against the object, I rotated it around so I could grasp it between my thumb and index finger. With a sigh of relief, I pulled out a one-inch gray piece of jagged razor.

"One down and two to go," quipped Cheryl.

I reinserted my right hand and resumed my meticulous exploration of the metal mutt's stomach. I ran my hand over the inside in every direction from his esophagus to his pylorus. I didn't feel a thing. My confidence from a few minutes ago evaporated. I started over and probed every crevice a second time. Nothing. *Where the heck were those other two pieces?*

I pulled out my hands and took a step back from the table. "Cheryl. I can't find those other two pieces."

"On the X-ray, those other pieces looked pretty big," she said. "I sure wouldn't want to leave them in there."

"I know. But I've felt around every which way, and I still can't find them. We need to find another way to get them out."

Then, a thought struck me! In veterinary school, I had a part time job helping in the study of sustained-release capsules in the rumen of cows. The rumen is the largest compartment of a cow's stomach. It's about the size of a fifty-five-gallon trashcan and helps mix up the plant material that a cow eats. This allows the natural microbes in the cow's digestive tract to break down and digest the material. Pharmaceutical companies were competing to make sustained release capsules that would provide maximum treatment duration when placed into the rumen of cows. To facilitate this study, there was a group of six "fistulated" cows. These cows had a permanent hole from the outside of their left abdomen into their rumen. The hole was closed with a large rubber plug like you would find in an outdoor sink. Once a week it was my job to round up the cows, remove their rumen plug, and reach around inside their rumen to fish out the drug capsules. There would be a representative from the pharmaceutical company who would measure the amount of drug dispensed from the capsule and then I'd put it back in the rumen.

However, there was another object sloshing around in the cow's rumen. A large football-shaped magnet about the size of a small cell phone. It was there to attract any stray staples or wire fragments that the cows would accidentally consume when eating off the ground. As part of the weekly process, I would grab the magnet, pull it out and clean off any metal debris before putting it back inside the cow.

"What if we used a magnet to fish them out?" I said. "I can hardly see anything in there, and I can't feel everything either. But a magnet might attach to those little buggers, and we could get them out that way."

"That might work," she said. "We must have some type of magnet somewhere in this building. Hold tight and let me go look."

Cheryl hustled out of the surgery room with a sense of purpose, leaving me and Ruger alone. Only his deep, steady breaths broke the 5am silence of the surgery room. I stood there with my gloved fingers interlaced in front of me and waited. I became aware of the ticking of the surgery room clock.

Each minute seemed like five. With no tasks to distract me, I had too much time to think. If I couldn't find those other pieces, this operation was a failure. Would this beloved dog survive my incompetence? I couldn't imagine calling Mr. Ada and explaining that after three hours of surgery, Ruger still had razor blades in his stomach. *Ugh!* I could faintly hear Cheryl rustling around in the treatment area. I could hear doors opening and closing as she searched around the deserted building looking for some type of magnet. I heard a few dull thuds and several moments later she reappeared in the surgery room. She had been running around in a tizzy for five minutes, and she was winded.

"Did you find one?" I said.

"Yes. I looked all over the flippin' place trying to figure out where I could find a magnet. Then I realized there was one right there on the treatment room desk. The inner lip of the paper clip holder is magnetized. So, I was able to get the magnet out of that."

She handed me a one-inch dark gray ring.

"Hmmm," I said. "That's what the magnet looks like from a paper clip holder?"

"Yep, that's it."

The magnet ring wasn't sterile, of course, but I wasn't in a position to be fussy at this point. The beauty of Cheryl's resourcefulness was that this magnet was like a large ring. I could easily slide it over the middle finger of my right hand and hold it in place by closing my fist. This left a decent-sized piece of the band protruding from the back of my hand. *This might really work,* I thought with some renewed optimism.

I shoved my Tolkienian *Ring of Power* back into Ruger's stomach and began rotating my fist around for the maximum coverage. I felt and heard an audible *clink.* Wherever that piece was hiding, the magnet found it and it stuck almost immediately. I pulled out my hand and sure enough, there was a half-inch metal shard stuck to the magnet. There were also a couple tiny metal slivers attached. I pulled the pieces off the magnet and pushed my hand back in. This time it took a bit longer. I fully explored the body and fundus of the stomach with nothing to show. I then changed the orientation of my arm and pushed my hand into the smaller pyloric region. *Clink.* Another piece snapped against the back of my finger. I gently pulled out my right hand and was rewarded with another large piece along with a few smaller shards also stuck on the magnet.

"That's it!" I proclaimed. "That ring magnet worked perfectly, Cheryl. Let's close up and get out of here."

It took me another twenty minutes to suture up Ruger's stomach and abdomen for the second time. It was a tedious job, but I felt relieved. We toted Ruger back to X-ray for the third time that night. When they came out, Cheryl and I both held our breath. Hooray, perfect! It was a thing of beauty. Not one single piece of metal was present. Even all the tiny slivers were gone.

We moved Ruger into a large bottom cage in the treatment room where Cheryl monitored him as he came back to consciousness. It was now 6 a.m. I plopped down on a roller stool at the long records desk in the treatment room. Under the dim lights, I could see Cheryl tending to Ruger off to my right. I needed to record the details of Ruger's treatment and I thought I might as well get it over with now. I set down his file and started to write, but there was something hard under the chart that was in the way. I lifted it up and under the chart was a jagged, clear chunk of plastic. I turned up the dimmed lights so I could get a better view. Under the brighter lights, I could see the entire desk was strewn with pieces of broken plastic and two hundred paper clips. I brushed away the debris so I could write in the chart then rotated around to talk to Cheryl.

"What the hell happened here? Did ya blow up the paper clip holder with T.N.T?"

"Not quite," she replied. "But when I saw that the paper clip dispenser held the perfect size magnet, I tried to pry it apart to get it out. That thing was really stuck in there. Then I realized the magnet was molded into the plastic. It wouldn't come out. I was in a big hurry, so I went to the tool shed and got a big-ass hammer. I then proceeded to *SMASH that thing to bits.* That got it out."

"Wow. Good job," I said. "The magnet worked perfectly, and you were able to vent your pent-up frustrations at the same time."

Cheryl gave me a big freckle-faced grin, her red ponytail bobbing up and down as she nodded. "Exactly!"

I picked up the larger bits of clip dispenser shrapnel and tossed them in the trash. I hunched over Ruger's chart to complete my notes.

When Ruger woke up, he looked around the room with wonderment and wagged his tail as if to say, *what the hell happened?* He was the lucky one. He slept through the whole darn thing. I called Mr. Ada at 9:30 in the morning. He picked up the phone on the second ring. Seven hours of sleep had done him good, and he sounded downright perky. I couldn't help being a little jealous.

"Good morning, Dr. Schmidt. Thanks for the call. How are you?"

Well, I feel like I've been run over by a city bus then thrown in the dumpster. At least that's what I wanted to say.

What I really said: "I'm fine, Kyle, thanks. I was just calling to update you on Ruger."

"Yeah, how's that goofy dog doing?"

"He's doing great. He woke up from anesthesia a few hours ago and seems to be happy. His abdomen will be sore from the surgery for about a week, but I was able to get all the metal pieces out."

I didn't bother telling Kyle that it took two surgeries to get the job done. I was too tired to get into the weeds on this and it didn't affect the outcome.

"That's great, Dr. Schmidt. Thank you. When can he come home?"

"He can go home now if you want. His post-op medications are ready, and he's had enough of this place."

Ruger went home an hour later and never looked back. If he ever ate razors again, it wasn't on my shift.

Later that morning, I was in the treatment room in between appointments. I'd had three more cups of coffee. I was unshaven, but I had changed into a fresh set of clothes and rolled on some deodorant. Reality was still fuzzy around the edges, but I knew I could survive until closing at 6 p.m. I'd experienced longer periods of sleeplessness in the army, and on those occasions, I was also freezing my ass off in the snows of Germany.

Dr. Carrol walked in and sat at the treatment desk. He was also seeing appointments that morning. He had a white coffee mug balanced in his right hand and two manilla charts in his left. He carefully placed his full mug down and pulled a pen out of his breast pocket. Evidently his plan was to write notes from his last couple of appointments and enjoy a quick cup of coffee. Dr. Carrol was my boss and one of two partners that owned Largis Animal Clinic. He and a buddy from vet school had joined forces and started this business over twenty years ago. He was a fit guy of average height and brown hair that was thinning on the top. When he found something amusing, he had a huge grin and a booming laugh that you could hear throughout the building. I watched out of the corner of my eye as he reached over to grab a paper clip. He looked confused when he noticed the dispenser was missing and in its place was an inch-high mound of multicolored paper clips.

"What happened to our paper clip holder?" he asked no one in particular.

"Cheryl smashed it with a hammer," I said. "It's a long story."

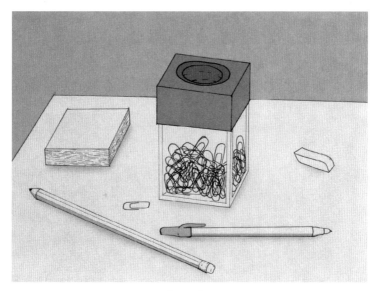

Paperclips

Author's note: For the rest of my career, I kept a sterilized pen magnet in one of the surgery room drawers in case I needed to find something metallic. It came in handy on several occasions.

CHAPTER 8

SHRED

"Dr. Schmidt, Dr. Lux needs your help right away!" Sabrina interjected as she leaned into the doorway of the doctor's office. "He's in room one."

What the heck? I thought. *Dr. Lux needs me?* Dr. Lux was a very experienced veterinarian. He'd been a fantastic mentor to me over the one to two years I'd worked with him. He'd never needed my help before. This must be bad.

Sabrina was a red-haired, freckled whirlwind of activity, and she wasn't waiting for an answer. I jumped up from my desk and hustled after her down the tiled hallway and towards the exam room closest to the lobby. I wasn't prepared for the shocking scene that greeted me. Dr. Lux was leaning over the exam table using his arms and chest to hold down a struggling, crying bloodhound. The dog's head was sitting in a puddle of bright red blood. I stood there for a moment, stunned, trying to figure out what I could do to help. The pathetic dog would moan, cry, then struggle to lift his head. When he succeeded, he would scream and throw his head back down onto the table. It was excruciating to witness. But the most astonishing detail of the scene was the industrial paper shredder attached to this poor pup's left ear. His big, floppy ear just disappeared into the serrated cutting wheels of the shredder.

Shannon, one of our most experienced vet techs, was pressing her upper body down onto the lower half of the dog, trying to keep him from getting up. Her eyes were wild, and her bangs flopped down and covered part of her face. There were two other people in the room: a man and a woman, who I presumed were the pet owners. The man was near the dog's head, and blood was smeared over the entire left side of his face. He'd been using the side of his head to help hold the dog down. He was trying hard to calm the panicking pooch.

"Toby, Toby. It's OK, buddy. I gotch you. You're going to be OK."

He wore a baseball cap and a plaid flannel shirt with a quilted vest. The dark-haired woman was standing with her back pressed against the wall of the exam room. She was as pale as her white sweater and had a look of anguish on her face. Blood was smeared across her entire front. That kind of blood was never coming out.

"Jeff!" shouted Dr. Lux. "We need to get this dog sedated right away before he does any more damage!"

"Got it," I said and ran out of the exam room.

I rushed into the treatment area. There, I reached for a three-cc syringe from a rack on the wall. I unscrewed the plastic cap from the syringe then removed the rest of the protective sleeve by slamming it down on the countertop. I grabbed a small glass bottle with a blue label, a sedative called medetomidine. *How much to give?* I'd only seen the frantic bloodhound for about a second. I did a quick guess on his weight. *One hundred pounds?* I drew up 0.5 milliliters of the clear liquid, tossed the bottle back on the shelf, and snatched a bottle of Butorphanol from the controlled drug drawer. I drew up another 0.5 ml of Butorphanol into the same syringe and ran back to the exam room. I'd only been gone for about thirty seconds.

"I've got it," I exclaimed as I reentered, breathless, into the exam room. There was more blood than when I'd left, and the screaming continued.

"Quick," said Dr. Lux. "Give it in his right thigh."

Shannon scooted over a few inches to create some space. I quickly felt for the meaty portion of the dog's right thigh. I rammed the needle in and pushed the plunger.

This sedative combination works fast, but it's not immediate. I took over holding the dog's head from the male owner. After about ninety seconds, I could feel the large dog's neck and shoulder muscles start to relax. His crying became less frequent and less vigorous. Everyone in the room relaxed a bit, sensing that the worst of the panic was over. Another two minutes and the poor bloodhound was lying calmly on his side, taking slow even breaths. It was still a bloody mess. The temperature in the room was sweltering due to the presence of five adults and one large struggling dog.

"OK," said Dr. Lux, addressing everyone in the room. "That's much better. Now we can work on getting this thing off him. He turned to the pet owners and said, "Mr. and Mrs. Bismarck, you can go home and get cleaned up. We'll take care of Toby from here. I'll call you as soon as we have him stabilized."

"OK, Dr. Lux. Thank you," said Mr. Bismarck. "We've got a ton of blood to clean up in our house and in our car."

"Do whatever you can for him," said Mrs. Bismarck in a quavering voice. "He's our baby." Poor lady. She was clearly in shock.

Mr. Bismarck gently put his arm around his wife and guided her out of the exam room. Sabrina showed up two seconds later with a large metal gurney.

"Alright," said Dr. Lux. "Let's slide him over onto the gurney and get him back into the treatment room. Sabrina, as soon as we get him back, grab an anesthesia machine and get ready to anesthetize him. Shannon, I'll need you to put in an I.V. catheter."

Three of us grabbed the gurney and started wheeling Toby into the treatment room while Sabrina led the way, opening doors as we moved. Shannon pushed from the back and Dr. Lux guided the gurney from the left side. My job was to stabilize Toby's head and keep the bulky paper shredder from pulling on him and inflicting further damage to his ear. The thing was heavy—at least ten pounds. I wondered how the Bismarck's had gotten Toby into the car and then into the vet clinic with this boat anchor hanging off the side of his head.

We got the limp lump of dog safely to the treatment area and got to work. He wasn't fully unconscious, but he was very sedated. He was also exhausted and wasn't struggling anymore. Dr. Lux took charge of the chaos and started barking out orders.

"Shannon, get a catheter into his front leg."

"Sabrina, get that mask on his face and turn the O2 and Iso all the way up."

Shannon got to work shaving his left front leg and deftly inserted an I.V. catheter.

Sabrina fitted a large plastic anesthesia mask over Toby's bloody snout. She held the mask with her left hand and turned on the oxygen and isoflurane gas with her right. I still couldn't let go of the shredder. If it slipped off the table, its pendulous weight might tear his ear completely off. Dr. Lux took a quick break to stop at a nearby sink and scrub the blood off his hands and face. He stripped off his blood-soaked medical coat and threw a scrub top over his short-sleeved dress shirt.

It took two minutes for Toby to drift off to dream land. It was a relief to see his muscles completely relax and his breathing even out. The poor dog had been through hell, and the pain must have been excruciating. With him asleep, we could take stock of the situation.

"What the hell happened here?" I was finally able to ask.

"Mr. Bismarck tossed a half-eaten sandwich in the trashcan in his office," said Shannon. "Toby tried to push his head in there to get at the food. But that waste basket had the paper shredder on top of it. When he poked his head in, the shredder grabbed his ear and sucked it in."

"That's awful," I said. "Poor Toby."

I bent over Toby to get a better look. His left ear had gone in the shredder for five full inches before it stopped. This left only two inches between the
shredder and his head. I grabbed a handful of gauze squares, soaked them
with hydrogen peroxide and started cleaning away the blood. Hydrogen
peroxide is great for this. This was the fastest way to get a good look at the ear.
Sure enough, the shredder had done its job. Cleaning off the blood revealed
the ear flap was sliced into about twenty symmetric ribbons. The portion
sticking out looked like five inches of furry fettuccine. It was a horrible site.

"Let's see what we can do to get this thing off him without tearing his
ear off," said Dr. Lux.

"What about just amputating the ear?" I said. "I don't think we can
salvage it at this point."

"Let's save that as a last resort. If we can get his ear out of this contraption, I think I can save it."

"OK," I said. "How do we get it out?"

"Sabrina, go get the toolbox," said Dr. Lux. "Maybe there's something
in there we can use to pry this thing open."

Sabrina took off like a bat out of hell. There was a small storage shed
behind Pacific Street Vet Clinic where the tools were kept. As she sprinted
out to get the toolbox, the double doors crashed open with a bang and then
slammed back behind her. Sabrina was the fastest tech at Pacific Street Vet
Clinic. In fact, she was the fastest tech I'd ever worked with. She took pride in
being able to do three things at once. She would insert an I.V. catheter while
holding an endotracheal tube and a syringe in her mouth. She would insert
the I.V. catheter, grab the syringe from her mouth to start administering
induction drugs. Two seconds later, she would take the endotracheal tube
from her mouth and slide it down the dog's throat while starting to shave
for surgery. Sometimes she would do this while answering the phone. If you
wanted a whole bunch of things done *right* now, Sabrina was your gal. There
was a price to pay for this speed, however. Sabrina was a natural force of
destruction. In her wake, she would leave a trail of discarded trash, spilled

liquids, and broken pieces of equipment. Whenever Dr. Lux heard something crash to the hospital floor he would yell out "Sabrina, what did you break this time?" He called it correctly about ninety percent of the time.

Ten seconds later, Sabrina crashed back through the double doors coming from the other direction. In her left hand she held the handle of a heavy black metal toolbox. She was halfway across the room when the lid came unlatched and the shiny box opened up, scattering the metal tools across the concrete floor. It made a horrific racket.

"Yep, that's typical Sabrina," quipped Shannon. She could get away with saying things like this. Sabrina was her best friend.

Sabrina skidded to a stop, bent over, and began rapidly throwing the assortment of tools back in the metal box. She was nonplussed by all the pandemonium. It was just a normal day for her. She'd also become accustomed to the teasing brought on by her tornado of a personality.

"She's noisier than two skeletons screwing on a tin roof," remarked Dr. Lux.

She finally replaced all the tools back in the box, picked it up, and bashed it down unceremoniously on the metal treatment table. A pair of pliers spilled out and landed next to Toby's head.

Dr. Lux and I started digging through the tools, looking for something to pry the paper shredder off Toby's mangled ear. Lux grabbed a large pair of adjustable pliers and tried to grab one side of the contraption to lever it apart. No luck. The shredder was too big and too irregular to grip it. He then pulled out a small pair of bolt cutters. After thirty seconds of trying to maneuver the bolt cutters, he gave up. The space between the shredder blades was too narrow and there was nothing substantial to grab onto. I found a hefty screwdriver and inserted it between the two rows of opposing circular blades next to Toby's ear. By twisting the screwdriver tip between the blades, I could create a few millimeters of space, but not enough to pull out the entire ear. I started to pull out the screwdriver and try something else when Dr. Lux said, "Hold on a minute. Leave that in there."

He found another large screwdriver and placed it in the small space between the blades. He wedged it in on the other side of the ear from where I'd placed my screwdriver, but he did so from the opposite orientation. We stood on either side of Toby's bleeding ear with the shredder between us.

"OK," he said. "You pry toward me, and I'll pry towards you."

We both started to gradually push in our respective directions. The shredder was slick with blood and sitting on a stainless-steel table. There was nothing to stabilize it in place and it started to slide around dangerously. If the shredder suddenly turned unexpectedly, it would further rip Toby's ear, completely defeating the purpose.

"Shannon, you hold one end. Sabrina, you hold the other end as steady as you can," ordered Dr. Lux.

We now had four people surrounding Toby's head. We were squished together shoulder to shoulder.

"Alright. Ready?" Dr. Lux said. "Sabrina and Shannon. You hold that thing tight and keep it from moving around. Jeff, when they're ready, you push from your side to pry it open, and I'll pry from my side. OK. One. Two. Three. Go!"

Shannon and Sabrina clamped down on the shredder, pinning it to the table and preventing it from spinning. Dr. Lux and I pushed in opposite directions to pry apart the blades of the demonic ear mangler. This thing was tough. I had no idea paper shredders were built so strongly. I thought that the contraption would come flying apart with this amount of leverage. Nope. It was built like a John Deere tractor. The four of us stood around Toby hunched over and sweating with looks of strained concentration on our faces. Painstakingly, the blade separated two, three, four millimeters apart. It looked like there might be just enough space to pull out the ear. But none of us had a hand free to pull it out! If even one of us let up with one hand, the blades would start to close, or the shredder would spin around, and we'd lose our progress.

"OK. Hold up for a second," said Dr. Lux. "Evelyn!" he called out to another one of the techs.

Evelyn, a short lady with wire-rimmed glasses and dark bobbed hair was on her break. Unfortunately for her, she'd made the mistake of hanging out in the back of the treatment area. She was having some tea and munching on a cookie. She'd was attempting to keep a low profile during the action but hadn't escaped the notice of Dr. Lux.

"Get over here, Ev. We need you," said Dr. Lux.

Evelyn gently set down her tea and grabbed a paper towel to cover her half-eaten cookie. She was less than thrilled at her recruitment into this bloody fiasco.

"When we get this thing pried open, I'm going to need you to pull his ear out of the blades," said Dr. Lux.

"Watch your fingers," I advised. *If there's one thing worse than having an ear stuck in a paper shredder, it's having an ear AND a finger stuck in a paper shredder.*

We now had five people around Toby. It was getting crowded.

"OK. Let's try this again," said Dr. Lux. "One. Two. Three. Go!"

Shannon and Sabrina clamped down on the shredder with all their might. Dr. Lux and I used the screwdrivers as prybars to force the blades open. The blades separated more easily this time. Maybe we were wearing it down. When we had about four millimeters of clearance, Dr. Lux said, "Pull it out, Ev!"

Using both hands, Evelyn grabbed the giant bloodhound ear and began to slowly pull it out as evenly as possible between the blades. A couple of times it got stuck, and Dr. Lux and I had to increase the leverage on our screwdrivers. But, inch by inch, she painstakingly removed the damaged ear from the shark's teeth of the shredder. *Success!* The ear was out. Evelyn's hands and wrists were covered with blood. With a disgusted look on her face, she left the table to go scrub her hands. Then she got back to her cookie.

Toby's ear looked like the fringe on an old cowboy buckskin jacket. But it was now free of the mangler.

"Whew . . .," said Dr. Lux. "Thanks, Dr. Schmidt. I think we can take it from here. Shannon, let's get him into surgery and put this poor ear back together."

I was now at least thirty minutes late for my afternoon appointments.

"Do you think you can sew that mess back together?" I asked.

"We'll see," he said.

I rushed off to clean up a bit. I needed to scrub my hands and grab a clean lab coat before resuming my afternoon appointment schedule. It was 3:30 p.m.

At 5 p.m. I had a brief break between appointments. I cracked open the door to the brightly lit surgery room and poked in my head to see how things were going. The room was silent except for the beeping of the anesthesia monitor and the steady hiss of Toby's breathing. Shannon had positioned herself near Toby's head so she could record his vitals. Dr. Lux was seated on a roller stool and hunched in concentration over Toby's ear. He didn't look up when I entered. His blue OptiVISORs covered his eyes, and his face was only inches from the tattered ear. He was using some *tiny* blue suture material to repair it. I could barely see the spider-web sized filament.

"How's it going in here?" I asked.

"Good," replied Dr. Lux. "I'm about halfway done."

"What is that suture you're using?" I asked.

"6-0 Prolene," he replied.

"Man," I said. "I'm impressed you can even see that stuff."

"The visors really help," he said.

"Well, good luck. I've got to get back to my appointments."

I checked back in on Toby at 6:20 p.m. I'd just finished my last evening appointment and I wanted to see how things were going with his ear surgery.

Dr. Lux was still in the surgery room working on him. He and Shannon were in the same positions as when I last saw them. I entered the room and peered over Dr. Lux's shoulder.

"Still at it, huh?" I said.

"Yep," he said. "Almost done. My neck and shoulders are killing me."

I moved a bit closer to get a look at Toby's ear. Dr. Lux was just finishing the repair on the last half-inch of the final laceration. There were hundreds of neat tiny blue sutures in place: row after row. The margins of the ear looked a little irregular, but overall, his repair job was masterful. I was amazed at the amount of patience and perseverance he put into saving this dog's ear. My expedient solution would have been amputating it, but he was really invested in this dog and was not giving up without a fight. He wasn't willing to let the ear mangler win the day.

As I watched, he carefully placed the last tiny suture. He'd been working on Toby's ear for three hours.

"That's it," he said. "All done. I'll put a wrap on his head to protect his ear and he can go home in the morning."

"Good job on that ear," I said. "I'm impressed. I didn't think you were ever going to get that thing all the way patched back together."

Toby went home the next day without incident. He looked a bit silly with a big bandage on his head, but he seemed OK with it. He wagged his tail vigorously and vocalized in his hound dog warble when the Bismarcks arrived to take him home.

Later the next week, Dr. Lux and I sat in the doctors' office together. We'd just finished up a hectic morning of appointments and were enjoying the chance to sit down and take a lunch break. On Dr. Lux's stocky frame was an unzipped light blue short-sleeve doctor coat with a maroon stethoscope hanging around his neck. He was a graying gentleman, but you could still see the hints of the full head of red hair he'd had in his prime. He was in the habit of walking around all day with a pair of OptiVISORs perched on top of his head. He would pop them down in front of his face at any moment if he needed to look at something close. The big myopic visors would give him a comical appearance. Mr. Magoo came to mind. He had a great sense of humor, and his clients adored him.

"Jeff, do ya remember the dog that got his ear stuck in the paper shredder?" he asked.

"Yeah, Toby," I said. "How's he doing?"

"Pretty good, I think," he said. "I saw him three days after the surgery and took his bandage off. The sutures were all intact and he seemed pretty comfortable. But I wanted to tell you he's coming in on Saturday to see you. "

"OK," I said. "You're not going to recheck him?"

"I'd like to," he said, "but they can only make it on Saturday and I'm off work that day. But I wanted to tell you, even if everything looks good and the ear seems to be healing OK, don't take *all* the sutures out. Just take out every other one . . . so half of them."

"If the ear's all healed up then why don't I just take them *all* out?" I said.

"Let me tell you a little story," he said.

Usually when Dr. Lux said he was going to tell me a story, what he meant was a really bad joke. So, I settled down in my chair, sipped on my soda, and braced myself.

There once was this old country vet who made farm calls. One of his favorite clients was a tough old man named Farmer Smith. The vet knew Farmer Smith had a magnificent prize-winning pig. Smith was so proud of this award-winning pig that he built a pen for him directly in front of his house. Anyone who visited walked right by the pig to get to the Smith's front door.

One day the vet was out to see Farmer Smith. He had to check on a cow with mastitis. When Farmer Smith came to the door, the old vet couldn't help commenting on the pig.

"That sure is a fine-looking pig you've got there," said the vet.

"He sure is," said the farmer. "He won first place at the Manitoba County Fair two months ago and the Chelsea Fair last month. The missus is so taken with him she insisted I build him a nice little shelter right there in front of the house. She's named him Stanley."

Farmer Smith then led the vet over to the sick cow and the old vet was able to get the cow successfully treated.

A month later, the old vet got a call from Farmer Smith. "I'll need you to come over and look at a horse for me," he said. "She's come up lame on her back right leg."

"No problem," said the vet. "I'll be out there first thing in the morning."

The next morning, the vet pulled up and parked his truck in front of the farmer's house. As was his custom, he stopped to admire Stanley—the most impressive pig in two counties. Stanley looked up from his trough and the vet couldn't help noticing he was missing part of a leg. His right hind leg from the knee down was gone. "Huh," he thought. "I wonder what happened to the poor guy?"

When Farmer Smith answered his door, the old vet couldn't help but inquire about the prize-winning pig. "I noticed that ol' Stanley is missing part of his leg," said the vet. "What happened to him?"

"Oh, nothing to be concerned about," said the farmer. "Stanley is doing just fine. Now let's go look at that horse I was telling you about."

Two months later, the old vet was called back to the Smith farm. This time it was to look at some sheep that were off their feed.

As the old vet walked up to the front door, Stanley was directly on the other side of the fence looking at him. The vet went over to pat Stanley on the head. As he was scratching the pig between its ears, he saw that the rest of his right leg was now gone—all the way up to his hip.

When Farmer Smith answered the door, the old vet just had to ask about Stanley.

"Mr. Smith," said the old vet. "I couldn't help but notice that your pig has lost the rest of his right leg. What happened to him?

"Oh, don't you worry about him," said the farmer. "Stanley does just fine on three legs. What I really need is for ya to come look at these here sheep. I don't know what's going on with them."

The old vet followed Farmer Smith out to the barn where he was keeping the sick sheep.

Six weeks later, Farmer Smith was on the phone again. "Doc, I need you to come out here for me. Matilda, my donkey, has just about tore off her ear. She must have caught it on a fence or sumthin. Can you get out here to fix it?"

"Sure," said the old vet. "I can make it out there at 4:30."

The old vet pulled up to Mr. Smith's house at 4:30 p.m. He was worn out. He'd been making house calls since early morning. His back was sore, and he had abrasions on both his hands. As he walked up to the farmhouse, he looked over to see how Stanley was doing. He really was a fine-looking animal. As Stanley turned to look up at him, he saw something new. In addition to missing his entire right hind leg, he was now missing part of his left front leg from the elbow down. What the heck was going on? He wasn't in the mood for any more of Farmer Smith's deflections.

He banged on Farmer Smith's door.

"Well, hello there, sir," said Farmer Smith in greeting. "Thanks a lot for coming out today. Poor Matilda is in a rough spot."

"Mr. Smith," implored the vet. "This is the third time now I've been out to your place and noticed that Stanley is missing a part of his anatomy. As your veterinarian, I demand to know what's going on."

"OK, OK," said Farmer Smith with an impatient look on his face. "I didn't mean for you to get all outta sorts. We all have a warm place in our hearts for that pig. The fact of the matter is, with a pig as good as Stanley, you just can't eat him all at once."

I sat there looking at Dr. Lux. I shook my head several times. I couldn't help but let out a bemused chuckle, but then, almost immediately, I felt self-conscious that I found this twisted story amusing. What did this say about me? Over the years I'd learned that veterinarians have a uniquely dark sense of humor.

"So, are you telling me that you don't want me to take out the sutures *'all at once'* because you want to savor the process and enjoy it over time just like Stanley's legs?"

"Not really. I just thought it was a pretty funny joke," said Dr. Lux. "I don't want you to take them out all at once because it's a fragile repair job. So even if it looks all healed, we need to be cautious. I'd leave at least half the sutures in for another week to make sure his ear doesn't fall apart."

"OK. No problem. I'll look forward to seeing him on Saturday."

The weekend came around and Toby's family arrived right on schedule. I'd never really seen Toby under normal circumstances. He was a big drooly goofball and very talkative. He would look at you, size you up, and then vocalize like crazy, *Arhh, Arhh, Roo, Roo, Roo.* When he didn't get the response he was looking for, he would try again. *Lahhhrrr, Larhhhrr, Gruff. . . .* I didn't know what the hell he was talking about, but he had quite the personality and you couldn't help but love him for it. With Mr. Bismarck holding him, I was able to get a good look at his injured left ear. It resembled a neatly plowed corn field with about ten rows of evenly placed tiny blue sutures. I flipped the ear over to look at the underside. It looked pretty much the same. I certainly didn't see any areas that looked infected or spots that were coming loose. The hair was just starting to grow back. Dr. Lux's work was magnificent.

Toby

"How is Toby doing at home?" I asked.

"He's back to his normal dopey self," said Mrs. Bismarck. "He gulps down his food like he's starving and barks like a maniac if he sees a squirrel. Although . . . he won't go *anywhere near* our office where the paper shredder incident occurred."

"Yeah, the famous paper shredder incident," I said. "He may be traumatized for life. I wonder if he'll ever be brave enough to go back in there?"

With Mr. Bismarck holding Toby's head and Mrs. Bismarck giving him treats, I started the laborious task of taking out the sutures. I was now glad Dr. Lux only wanted half of them removed because there were oodles of them in there. It would have taken forever. I borrowed Dr. Lux's OptiVISORs for this project. In between treats and head shakes, I slipped the hooked end of the suture removal scissors under a tiny stitch and snipped it. I then used a small pair of hemostats to pull out the suture. In the end, I estimated that I removed four hundred sutures, and it took about a half hour. There was a pile of little blue pieces on the floor by my feet. We had to stop a few times because Toby needed a break. He could only stand still for so long.

When I was finished, I stood back to admire the job.

"Dr. Lux sure did a nice job on that ear," I said. "I honestly wasn't sure he was going to be able to save it, but it's looking almost normal. He only wanted me to remove about half the sutures today. He wants to personally recheck him next week to make sure it's healed properly before he takes out the rest."

"I'd assumed Dr. Lux was just going to have to cut his ear completely off," said Mr. Bismarck.

"Me too," I said. "Instead, he spent about three hours putting that ear back together."

"Well, we are both really grateful to Dr. Lux for doing such an amazing job," said Mrs. Bismarck. "Toby would have looked pretty funny with just one ear."

"Yep. I'll let him know," I said. "He is an impressive surgeon. He'll be happy to see him next week and see how well his ear is healing."

Later, alone in the coffee room, I had a chance to reflect on Toby's case. If I'd been the only vet on duty that day, Toby would be running around with one ear. He would be perfectly healthy but disfigured for the rest of his life. I didn't believe his ear could be saved. Fortunately for Toby, he was cared for by Dr. Lux. He had the skill, fortitude, and patience to save his ear. I'd been educated by the best vet school in the country, but I still had a lot to learn from an old vet with a questionable sense of humor.

A week later, Toby wagged his way back into the clinic. He greeted the front staff with *Roo, Roo, Lahharr, Arhh, Arhh.* That's bloodhound speak for *I'm here for my appointment with Dr. Lux.*

Dr. Lux patiently removed the rest of his sutures and gave Toby a treat from the jar sitting on the countertop. After that, Toby became a regular at Pacific Street Vet Clinic. We'd see him at least twice a year for health checks and vaccinations. His shredded ear went on to heal nicely, but it was never quite normal. The linear scars formed neat cornrows and the regrowth of fur never completely covered them. But through the process, he'd become somewhat of a celebrity. *"The dog who got his ear caught in a paper shredder."* Dr. Lux saved that shredder. It's held in a special place in his museum of bizarre veterinary memorabilia.

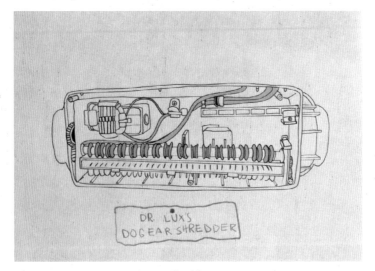

Shredder

CHAPTER 9

So, You Wanna be a Vet?

"**H**ey, Doc. What the hell is goin' on out there? I've been waiting for twenty minutes," said the black leather–clad pet owner in exam room two.

"I'm very sorry, Mr. McFarland," I said to what appeared to be a permanent scowl on his face. "The last appointment I saw . . . man, that dog had a lot of problems and the owner wanted to describe them *all* in detail."

Mr. McFarland sat on the hard wooden bench in exam room two at Pacific Street Vet Clinic. He was sitting at an awkward angle. His posture suggested he wanted to lean back, but the narrowness of the bench made this precarious. His arms were crossed over his chest, and he didn't look so happy.

"Well, you should just tell 'em they've got thirty minutes and then they need to get the hell outta there," he said. His sparse cropping of white hair and angular features added extra authority to the statement.

I couldn't help but grin at this declaration. He cut straight to the point and didn't have much of a filter. It was rather refreshing compared to the common chitchat the rest of us felt compelled to take on. He either wasn't aware of this custom, or, more likely, just didn't give a damn.

"Well," I said, enjoying the irreverent path this conversation was taking, "Don't you think they might get upset and never come back?"

"That's *their* problem," he replied with a snort.

I'd never met Mr. McFarland before. He wore black jeans, black leather boots, a black t-shirt, and a black leather motorcycle jacket.

"I'll take that under advisement," I said. "It certainly *would* help keep my appointments on time."

"Damn straight," he said.

I decided on a change of subject. "That's an awesome-looking golden retriever pup you've got there. What can I do for him today?"

"His name is Mac. He's four months old. I've only had him for about six weeks and he's pretty much a royal pain in the ass."

For the second time, I found myself grinning at his gruff assessment.

"So, does he just need his last series of puppy shots?"

"Yeah, and maybe a prescription of Xanax for him . . . and Dilaudid for me," he said. "This dog's got so much energy; he's driving me bonkers."

I looked down at Mac. He noticed me gazing at him and went into a spasm of uncontrolled wiggles. His tongue lolled out to one side and swayed in unison with his whipping tail. He was a gorgeous young dog with an alert, intelligent, kind face, and a beautiful glossy golden hair coat. He was so damn happy he couldn't control himself. When I looked at him, he got so excited he would shake his whole body and make warbling noises in the back of his throat.

"See what I mean about this dog?" said Mr. McFarland, making a gesture with both hands as if he was giving me a present. "Mac's a total nutcase."

At the mention of his name, Mac reared up on his hind legs, put his front legs on Mr. McFarland's lap and started covering his neck with a flurry of slobbery kisses.

"Awww . . . ugghh . . . arrgghh," exclaimed Mr. McFarland as he pushed Mac away.

I stood leaning against the exam room door, thoroughly enjoying the spectacle and the faux outrage by Mr. McFarland. It was clear that he was smitten with Mac and truly loved the affection. "It looks like you happen to have a really healthy, smoochie, young golden retriever," I said. "That's how they act. The challenge is going to be finding something for him to do and keep him occupied."

Mac was hard to resist. He wanted so badly for someone to play with him and pet him. He was bursting at the seams. I sat down on the linoleum floor to oblige. I rubbed him on his head and shoulders and let him lick me a little. I tousled his hair, rubbed his nose, and then playfully pushed him away. He thought this was a wonderful game, reared up on his back legs and came back for more. This time he made a playful growl and went into a downward dog pose before he pounced. His tail whipped about, betraying his mock aggression. He was hilarious. I wrestled around on the floor with him for about thirty seconds before I stood up and got down to business. Mac looked crestfallen that I'd interrupted his game.

"He's a great dog. You're gonna have a lot of fun with this guy."

Mac was in the clinic for a simple visit that day: a "get to know you" type appointment. I did give him a rabies and a DHPP vaccine. He took both injections without a flinch. He was more excited about the human interaction than being worried about the little poke in the nape of his neck. At every opportunity, he would turn his head and give me a smooch on the cheek or neck. We started Mac on an oral monthly medication to prevent heartworms, as well as a monthly topical medication to control fleas and ticks. We discussed transitioning him from puppy food over the next couple of months to an adult dog food. Our last topic of discussion was getting him neutered, or castrated, as it's termed for male dogs.

"So, you just wanna cut his nuts off?" said Mr. McFarland.

Once again I was taken aback by his brusqueness. Refreshing? I guess, but he was a hard guy to read. I was on uncertain ground but decided to forge ahead.

"Well, more or less," I said. "But it's not really that bad. They're fully under anesthesia for the procedure. We send them home on pain meds. Most of the time they're back to normal the next day. It's not a mandatory procedure, but with most dogs it makes them better pets."

"Like, how?" said Mr. McFarland.

"Well, they're less likely to get loose and roam the neighborhood. When a female dog goes into heat, the local male dogs go crazy if they're not neutered. Even easygoing, mellow dogs will break out and try to find her. I've seen male dogs hurt themselves trying to escape. They'll break through windows and climb over fences. One time I had a sad situation where a frenzied male dog accidentally killed himself. He was tied up by his neck with a rope in the front yard. He pulled and twisted so hard to escape that he strangled himself. Getting them neutered also makes them less territorial. They get in less fights and are less likely to urine-mark on every tree and bush. And . . . they're less motivated to hump the legs of your guests when they come over for dinner."

My last comment seemed to get his attention. Mr. McFarland pursed his lips and slowly shook his head.

"Yeah. He's already starting to do that. My wife, Lori, absolutely *hates* it. OK, doc. I'll think about it and get back to you. When would this need to be done?"

"Sometime between six and twelve months of age would be reasonable," I said. "If you want, I'll just set a reminder in our computer system. We can meet to talk about it again at that time."

Mr. McFarland stood and picked up the end of Mac's leash in preparation for leaving. "So, I guess today's visit is free, since you were twenty minutes late?"

"Sorry, my friend. Nice try, but that's not the way it works," I said. "You've got an awesome dog there, though. I'll see you in a couple of months."

We shook hands. Mac wagged his tail and pranced in excitement. Mr. McFarland headed towards the reception desk where he could pay his bill and lambast the office staff for a few minutes.

One week later, I got a phone call from Mr. McFarland. I was sitting in the doctor's office at Pacific Street Vet Clinic. The office had a large built-in desk that wrapped around three sides of the room. My workstation was on the right side, in the back, against the windows to the parking lot. I was in the midst of struggling and cursing at my new computer. It had the outside dimensions of an eight-by-ten-inch piece of paper and was only one centimeter thick. It was very stylish and cute, but a god-awful pain in the butt to operate. This was a new type of gizmo that worked both as a laptop and a tablet. The clinic had proudly purchased ten of them, being quite pleased with their techno-savvy. When the device was in laptop mode, you could twist the screen then fold it over the keyboard to make a compact tablet. The screen was touch-sensitive and came with a stylus that would convert handwriting directly to text. The concept was ingenious, but it was quickly apparent how awkward it was to use. The keyboard was about the size of a cell phone with the keys squished impossibly close together. A pixie elf would find it just about the right size. I discovered, to my dismay, what happens when you accidentally touch the screen while typing. It would highlight, then delete *everything* you just entered. It was infuriating. I was in the process of retyping a record for the *second* time that afternoon when the overhead speaker crackled to life.

"DOCTOR SCHMIDT, I HAVE AN ANTONY MCFARLAND ON LINE THREE WANTING TO SPEAK WITH YOU."

Uh-oh, I thought. It struck me as ominous since I'd seen him so recently. *I hope everything is OK with Mac.*

I picked up the receiver and tapped the blinking button for line number three. "Hello, this is Dr. Schmidt," I said into the receiver.

"Doc, this is Antony McFarland," came over the speaker.

"Hi, Mr. McFarland. What can I do for you?"

"Doc, please just call me Antony," he said. "Mr. McFarland is my dad. He was a mean old bastard and he's been dead for ten years now."

"OK, Antony," I said. "How can I help you? Is Mac doing OK?"

"Yeah, yeah, yeah," he said. "Mac is fine, but he's still a big pain in the ass. Yesterday he dug a two-foot hole in my back lawn. Then he ran his muddy ass inside and rolled around on my new carpet. But that's not the reason I'm calling you. I wanted to let you know that I really appreciated the way you handled my dog the other day. It was great the way you got down on the floor and played with him. You're the only vet I've ever seen that does that."

Wow. A compliment from Mr. McFarland? He was such a hard nut to crack. Sarcastic one moment and now complimenting me. I was honored.

"It was my pleasure, Antony. He's a great dog. I was just having some fun with him."

"He loves you, Doc. I've never seen him get so excited around someone before. Even my daughter . . . she plays with him a lot, but not as crazy-playful as the other day with you."

"He does like to play kinda rough," I said. "I just indulged him a bit."

"Well, he loved it, Doc. I was happy to see him so comfortable with you. You're going to be my vet from now on."

I was pleased that I'd won over Mr. McFarland. He didn't seem the type to trust people readily. It was an honor, but I'm not sure the reception staff would share my sentiment.

"Well, thanks a lot. I appreciate that." *Was this the whole reason for the call?*

"Hey, Doc, I do have a really big favor to ask of you."

Uh-Oh. Here it comes. I was pretty sure he didn't call just to tell me what a great guy I was.

"It would mean the world to me if you could talk to my daughter about being a vet. She's really into animals and thinks she'd like to be a vet someday."

I paused before answering. *This could get messy.* There were little favors and big favors, and this was leaning into the big favor category. But how could I refuse helping a young kid that loved animals?

"Sure. I guess I can do that for you. How old is she?"

"She's sixteen. She's a junior at Oakdale High School."

"Just let me look at my work schedule for the next couple weeks," I said.

Being very careful and using the back of my pen so as not to anger the fussy computer gods, I typed a few keystrokes on my new miniature laptop. On my third keystroke, I accidentally hit two adjacent keys at the same time. The entire screen went blank, then defaulted back to the reboot screen of Windows 98. *Shit . . .*

"Hold on a minute," I said over the phone. "My damn computer just rebooted, and I have to start all over."

"No prob, Doc. Take your time," he said.

While I was waiting, I asked a couple more questions. "So, what's your daughter's name?"

"Alex. Short for Alexandria."

"Has she read any of those James Herriot books?" I asked. "Those books give a lot of good insight into vet medicine."

"Doc. She fucking loves those books," he said. "Her grandmother gave her the full set when she was eight years old. She read them all in a month."

"All right," I said. "I've got my work schedule back up. How about this Saturday at 12:30? I have a lunch break and then I don't have another appointment until 2:30. Does that work OK for the two of you?"

"That's perfect, Doc," he said. "We'll be in the lobby of your office at 12:30 sharp. I really appreciate it. I owe you one."

Mr. McFarland could be quite charming when he chose even if it was in a cracked dry leather sort of way.

"Nah, it's not a problem. I'll see ya this Saturday."

Saturday at 12:20 p.m., I was sitting at my desk once again fighting with my nano computer to record the exam findings for Brutus the mastiff. I was contemplating chucking the sleek, aesthetic piece of crap into the dumpster when my phone intercom chirped to life.

"Dr. Schmidt, Mr. McFarland is here with his daughter to speak with you."

"Got it, Kim." I replied. "I'll be out there in a few minutes."

As I finished writing the last of the exam results for Brutus, I couldn't help but picture his most striking feature: a beach-ball sized head. It must have weighed forty pounds. Brutus would use his head like a battering ram to butt against your hips for attention. When he got his way, and the petting ensued, drool would spill over the sides of his mouth like an overfilled water trough. My pant legs were still damp.

I took off my blue doctor's coat. It was smeared and stained and hairy. If Alex was interested in being a vet, this was exactly the look that might gross her out and change her mind.

I walked out into the treatment room and headed through the clinic toward the lobby. The reception lobby of Pacific Street Vet Clinic had been recently remodeled. It looked new and clean and sharp, but it was still very bare. Corrugated metal siding covered the front of the reception desk and there was a single anemic-looking plant in the corner. The owner hadn't added any décor yet, so it looked like an abandoned house. There were two rows of flat benches and Antony and Alex stood up from one of them when I entered.

I could tell right away that Antony's whole demeanor was different around his daughter. Gone was the black leather ensemble replaced with stylish blue jeans and a long-sleeved white button-down shirt. As his daughter got up, he motioned as if he was going to support her arm if she needed assistance, but she didn't. She was a fit, athletic girl who was perfectly able to get up on her own.

"Doctor Schmidt, this is my daughter, Alex," said Antony with considerable pride.

"Hi, Alex. Nice to meet you." I said as I extended my hand to shake hers. "Your dad says you're a pretty motivated young lady."

Alex held a camel-colored portfolio in her right hand. She had to switch it to her other hand to shake. She was dressed very sharp as if for a job interview. *Good for her,* I thought. She's taking this very seriously. She wore tasteful khaki trousers, a crisp white blouse, and a striking blue blazer the color of the sea. She had dark hair and dark eyes. She was well-composed and attractive. I could see why her dad was so proud of her. Antony obviously adored her.

"I met your new dog, Mac, a couple weeks ago," I said. "He seems perfect. What a sweetie. I'm jealous."

"Thanks, Dr. Schmidt," said Alex. "Yes, we love Mac. He's a riot. And thanks again for meeting with me and agreeing to answer some of my questions."

"My pleasure. Why don't we go into one of the exam rooms so we can sit down and talk?"

"After you, Doc," said Antony, gesturing forward with both hands, as if he owned the place.

I escorted Antony and Alex down the hallway. To the right was a row of identical wood-paneled doors each with a number on them. I opened door number one and peeked inside. The floor was covered in clumps of dog hair, the countertop was smudged with some unknown brown substance, and there were used vaccine vials still on the exam table.

"Nope," I said, "Not that one. It still needs to be cleaned. Let's try number two." I pushed open the door to exam room two. It looked neat and tidy. "This looks good. Let's give this a try."

I held open the door. Antony and Alex sat next to each other on the narrow, uncomfortable bench against the far wall. I pulled up a rolling exam stool and sat across from them.

"So, you wanna be a vet?" I commented, looking at Alex.

"I'm seriously thinking about it," she said. "I read all the James Herriot books and I loved them. I just love being around animals and caring for them. I think it might be a very rewarding career for me."

"That's great. I've been a veterinarian for about ten years now and I can tell you it's never boring. There's always some new problem to solve. You get to see a wide variety of furry creatures . . . and you meet some pretty *interesting* people—like your dad," I said with a grin.

"Yes, interesting would be *one* word for it," said Alex as she contemplatively looked over at Antony.

"So, what made you want to be a vet in the first place?" Alex asked me.

I paused for a moment, leaned back, and pursed my lips. This was a question I hadn't thought about in a long time. In any profession, one gets tangled up in the daily particulars of the job. I would complete task after task, see client after client, patient after patient. At the end of the day, if I'd checkmarked all the boxes, I felt a sense of satisfaction. I was busy *every* day. I worked four twelve-hour days and one overnight shift a week. I had a wife and two daughters at home. I also had two cats and a dog. It's not very often that I stopped to think, *Well, how did I get here?* The old "Talking Heads" song came to mind, and I grinned inwardly, remembering the quirky lyrics . . . *and you might find yourself behind the wheel of a large automobile.*

"That's a good question. It's not something I think about much these days." I paused hoping I could find some meaningful response. Then an image began to materialize in my head, and I heard myself say . . .

"When I was about eight years old, there was an incident I remember quite clearly. My family lived on forty acres of land in Scottsdale, Arizona.

We had a family dog named Gobi. He was a Samoyed. Are you familiar with Samoyed breed dogs?"

"Yes," said Alex. "They are big, fluffy, white dogs, right?"

"Right," I said. "They're big, fluffy, white dogs. They come from the Gobi Desert in China. The temperatures there are brutally cold, so they have super thick, beautiful white fur coats to keep them warm. We first got Gobi when we lived in the Sierra Nevada Mountains, but then we had to move to Arizona when he was about four years old. Arizona's a terrible climate for a Samoyed. It's way too hot for them, but he made do. He was a trooper."

"At this same time, we also had a horse named September. We took care of her for a couple of years while her real owner was going through a rough patch. September was a beautiful chestnut horse, an American Saddlebred. She was very gentle and sweet. She was also a trained competitive jumping horse."

Me & September

"How long did you live in Arizona?" asked Alex.

"For about three years. My family was used to the cooler climate of the mountains, and it was just too hot and miserable there. We moved as soon as my mom finished nursing school and got a job back in California."

"Anyways, one day I was riding September out in the desert around our house. I wasn't a very experienced horseman, but September could tell that, and she took it easy on me. She was remarkably gentle for being such a huge creature. Gobi was trotting back and forth around us as we weaved around the creosote bushes. He'd entertain himself by chasing lizards and mice that popped out of their holes. At one point in the ride, we came up to a dry creek bed in the desert floor. It was about three feet deep and fifteen feet wide. The banks of the gulch were gently sloped, so I figured we would walk through without incident. The problem arose when my plan for crossing the dry creek bed and September's plan diverged. As we moved toward the edge, I assumed she would mosey down the bank, cross the floor, and walk up the other side. She disagreed and thought this was the perfect opportunity to show off her competitive jumping skills. Just when we reached the lip of the bank, she gathered up her haunches and gracefully launched herself five yards to the other side. I was caught completely off guard and tossed six feet in the air. I yelled in surprise as I flew through the air, then landed with a loud *oooff* sound flat on my back on the floor of the creek bed. The wind was completely knocked out of me. I was on my back in the dirt moaning and gasping for several minutes. I felt horrible, and thought I was going to die. I could tell Gobi was scared, but he ran to my side and nuzzled and licked me. September stopped on the other side of the creek bed. She glanced back at me lying in the ditch and started nibbling at some shoots of greenery sprouting out of one of the nearby bushes."

I chose this moment to pause and catch my breath. Both Antony and Alex were leaning forward and staring at me intently.

Alex chimed in. "I've been thrown by a horse while riding too. Last year in Santa Barbara. It's a long ways down. It hurts."

"Yeah. No kidding," I said. "I couldn't even move for a couple of minutes. But, unbeknownst to me, one of our neighbors, Larry, saw the whole thing happen from his backyard. He ran out across one hundred yards of dirt in flip-flops, shorts, and a t-shirt to make sure I was OK. But when he got to the creek bed, Gobi wouldn't let him *anywhere* near me. He stood directly between me and Larry, snarling, barking, and lunging whenever Larry tried to approach, even though he knew him well. Larry was a good friend of the family and hung out with my dad. But because I was injured and lying on the ground, Gobi was not letting him get close to 'his kid.' His face was one big, menacing snarl."

Antony's elbows rested on his knees, and he held his chin with both hands. He was clearly anticipating the part of the story where Gobi tore off my neighbor's arm. Alex had her portfolio opened on her lap and appeared to be scribbling some notes.

"Larry tried talking to Gobi to calm him down. '*Hey Gobi, buddy. It's OK. I'm just here to check on Jeff.* You know me. We're friends, right?' he said."

"Nothing doing. Gobi was *not* Larry's friend on this day. With his lips pulled back in a snarl, his teeth looked huge. He was scary as hell. Even I was afraid of him. Gobi wouldn't back down an inch. This went on for a few minutes until my dad arrived. He'd been outside and heard all the commotion. As soon as he showed up, Gobi completely changed his demeanor. He stopped barking and started wagging. He backed away and let my dad and Larry come over to check on me. I was basically fine—bruised and embarrassed, but no serious injuries. We grabbed September by the reins and slowly walked the hundred yards back to the house."

I leaned forward on my stool. "Here's the thing, though," I said. "In that moment, I felt a huge surge of pride and love for that dog. When it came to his family, there was no middle ground. His fear and anger may have been misplaced, but he was willing to protect me to the death. His loyalty was etched in granite. He proved he was much more than just a furry sidekick. He was instead an incredibly noble creature worthy of love and respect."

I paused again. I needed to stop and gather myself a bit. I was surprised, and a little embarrassed, at the amount of emotion this story brought out in me.

"I can't say for certain that was the moment I decided to become a vet," I said. "But it was a big factor. That's a kind of love and loyalty you don't see every day. It's an incredible thing to witness."

Gobi

"Wow," said Alex. "That's a good story. Can I ask you some questions about your schooling?"

Relieved to move on to a less emotional topic, I sat up straighter on my stool, took a deep breath, and crossed my arms over my chest. "Sure. What would you like to know?"

We went on to talk for another forty-five minutes. I told Alex that to get accepted into vet school, she needed to be a dedicated student. She needed pretty near straight A's across the board. Vet school applications were extremely competitive. At that time there were only twenty-seven vet schools in the country. California only had one, U.C. Davis. The vet program at Davis received around five hundred applications each year for 125 positions. She especially needed to excel in math and science. Chemistry, organic chemistry, biology, anatomy, calculus, physics, microbiology, virology, physiology were also all on the menu. I *loved* this stuff. I got excited just talking about it. But with most people, when you talk about these subjects, their eyes just glaze over. Alex seemed to take it all in.

Alex was obviously a smart, motivated young lady and she'd grilled me pretty thoroughly. When I was done answering all her questions, we stood up to leave. She'd taken a few notes during our talk, and it took her a few moments to pack up her belongings. Her demeanor reminded me of an attorney after finishing her final arguments before the court.

"Wow, thanks, Doc. That was great," said Antony.

"Yeah, thanks, Dr. Schmidt. That was super helpful," said Alex.

"It was a pleasure to meet you," I said. "If you have more questions, feel free to call me or email me. Antony, let's get Mac back in here in a couple of months to talk about his procedure."

"Will do, Doc," he said. "Again, thanks so much. I owe you."

"Happy to help, sir. See ya soon," I said as I escorted them out to the lobby.

I didn't hear from Antony for a couple of months. Then one day, on a Wednesday afternoon, I saw his name on the appointment schedule. He was bringing Mac in for a neuter consultation.

At 3:05, Shannon approached me in the treatment room. She was holding a clipboard in her left hand. "Hey, Dr. Schmidt," she said. "I have your three o'clock appointment in room one. It's Mac McFarland. Mr. McFarland says he's here to get Mac's balls *chopped off*." Shannon was a sweet person and a dedicated vet tech, but I could tell from the look on her face she didn't appreciate Antony's crassness.

"OK," I said. "I'll be right in there. Give me a minute. I just need to go grab the meat cleaver."

When I opened the exam room door, Mac was waiting directly on the other side to greet me, all grins and wags. Even though I'd only seen him once before, he acted like I was his best friend. I got down on my knees and gave him a hug and let him lick my face. He was one of the happiest, friendliest dogs I'd ever seen. He'd also gained about twenty pounds since I last laid eyes on him. He still had a little bit of puppyness about him, but it was mostly being replaced with the physique of a gorgeous adult golden retriever.

"Hi, Antony. Good to see you," I said. "How's it going?"

"Pretty good, Doc," he said as we shook hands. I noticed Antony was back to his uniform of black boots, black jeans, and motorcycle jacket. But today he was wearing a snug white t-shirt. He was a fit, muscular guy. Especially considering his age. "I'm just here to plan for Mac's surgery."

The main purpose of this consultation visit was to make sure the pet owner understood the process and had an opportunity to ask questions. I gave Mac a cursory exam, which mostly consisted of him romping around the exam room and licking me on the face. I listened to his heart and lungs. I pried open his mouth so I could check to make sure nothing was amiss. At one point, he flopped over on his back so I could rub his tummy. This was convenient since I did need to confirm that he indeed had two descended testicles. I'd made the error of not checking before with other dogs. It was embarrassing on surgery day to realize the patient only had one descended testicle. I'd have to call the pet owner and explain that the ensuing *Easter Egg Hunt* to find it would now make the bill three times more expensive.

"All right, Antony. I've got Mac scheduled for surgery for next Tuesday," I said. "Just don't feed him anything that morning so his stomach is empty. Drop him off between seven and nine in the morning."

"No problem, Doc," he said. "We'll be here."

"By the way," I said. "I haven't seen you since we talked with Alex. Whatever came of that? Does she still want to be a vet?"

Antony paused for a moment and got an odd look on his face. "Doc, I'm grateful for you taking the time to talk to my daughter like that. It means the world to me. But that's kind of a long story. I'll tell you what. Why don't we meet someday when you get off work? I'll buy you a drink and we can talk about it."

I hesitated a bit at his offer. Seeing Antony on a professional level to care for his dog was one thing. Consulting with him and Alex for a career-counseling session was another. Meeting him after hours for a drink was taking things to a different, and potentially uncomfortable, new level. My staff was already giving me grief over his *rough around the edges* approach to, well, everything. On the other hand, I was intrigued. What made this odd character tick? I had to say something quick. I didn't want my pause to be too obvious.

"Sure, I'm game," I said. "I'm available most days after work. I'm usually done by 6:30 or 7." I wrote my cell phone number on the edge of the check-in sheet and tore off the corner and handed it to him.

Antony took the scrap of paper and shook my hand. At the same time, Mac licked me on the wrist. "I'll check my calendar for the next couple weeks, Doc, and hit you up," he said. "Probably after Mac's all done with his nut job."

"Yep, Sounds good to me. See ya next week," I replied.

Mac's surgery went fine. He was healthy as a horse and just about the most cooperative doggy patient you could hope for. He thought the vet clinic was a wonderful place and all the employees were specifically hired just to play with him. We were all his best friends. Even after his procedure, groggy and lying on his side recovering from anesthesia, all you had to do was look at him and he'd start thumping his tail. He was a keeper.

I met Antony in the lobby that afternoon when he was there to pick up Mac and take him home.

"I love what you've done with the place, Doc," said Antony gesturing to the lobby as he stood to greet me. "You've really been working on the décor."

His deadpan expression didn't help me interpret the comment. However, considering the source, I assumed this was sarcasm. We had actually added another anemic plant and an end table in the corner.

"Yeah, Martha Stewart's got nothing on us," I said. "We've been decorating all weekend. By the way, Antony, Mac did great. No problems at all. He likes this place and thinks it's really fun."

"Even now?" he asked.

"It seems so. The first thing he did when he woke up was wag his tail. He's been wagging and wiggling all afternoon. He certainly doesn't seem to hold a grudge."

"I don't think I'd be so accommodating if you cut *my* balls off," he said.

"Yeah, but he's a lot nicer than you," I said with a smirk.

"Yeah, that's definitely true," he said.

"Hey, Doc. Are you still up for that drink?" he asked. "I'm thinking this Friday night might work. Lori is out of town on business so my evening's free."

"Sure," I said. "I think that'll be fine. I don't have to work the next day, so that makes it easier for me. Where should we meet?"

"Don't worry about that, Doc. I've got a really cool place. I'll just come by around 6:30 and pick you up. When we're done, I'll just drop you off back here."

"Sounds good," I said. "See ya Friday."

Friday evening came around and I met Antony in the vet clinic right on time.

"Hey, Doc. Ready to roll?"

"Yes, sir. I'm ready."

"Alright, your chariot awaits," he said as he held open the door.

He wasn't kidding about the chariot. His car was parked front and center right outside the lobby door. It was a beautiful silver Mercedes sports coupe. It was elegant and bad ass all at the same time.

"Wow! This is your car? It's gorgeous. What model is it?"

"A 2005 Mercedes SL500," he said.

If Antony was trying to impress me, he succeeded. I'd never been in a vehicle like this one. The sleek silver car was eye-catching. James Bond would look right at home behind the wheel. I was already having fun.

Antony relished pushing the performance of his three-hundred horse-power sports car. His foot was on the accelerator or the brake for the entire trip while I held on like a kid on a roller coaster. I was trying hard not to show my alarm. At one point, I glanced over at my right hand gripping the passenger side grab handle to see white knuckles and the tendons in my arm protruding. I forced myself to relax my grip, understanding that if we smacked into a light pole going eighty, the extra-strength hold wasn't going to save me.

After reaching the restaurant in five minutes despite it being ten miles away on city streets, Antony pulled into the parking lot and whipped his steed into a parking spot on our left. I inwardly sighed in relief. I needed a strong drink after that jaw clencher of a ride.

"Here we are," he declared. "This place is pretty dope. Nice bar and they make their drinks strong."

I looked out the windshield at the elaborate multi-colored neon sign and was surprised that I'd never heard of this place before. Cha-Cha's Cocina Mexicana restaurant. My kind of place. I loved Mexican food.

It took a concerted effort just to boost myself out of the little Mercedes. It was so low that my wallet almost touched the ground. We walked over to the huge, ornate, double wooden doors and Antony held one side open for me. Once inside, it took a few seconds for my eyes to adjust to the dim lighting and take stock of the place. Antony was right. This place was cool. There was a myriad of artwork and sculptures in every nook and cranny. A creepy three-foot-high smiling pig statue greeted us in the entry. Stained glass lamps hung from the ceiling. The front of the check-in desk was covered in multicolored pastel ceramic butterflies. Sparkly blown glass flower arrangements were scattered about. The ceiling was crisscrossed with huge wooden beams. And the bar . . . the bar was impressive. It was at least forty feet long and curved around in a graceful "L" shape. Instead of traditional bar stools, the bar was surrounded by dark tanned-leather bar-height chairs. Behind the bar was a display of hundreds of tequila bottles. The lighting in the bar was even darker than the entry. It was like a scene from a Quentin Tarantino movie. I half expected to see Antonio Banderas downing tequila shots in the corner.

"Let's head over to the bar," said Antony, gesturing in that direction.

The bartender saw us heading over and gave us a quick smile and waved. She was an attractive young woman with long blond hair and dressed all in black.

"Hey, Antony," she said. "How's it goin'?"

"It's going good, Darlin'," he said. "This is my friend Dr. Schmitty. Set us up with two margaritas on the rocks. Patron tequila . . . and don't hold back on us."

"You got it," she replied.

"Wow, this place is cool," I said. "And the bartender knows you by name? I'm not sure if that's a good sign."

"Yeah, I come in here from time to time. I like the vibe."

The margaritas arrived in thirty seconds. They were BIG. After the harrowing ride over and a long day at work, I was ready to smooth off the edges. I was tempted to stick my whole head into the spacious opening of the extra wide glass. "Cheers, Doc," said Antony.

We carefully clinked glasses. "Cheers," I said. "Thanks for the drink."

I determined the glass was too big and tipsy to lift going forward, so I rested my elbows on the bar to maneuver into position, slurping the top-heavy margarita with a straw.

"So," I said. "What's the deal with Alex? Does she still want to be a vet? Did anything come outta that?"

Antony looked at me. He paused, grimaced, and took a gulp of his drink.

"Well, Doc. After that discussion, Alex decided she's definitely *NOT* going to be a vet."

"Really?" I wasn't completely surprised. I'd never been a great salesman. "When did she decide that?"

"On the car ride back from your clinic," he said.

I had to catch myself from spitting up my mouthful of margarita. A little may have come up into the back of my nose. The abruptness of his answer and the abruptness of her decision struck me as funny.

"So, I take it she wasn't *real* impressed by my story about Gobi?"

"Doc, Doc, Doc." At this point Antony put his drink down and put his right hand on my shoulder. "You know I have nothing but respect for you, brother. So, no offense intended, but that story was crap . . . just way too weepy for her. You realize you were talking to *my* daughter." On the word "*my*" he gestured by raising both his hands, bending his elbows inward and tapping his chest with his fingers. "She's not interested in all that mushy emotional stuff. She just wants the cold, hard facts, and what obstacles she needs to clear to reach her goal."

I was a *little bit* hurt. I thought it was a pretty good story. I took another sip of my margarita. I had a feeling I was going to need it. "Ahhhh, I'm sorry about that," I said. "That's not what I was going for. I was trying to be encouraging, but realistic. I must have been too harsh about all the science stuff and the grade requirements. I didn't mean to talk her out of it. I feel bad if she gave up her dream because of me."

Antony made several exaggerated shakes of his head. The tequila was starting to kick in.

"No, no, Doc," he said. "You're not getting it. The talk was *PERRRFECT*. It's *exactly* what she needed. I knew her math and science wasn't good enough to get her into vet school. She's a smart kid, but that stuff is not her strong suit. After that talk, Alex realized it as well. She's already moved on to a whole different career plan."

Our conversation was interrupted by Antony's cell phone buzzing in his pocket. He took it out and looked at it. "Scuze me, Doc. It's Alex. Let me get this real quick."

"Hi, Memee, how's it goin' sweetheart?" he said into the receiver. "Naw. Don't wait for me. I'm at dinner right now. Yeah. Mexican food. I'm here with Doc Schmitty. We were just talkin' about you. Alright, Memee. Love you too. See ya in a couple of hours."

He hung up and put the phone back in his pocket.

"That was Alex?" I said. "Were her ears burning?"

"Yeah, that was her. She was just wondering where I was at."

"You call her Memee?" I said. "Why do ya call her that?"

Antony turned to me and thrust out his chest. "I call her Memee because she is a huge part of *ME*." With forced slowness, he raised his arms and bent his elbows for the second time. But this time he hit his chest with both fists two times. He thumped his chest with authority. I wondered if tomorrow he'd remember how he got those bruises. "Me-me" he said. "Get it?"

"Oh, I see," I said. (I'm not sure I really did see). "Well, I'm sorry again that I dashed her dreams. I feel kinda bad about that."

Antony looked at me with an intense stare. "No, Doc. I can't thank you enough. You saved her a fuck-ton of wasted time and energy and frustration by being upfront with her. And you saved me a shitload of tuition money. You're a standup guy. Hey, let me buy you dinner."

Antony

We hefted our margaritas and headed over to a table. It was the beginning of a long, and awkward friendship.

CHAPTER 10

Watson

"I thought I was going to have to give him the Heimlich," explained a distraught Mrs. Emerson. "I've never seen a dog salivate so much. He'd just been running around off the trail like he normally does, but when I caught up to him at the next bend, I saw he was on the side of the path all hunched over. He was drooling and pawing at his face. I was afraid he might be choking, so I ran over to him. But when I got there, he seemed like he was breathing all right. Just something was hurting his face."

Poor Mrs. Emerson was obviously frightened. Her face was tensed up tight in a grimace and as she spoke, she vigorously wrung her hands. The arms of her Oakley sunglasses were tucked down into her white Spalding visor, and they bobbed precariously on the top of her head. I was afraid they might shake loose and crash to the floor. Those suckers were expensive. She'd been out for a trail run and her outfit showed it, gray running shorts and a light blue t-shirt. Her relaxing morning outing had taken a bad turn thanks to her dog's shenanigans.

It was a hot summer morning, and we were tucked away in exam room number one at Oak View Vet Clinic. The air conditioner was already blasting.

The subject in question was Oliver. He was a fit, glossy, German short-haired pointer weighing in at seventy pounds. As he shuffled around in front of me, I could easily see the banded ripples of muscles under his skin with zero fat. His squared off regal features would ordinarily be quite handsome, but right now the elastic strings of drool dangling from his lips kind of ruined the effect. As I glanced at him, he crooked his neck sideways and made an odd open-mouthed chewing motion with his jaw. He was breathing fine, so there was no immediate danger.

Mrs. Emerson continued. "I was only about five minutes from the parking lot, so I rushed him back to the car. Then I drove him straight over. Do you think he was stung by a bee, or bit by a snake?" In her fright, she had Oliver's leash wrapped too tightly around her left hand and her fingers were turning purple.

"Hmm, that's certainly possible," I said. "That Secret Ravine area is well known for rattlesnake bites this time of year." I felt like I was getting ahead of myself. I hadn't even touched Oliver yet, so at this point, it was all speculation. "Let me take a look at him."

As I approached Oliver, he dipped his head down and reached up with his right leg to push along the side of his face with his foot. He then wagged his tail-nub several times. It was a half-hearted greeting, but he was obviously a pretty friendly dog—just distraught by whatever was going on with him. I cupped his head in both my hands to get a straight-on view of his face and eyes. I was looking for any signs of asymmetry or swelling. He looked symmetric to me. Next, I ran my hands over his muzzle, his forehead, his lips, and his chin. I paused at each region to give his face a gentle pinch or poke. One of the distinguishing signs of a rattlesnake bite is excruciating pain. Putting pressure on the region of a snake bite will elicit a dramatic response. Usually the dog will cry, wince, and jerk away from the touch. I'd expect to see some swelling and bloody puncture holes as well, but occasionally they're difficult to find. Sometimes the pain precedes the swelling and other times it's the reverse. Stings from bees and wasps hurt too, but not *nearly* as bad.

"Well," I said. "It doesn't look like a rattlesnake bit him. Thank goodness. There's just not enough pain and swelling for that. Maybe he's got something stuck in his mouth."

The masseter muscles of dogs are the strongest muscles in their body. Their jaws can exert an extreme amount of force. In a battle of strength between human hands and a dog's jaws, it was like Peewee Herman wrestling Hulk Hogan. I wouldn't stand a chance. However, with proper technique, sometimes you can get a quick look. With my left hand, I reached around Oliver's muzzle and grabbed behind his canine teeth. With my right hand I pulled down on the front of his lower jaw to pry his mouth open. This method allowed me to get decent leverage on his mouth without my fingers protruding dangerously between his teeth. I had to do this quickly. Most dogs will only give you a couple seconds to peek in before they slam shut. It's a good idea to have your fingers clear when this happens.

Oliver was reluctantly cooperative, allowing me to pry his mouth wide open. On the roof of his mouth, wedged in crossways between his molars, was some sort of dark brown stick. I was just about to maneuver into position to grab it when Oliver chomped his jaws together like a bear trap. I lost my grip as the fingers of my right hand gave way with a loud clack of his teeth.

"I can see the problem, Mrs. Emerson. Somehow Oliver got a stick wedged in between the molars of his upper jaw. He'll be fine. We just need to get that thing out of there. Let me try a different approach."

I fished around in my pocket and pulled out a pair of mosquito forceps. These steel instruments were like a small pair of pliers, often handy for removing splinters, burrs, or foxtails. With the looped handles in my right hand, I positioned the forceps to grab hold of the stick. With my left hand, I again reached around Oliver's muzzle behind his canine teeth. In this manner, I could get a little control of his upper jaw. Then, using the middle and ring fingers of my right hand, I pried his mouth open. I could clearly see the ugly splintered stick crammed against the roof of his mouth. It must have been driving him crazy. Still, I only had a moment to get the stick out before he'd reach the end of his patience and slam his mouth shut again. As soon as I got his jaws apart, I reached in with the forceps, grabbed the stick, and gave it a hard tug. The stick didn't budge. The jaws of the forceps lost their grip on the mucus slimed chunk of wood and slipped out of his mouth. Oliver immediately snapped his mouth shut.

"That stick is really wedged firmly between his molars, Mrs. Emerson. Even with the forceps, it's not coming out. I think we're going to have to sedate him so he'll hold still. That'll give me more time to pry it out. Does that sound OK to you?"

"Oh, yes," replied Mrs. Emerson. "I'm just relieved it's not something more serious. I have the time. I'll just sit with him while you get that done."

"OK. Let me go draw up that sedative shot, and I'll be right back."

When I opened the door and stepped out, I saw Maggie, my white-haired office manager, waiting outside. She was leaning against the wall of the hallway tapping her foot impatiently. When she spotted me, she pushed away from the wall and straightened up. I could tell she'd been waiting for me and I was immediately on guard. She didn't normally hover like this unless there was something really important.

Maggie was seventy-two years old. She'd been my *right-hand-man* for two years, ever since Dr. Lux and I had moved from Pacific Street to Oak View. She was a bundle of energy and keenly alert. Her finger was on the pulse of all the workings of the clinic. She fought off the chaos so Dr. Lux and I could concentrate on the medicine. Without her constant vigilance, the place would unravel. I may have been a decent veterinarian, but I was a terrible businessperson. She made sure the bills were paid, the phones were answered, and our clients were happy. She'd lived in the community for most of her life and knew everybody. If you wanted any local gossip about the town mayor or the high-school football coach, Maggie was your gal. She'd probably been their babysitter in grade school.

"Dr. Schmidt, Mr. Clarke came in about fifteen minutes early for his appointment with Watson," she said. "He's pretty worried about him. I told him you'd be in to see him as soon as possible. I put him in room five."

Mr. Clarke was a V.I.P. at Oak View Vet Clinic. Dr. Lux had been his vet for over twenty years and the Clarkes had remained loyal despite the move to our new practice. He and his wife were dedicated dog lovers, and it was clients like the Clarkes that kept Oak View afloat during the lean years when we first opened. They were both devoted to the local golden retriever rescue group, but Watson was one of their personal dogs. He was an absolute sweetheart. They'd rescued him from a terrible home over three years before. Maggie didn't give this kind of attention to every client, but the Clarkes were special and she wanted to ensure Watson was well cared for.

"What's wrong with him?" I asked.

"He's just acting kinda lethargic," she said. "He doesn't look too good."

"OK," I said. "I need to sedate the dog in room one to pull a stick out of his mouth. As soon as I do that, I'll go check on Mr. Clarke just so he knows I'm paying attention."

"Thanks, Dr. Schmidt. I'll go back in and tell him I talked to you."

I turned left out of the treatment room, then turned right and walked past the doctor's office. I had to take a quick sidestep to avoid slamming into Dr. Lux barreling out of the office. His head was down, and he was wearing a blue surgery scrub top with his trademark OptiVISORs snugged down on his head.

"Hey, Dr. Lux," I said in passing. "Just FYI. Watson Clarke is here today. Mr. Clarke thinks he's feeling sick."

"OK," he said. "Thanks for letting me know. Just keep me in the loop and let me know if you need my help."

"Yep. I will," I said.

As I entered the treatment room, doctors and techs were scurrying all over. Sabrina was cleaning a lab's teeth at the dental station. Correen and Loren were inducing anesthesia on a Rottweiler for a knee surgery on prep-table number one. On prep-table number two, Adam and Dr. Wilson were holding a Brittany Spaniel to look in his ear. Just when I thought there couldn't be any more action, the back door flew open. Carl from the anesthetic gas company was carting in a new green H-tank to resupply our oxygen. Truth be told, I enjoyed the mild chaos. Things were getting done and pets were getting treated. It was good for my soul.

I took a circuitous route around the melee towards the four-foot-high shelf of injectable meds. I drew up 0.4 milliliters of Domitor and 0.4 milliliters of butorphanol in the same syringe. These two drugs, when combined, made a safe and potent sedation combination. When given in a muscle or a vein, the patient would get very limp and groggy within minutes. The nifty part is that when the procedure was complete, a reversal drug could be administered that made the patient ready to go in less than ten minutes. I wove my way back through the throng of people and pets back to Oliver's exam room with the syringe.

"Alrighty, I'm back, Mrs. Emerson," I said. She'd released the stranglehold on Oliver's leash and removed her cap and sunglasses to place them on the chair next to hers. "This should do the trick. This injection will take about ten minutes to kick in. It'll make him pleasantly calm and sleepy so I can pry that stick out of his mouth for you. When we get it out, there's a reversal drug I'll give so he can wake up and go home. The whole thing should take less than a half hour."

Mrs. Emerson was checking messages on her phone. I'm not sure she heard anything I'd just said.

"Could you please hold him steady for a second. Just grab his neck and head and give him a big hug."

She reached around Oliver's muscular neck with her right arm and hugged his face up against her cheek.

"OK. Ready? One. Two. Three. Poke." I gave Oliver the injection in the outer portion of his right thigh. He flinched a little, but it wasn't a big deal. German shorthaired pups are notoriously tough.

"OK, you can let him go now. I'll dim the lights for some mood lighting to help him get sleepy. He'd probably like it if you just petted him for a bit. I'll be back in about ten minutes to fix him up for you."

"OK. Thanks, Dr. Schmidt." She sat down cross-legged on the tile floor and Oliver plopped down in her lap. "See you soon."

I closed the blinds and turned down the lights. "You may both be asleep by the time I come back," I said. "Nighty night."

I quietly eased the door open, let myself out, and closed it behind me. Now to see Mr. Clarke.

"Hey, Jerry. How are ya?" I said as I entered exam room five on the opposite side of the building. Mr. Clarke was a tall, lanky, friendly guy who liked being called by his first name.

"Hi, Dr. Schmidt," he said boisterously as he stood up to shake my hand. "I'm doing well, but Judy and I are worried about our boy here."

"Yeah, Maggie told me you were concerned about Watson. What's going on?"

As I spoke to Mr. Clarke, I sat on the floor of the exam room. I'd seen Watson many times before and knew him well. He was just about the friendliest dog I'd ever met. He liked to come up within an inch of my face, look me in the eye, and then give me a dainty lick on the cheek. It was the Watson handshake. Sometimes he would give me an actual handshake by lifting his left paw to grab. He was a big, solid, reddish-colored golden retriever. Today there was no handshake.

"He's just been moving really slow, like he's tired all the time," said Mr. Clarke. "Yesterday it took him five minutes just to climb the stairs from our backyard up to our deck. He also isn't eating with as much gusto."

"Hmmm . . . any other symptoms? Is he coughing? Vomiting? Diarrhea?" I asked.

"Nope, nothing like that," replied Mr. Clarke. "Although, I do think his belly looks rather swollen."

I leaned back away from Watson to get a better perspective. Uh-oh . . . Mr. Clarke was right. The bottom bulge of Watson's belly was drooping to the level of his knees. He also protruded a bit more out to the sides. I didn't like this observation. A swollen belly can indicate a great many things and they're almost all bad. An unwelcome cloud of gloom blew in and hovered over my head.

"Alright. Let me take a closer look at him," I said.

I pulled my stethoscope from around my neck and adjusted the earpieces into my ears. I placed the diaphragm of the scope on the left side of his chest between the fifth and sixth ribs. I then moved it around until I could easily listen to his heart. Watson wagged and licked me on the forehead. His heartbeat with a nice steady "lub-dub" sound at around sixty beats a minute. No murmurs or abnormal rhythm. I switched the stethoscope around to his right side and listened again. Same thing . . . perfect. I then changed the position of the scope and listened to his lungs. It sounded like a light breeze going through the leaves on a fall day.

"His heart and lungs sound good, Jerry."

I next looked in his mouth, concentrating especially on his gum color. A swollen belly can mean it's filled with blood, and this can manifest as pale gums. Watson's gums looked great. He had a little bit of calculus on his teeth and some mild doggy breath . . . no big deal. I already knew his temperature was normal. Shannon, my technician, had checked that and dutifully noted it in his record. I next moved in to get a feel of that round tummy. I stood over Watson from behind and placed my hands around his abdomen. Then, gently at first, I began pushing and prodding to get a feel for what was in there. His tummy was big and hard. This wasn't right. Due to the distention, I really couldn't palpate any of his internal organs. The handling didn't noticeably bother Watson—but he was such a good-natured chap that I worried his tolerance was just him trying to please me. Sometimes being stoic and cooperative wasn't a good thing.

I stood back up to address Mr. Clarke. I couldn't mask the concern on my face. "Well, Jerry, his gum color is good, and he doesn't seem to be in any pain. But you're right; his belly is swollen and that worries me. The quickest way to see what's in there is to do an ultrasound. I could start in thirty minutes or so if that's OK with you. I do have another dog sedated in room one. So, I'll need to go attend to him first."

"Sounds good to me," Jerry said cooperatively. Like pet, like owner, I guess. Watson must be a good influence on him. "Do you want to take him now?" He held out Watson's leash like he was handing over the keys of his sports car to the valet at the Ritz-Carlton. "He's all yours."

"Sure," I said. "I'll take him now and Shannon can prep him for the procedure. We must get his belly all shaved so I can see in there. While she's doing that, I've gotta go pull a stick out of a dog's mouth."

"Ouch," said Jerry. "That sounds rough."

"Nah . . . he'll be fine. If you don't mind waiting in here for a bit, I'll let you know what I find."

"Sure thing, Dr. Schmidt. I've got some phone calls I need to make."

Mr. Clarke owned several small businesses in the area. He was in high demand. I'm sure today's surprise trip to the clinic really disrupted his schedule. But he was cheery about it. He always put his dogs first.

I led Watson out of the room and found Shannon. She was filling a prescription in the pharmacy, visibly counting out sixty tiny Lasix pills, so I let her finish the math before I spoke.

"Shannon, I've got Watson with me. Mr. Clarke is waiting in room five. I'm kinda worried about this swelling in his belly," I said. "Can you get him shaved up for an abdominal ultrasound while I go back into room one?"

"Sure," she said, "I'll take him." She looked down at Watson. "Ooh, you're right. His belly is big. I didn't notice that before. Crap."

"Yeah," I said. "I don't like it either."

"Are we going to sedate him for the ultrasound?" she asked.

"I don't think we need to," I said. "It's Watson."

"Yeah, you're right. I'll get him ready and meet you in there."

"OK, I'm headed back to Oliver." I said. "It'll be a few minutes."

I trudged back across the clinic dodging hurried vet staff along the way. I was worried about Watson. *He's a great dog, and the Clarkes loved him to death.* The Clarkes were also tremendously supportive clients. I *really* didn't want to let them down. There sure was a lot more simplicity and satisfaction just pulling a stick out of a dog's mouth. That was more my speed.

I knocked lightly on the door of room one before easing it open. It was as pleasantly dim and quiet as I'd left it: a little oasis of peace and quiet amongst the hubbub of the busy clinic. *I wonder if I could get away with hiding out here for twenty minutes to catch my breath?*

Mrs. Emerson looked up from where she sat on the floor. Oliver was conked out on her lap. A rough snore emanated from the relaxed dog, his lips gently flapping in the breeze as he exhaled. A trickle of drool ran out of the corner of his mouth and down his owner's bare left leg.

"I think your sedation worked," she said with a wry grin perfectly timed to Oliver letting out a particularly loud snore.

"I think you're right," I said. "He looks pretty content. Now let's see if we can get that darn stick out of there."

With Mrs. Emerson holding Watson's head, I sat down on the floor and opened his mouth. It was *much* easier this way. I gently wedged a mouth gag around his canine teeth so he couldn't chomp down on my fingers. Even in his relaxed state, he could still do some damage. Mrs. Emerson played the part of vet assistant and directed a penlight at the back of his mouth.

"Wow! Now I see it," she said. "That thing is huge. How did he get that stuck in there?"

"Who knows," I said. "If it wasn't for dogs eating goofy things, we vets would be out of business."

With Oliver's mouth pried open and Mrs. Emerson holding his head, I reached towards the back of his mouth and got a hold of the stick with my forceps. But the stick was wedged in tight. I wasn't able to just pull it straight out. I had to twist it and pry it to work it loose. Finally, the chunk of stick popped out with a satisfying *THUNK*. I held it up like the catch-of-the-day in front of my face.

"There it is," I proclaimed proudly, holding it up in my forceps. "Do you want to keep it?"

Mrs. Emerson gave me an odd look. *Just what kind of a weirdo am I dealing with here?* "Uhm . . . no. That's OK, Dr. Schmidt. You can just throw it away," she said.

"It just goes to show, when you have a problem like this you just have to *stick* with it," I said.

"Uhhh . . . yeah, right," she said. I'd evidently misjudged my audience. Now she was truly convinced I was a whack-job. This wasn't her idea of a humorous situation.

"OK, Mrs. Emerson. I'll give Oliver an injection of Antisedan in his thigh. This drug will displace the sedative molecule from its receptor and get him to wake up. He'll be up in about ten minutes. I'll have a vet tech come check on him in a little bit to make sure he's safe to go home. He should be fine now that we removed the stick."

I patted Oliver on the head and stretched up from my hunched position to turn the lights back on.

"Have a good rest of the day, Mrs. Emerson," I said as I reached towards the doorknob.

"Thanks, Dr. Schmidt. You too," she said.

I left the peaceful sanctuary of room one and re-emerged into the clamor of the busy vet practice. The noise, activity, and smell hit me at once and my tranquil moment came to an abrupt end. I found Shannon waiting for me in the ultrasound room at the other end of the hospital. She'd been busy.

Watson was lying on his back in a padded blue foam trough. The trough was on top of a stainless-steel electric lift table, making Watson hover at about three feet off the ground. "OK, we're ready for ya," she said as I walked in.

Even upside down, Watson was friendly. He half-heartedly wagged his tail when he heard me enter the room. In this supine position, his tongue lolled out of the side of his mouth and nearly touched his left eye. His belly was shaved as bald as a billiard ball and his white skin shined with the alcohol and ultrasound gel Shannon had applied. In this position, the distension of Watson's abdomen was even more apparent. In retrospect, I should have noticed it right away when I first saw him. This whole situation was making me uncomfortable. Part of me didn't want to look in there. I was afraid of what I would find.

"Did he give you any trouble?" I asked.

"Nah," said Shannon. "He practically climbed up there and shaved his own tummy. He's a super good dog."

Upon hearing the compliment, Watson lifted his head a little, looked at Shannon, and wagged his tail again. Part of him was just enjoying the attention.

"OK. Thanks for getting him all ready. Let's take a look in there and see what we find."

I lifted the five-to-ten-megahertz ultrasound probe and adjusted the depth settings. I dimmed the lights and placed the blunt end of the probe on his abdomen with my right hand. This kept my left hand free to adjust the settings as needed.

Shannon and I leaned in closer to get a good look at the monitor. Oh, boy . . . Watson's intestines were floating in a sea of liquid. Wispy strands of mesentery tissue swayed gently back and forth in the fluid. It reminded me of Jacques Cousteau's underwater footage of a kelp bed. The good news was, it didn't look like blood, which is cellular and has a murky, viscous appearance on ultrasound. Ultrasonic waves easily penetrate water without any reflection, giving it a jet-black appearance. This fluid looked more like that. But where was this fluid coming from? So far his organs looked OK. I carefully scanned both his kidneys. They were normal, healthy dog kidneys. I methodically moved on to scan the rest of his organs. Intestines, normal. Bladder, normal. Spleen, normal. Liver. . . . *Oh shit*, I thought to myself. His liver looked awful.

"Shannon, are you seeing this?"

She was standing on the other side of Watson, holding his front legs, and petting him on the head.

"Yeah," she said. "What the heck is that? It looks like the surface of the moon."

"That's his liver," I said. "It looks like it's full of holes."

I slowly scanned Watson's entire liver from his right side to his left. The entire liver was full of craters. Normal liver tissue should be a nice even shade of gray. Small arteries and veins (which appear black on ultrasound) criss-cross throughout the tissue. What I was seeing was *highly* abnormal. Watson's liver was pockmarked with hundreds of black holes, ranging in size from five millimeters to five centimeters. It was awful. I felt my heart sink. These lumps of abnormal tissue almost always meant cancer. Lymphosarcoma, a lymph node cancer, had this appearance. Hemangiosarcoma, a type of blood vessel tumor and histiocytic tumors, could also look like this. It's unheard of for this to be something readily treatable. Poor Watson. Poor Mr. Clarke. There likely wasn't anything I could do for this pup. I felt defeated.

I carefully replaced the ultrasound transducer back in its slot and paused to gather my thoughts. I took a deep breath and slowly let it out. "This looks terrible, Shannon. It's gotta be some type of cancer. We may be putting Watson to sleep today."

The look on her face said it all. Shannon was a softy and cared about all the animals we treated, but she especially loved this kind-hearted dog.

"Let's get him down and I'll go break the bad news to Mr. Clarke."

Shannon wordlessly pushed the toggle lever that lowered the table to the ground. We helped Watson get back to his feet. He wagged and grinned at us without any concern. He just didn't look *that* sick. At that moment, I'm pretty sure I felt worse than he did.

"Just keep him here for now and pet him," I said. "I'll go talk to Mr. Clarke and see what he wants to do." Shannon sat down on the floor next to Watson, pressed his head against her chest and started scratching him behind his ear. Watson leaned into her, relishing the affection.

I left the ultrasound area and went directly back to the exam room where Mr. Clarke was waiting. He was on the phone when I came in. He was talking to a business associate. He recognized in my expression that there was something serious at hand. He cut the conversation off quickly.

"Stan, the vet just came back in the room, and I need to talk with him," he said into the mobile phone. "Yeah, something's wrong with Watson. Yes. Thanks, Stan. I'll call you back as soon as I can." He punched the button to end the call and looked at me. "Dr. Schmidt, you look worried."

I've learned over the years that when you have bad news, it's best to just get right to it. These conversations were always difficult. Hemming, hawing, and procrastinating never helped.

"Yep. It's not good news, I'm afraid." Mr. Clarke sat back in his chair, put both hands on his thighs and took a deep breath. "OK. Lay it on me," he said.

Mr. Clarke

"The ultrasound shows Watson's belly is full of fluid. There must be one to two gallons in there. This is causing a fair amount of pressure and making him uncomfortable. From what I can tell, the fluid is coming from a diseased liver. On ultrasound, his liver is full of holes. It looks like Swiss cheese. It's highly abnormal."

"Do you mean like cirrhosis of the liver?" said Mr. Clarke. "I've told Watson he needs to slow down on his drinking."

I smiled a little. It was a noble attempt at humor considering the circumstances. "No. I'm afraid not. Those holes in his liver aren't really holes, that's just the way they look on ultrasound. They're likely growths of abnormal tissue. I'm afraid that nine times out of ten, they are pockets of cancer."

I gave Mr. Clarke a moment for this to sink in. He seemed a little stunned. Watson wasn't that old and he'd looked great when I last saw him in the spring. We'd both assumed this conversation would be *years* down the road.

"So, are you *sure* it's cancer?" Mr. Clarke asked, hoping for a loophole.

"No, I'm not. The only way to know for sure would be to get a sample of liver tissue . . . and maybe some of the abdominal fluid. I'd send it out to a pathologist. They would examine the samples under a microscope and look for cancerous cells."

"In situations like this, have you ever had it come back as anything *but* cancer?" he asked.

"No. I'm afraid not," I said. "In my personal experience, it's always turned out to be some type of cancer."

"Oh no," said Mr. Clarke with a beaten look on his face. "This isn't what I was expecting. He's only seven years old."

"I know. I wasn't expecting this either. I'm sorry."

"If you drain off that fluid, will he feel better?"

"Yeah, I think so," I said. "It won't do anything to cure him, but it might buy you some time to think it over."

"But to really know if it's cancer, you'll need to submit some tissue, right?"

"Yes, that's correct. They may get a diagnosis from just the fluid, but most likely they'll need to see some tissue samples of the liver as well."

"And for that you'll have to do surgery?"

"Nope. I can just get some aspirates from those liver lesions with a long needle. I don't think surgery is needed. At least not yet. I can do that right now if you want to go that route."

"And he could go home with me today?"

"Yep."

"OK, Dr. Schmidt, I have complete faith in you. Here's what I'd like to do. Please drain off as much of that fluid from his stomach as you can and submit some to the lab. Get some cell samples from the liver as well. I've got to go to work for a few hours. Would it be OK to pick him up at four?"

"Yes," I said, "that should be fine."

"I know it's a long shot, Dr. Schmidt, but that dog is one of the best goldens we've ever had. Judy and I aren't ready to give up on him quite yet."

"I can certainly understand that," I said. "He's a gem."

Mr. Clarke stood up, put on his windbreaker, and pocketed his phone. He reached out his right hand to shake. "Oh, and one more thing," he added. "Could you please let Dr. Lux know what's going on? He's been our vet for twenty years. Judy and I really respect his opinion."

"I'll certainly do that," I said. "I already told him Watson was here and that I'd keep him apprised."

"Thanks a lot, Dr. Schmidt," he said as we shook hands. "I know you really didn't want to tell me that bad news. You have a really tough job sometimes. I appreciate your candor. Please take care of my boy."

"I sure will, Jerry. Thank you," I said as we left the exam room together.

Shannon was waiting with Watson back in the ultrasound room. I could tell she was expecting the worst when I returned. "How'd it go?" she asked tentatively.

"Pretty good, I guess. I still think it's looking pretty gloomy, but his dad isn't ready to give up yet. He'll live to see another day. We're going to drain his abdomen and get some needle aspirates of the liver."

"What a relief," said Shannon. She performed a dramatic wiping of her brow. "I really did NOT want to have to put Watson to sleep today."

"Yeah. Me neither," I said. "Now let's get ready to do this. I think we should sedate him a little. It's going to take some time to drain off all that fluid. We'll need to get out the suction pump, tubing, and some big needles.

Once we get rid of the fluid, I'll need some twenty-two-gauge needles to get the liver samples."

"I'm on it," said Shannon.

She wasn't kidding. Shannon did not screw around when she was on a mission. She did all the ordering for the clinic and knew exactly where everything was kept. She started opening cabinets, pulling out drawers, and grabbing supplies. She was a model of efficiency. I couldn't ask for a better helper.

Ten minutes later, we were ready to go. Watson was on his back on the ultrasound table again. This time he was snoring, and his tongue *was* touching his eyelid. I'd administered 0.3 milliliters of butorphanol and 0.3 milliliters of medetomidine intravenously to make sure he was relaxed and comfortable. Shannon had the suction pump on the floor connected to five feet of sterile tubing. Next to Watson was a pile of scary looking, fourteen-gauge needles. It was necessary to use big needles to drain fluid like this. The large lumen was less likely to get clogged and it made it more efficient to suction off the fluid. Draining abdominal fluid with a dainty needle could take hours. I'd tried to do it before, and it was a frustrating waste of time.

Using a Sharpie, I marked four dots on Watson's belly, one on each quadrant of his abdomen. These would serve as markers so I would later know where to poke. Next, I drew up three milliliters of lidocaine to numb the region for the needle pokes. For smaller needles, the local anesthetic wasn't necessary, but to insert these harpoons, I had to be rather aggressive. It took some significant stabbing force to fully puncture the abdominal wall. I injected 0.7 milliliters of lidocaine in the subcutaneous space under each of my Sharpie marks. We waited a couple of minutes for the numbing agent to do its job.

"OK, Shannon. Are you ready?"

"As I'll ever be," she quipped.

"Is Watson doing OK?"

"Yeah. He's out like a light," she replied.

I donned some sterile gloves and Shannon popped open one of the large bore needles from its protective sleeve. With the sterile needle in my right hand, I held the ultrasound probe in my left and placed it on one of the Sharpie dots. I found a fluid pocket in the neighborhood of the dot so I could insert my needle through the numbed area. No problem there. I didn't have to be very precise at this point. There was fluid *everywhere* in his abdomen. Aiming for the dot, I pushed the large needle into his abdomen with a firm thrust. Watson lifted his head slightly for the needle poke, then rested it back down and resumed his deep breathing. Pale yellow fluid instantly started pouring out of the needle. Shannon flicked the switch for the suction pump, then attached the end of the tubing to the end of my needle. Fluid leapt into the tubing and streamed into the one-liter glass receptacle on the floor. The loud noise from the pump was unnerving in the small room. It sounded like we were in the engine room of the *Titanic*. The grating rumble of the motor filled the room and made it difficult to communicate.

"OK," I shouted to Shannon. "GET COMFORTABLE. THIS IS GOING TO TAKE A WHILE."

Shannon and I stood there in the dim room. My job was to keep the fluid flowing into the tubing. Occasionally a strand of mesenteric fat would clog the needle. I could see this on ultrasound. Shannon would turn off the pump and I would readjust the needle so we could resume the suction. Shannon was keeping her right hand on Watson to make sure he didn't move. With her left hand, she supported the suction tubing. Her job was to keep a close eye on the suction container to make sure it didn't overfill. If the container got too full, it would suck fluid into the motor and destroy the pump.

"I'M STOPPING THE PUMP," yelled Shannon. "WE'RE ALMOST FULL. THAT WAS 750 MILLILITERS AND IT TOOK ABOUT SIX MINUTES."

She reached down and turned off the pump. Suddenly it was quiet. What a relief. Shannon disconnected the lid from the top of the glass jar. "Give me a sec to go dump this," she said.

"OK, but save at least sixty milliliters so we can submit it to the lab," I said.

"No problem." She lifted the container and carried it out to dump in the treatment sink. She returned a moment later with an empty suction jar and we started the process all over again. I'd kept the same needle in the same spot. There was no reason to change positions yet. It was working well.

"OK. Turning on the pump," she said.

I grimaced a little, bracing myself for the noise.

The next 750 milliliters were drained easily. It only took another four or five minutes. Shannon emptied the container while I removed the old needle and started with a fresh one in a new location. The brief respite from the noise was interrupted again by the pump. I was getting awfully tired of that thing. My stress level was already at yellow alert and the cacophony of noise was pushing me into the red.

At some point, Dr. Lux wandered into the room. "WHAT'S GOING ON IN HERE?" he shouted over the thrumming of the pump. "IS THAT WATSON?"

"YES," I said. "HIS BELLY IS ABSOLUTELY FULL OF FLUID. WE'RE DRAINING IT TO GIVE HIM SOME RELIEF."

"DO YOU KNOW WHERE IT'S COMING FROM?" said Dr. Lux.

"I THINK IT'S FROM HIS LIVER. HIS LIVER LOOKS TERRIBLE. IT'S FULL OF HOLES. I'M AFRAID IT'S CANCER. BUT MR. CLARKE ISN'T READY TO GIVE UP YET."

"NAH," said Dr. Lux, "THEY LOVE THAT DOG TO DEATH. AND I'VE KNOWN THEM FOR YEARS. THEY DON'T GIVE UP EASY."

I just nodded my head at this comment. I was tired of screaming. Dr. Lux gave me a thumbs-up and left the room. I suspect he wanted to escape the din as well.

It took another twenty minutes and three more trips to the sink to finish the job. I'd used five needles and all four of my lidocaine spots. The ultrasound showed there was still some residual fluid in his abdomen, but not a significant amount. Watson's tummy shrank like a pregnant woman after having a baby, relieving all that pressure. The ungodly suction pump was shut off. Now on to phase two. We needed aspirates of his liver.

Using a surgical drape, Shannon cordoned off a section of the X-ray table behind me. She'd laid out five, twenty-two gauge, one-and-a-half-inch needles. Next to those were ten microscope slides, laid out in an orderly row like little soldiers. She'd also opened a pack of sterile surgeon gloves for me.

I cleaned off the ultrasound gel from Watson's belly and applied a generous dousing of alcohol. The alcohol would form a contact medium between the ultrasound probe and his skin so I could better visualize his liver. I'd have to work quickly or reapply frequently, because it evaporated fast. Holding the probe in my left hand, I placed it directly behind his ribs. In dogs, the liver is tucked tightly up under the ribs in the most forward part of the abdomen. In some dogs it's difficult to reach the liver with a one-and-a-half-inch needle. Luckily, it wouldn't be a problem for Watson. His liver was swollen with disease and extended well past his ribs, making it easily accessible. I found an area of the liver close to the surface and containing one of the larger diseased sections. With my gloved right hand, I guided the needle through his skin and into the liver at a forty-five-degree angle. The needle tip appeared on the screen as a bright reflective line. The tip could be seen penetrating the center of the liver mass. I made six or seven quick jabs in and out of the mass. This sewing machine motion would pack some of the liver cells into the needle. I removed the needle and passed it to Shannon, being careful not to touch my sterile glove to her hand. Shannon took the needle and attached it to a six-milliliter syringe filled with air. She poised the needle tip over a slide and then pushed the plunger of the syringe, jetting any cellular material from the needle onto the slide. Her efforts resulted in a small red blob of thick goo in the middle of the slide. She then took another slide and laid it down on top of the first one. Quickly, she pulled them apart. This motion smeared the blob of cells transforming it into a thin layer across the original slide. The pathologist would later stain this layer of cells to examine them at the laboratory.

Shannon and I repeated this process four more times, resulting in a row of five bloody slides laid out on the table. I always like to submit at least four slides to give the pathologist the maximum chance to get a diagnosis. Nothing was more frustrating than going through this procedure only to have the pathologist get back to you three days later and say that your samples were inadequate. Shannon packed the slides in a plastic holder to send out to the lab.

"I think we might be done," I said. Watson, who hadn't moved a muscle for thirty minutes, groggily wagged his tail and lifted his head to look at us. It was eerie how well he seemed to understand us.

"Thank goodness," said Shannon. "I'm about done with this project."

"Yeah. Me too," I said. "Let's find him a cozy cage with a big blanket and let the sedation wear off."

As Shannon got Watson situated, Maggie approached me in the treatment room. She was wearing a thick gray sweater with reading glasses hanging from a chain around her neck and a look of concern on her face. As she crossed her arms over her chest, she leaned back against the edge of one of the treatment sinks. Something she did often, and it always made me nervous. The treatment sinks were big, heavy, stainless-steel chunks of metal, but they were not anchored to the ground. If you put too much weight on them they would shift. I'd saved Maggie from falling in this fashion on at least three separate occasions—but she insisted on doing it anyway. She was a stubborn old lady and didn't like anyone telling her what to do. I wasn't going to mention it again, but I edged a little closer so that I could grab her if need be.

"So, Dr. Schmidt, what do you think about Watson?"

"It's not good," I replied with a sigh. "His belly was full of fluid. Shannon and I just drained off two gallons. And his liver looks really bad. I got some samples to send to the lab, but I bet it's going to be some awful type of cancer."

"Ahhh, that's too bad. That couple loves their goldens. They've had goldens going back to when Dr. Lux and I worked at Placer Vet Clinic."

"Yeah, I know. They're pretty terrific pet owners. Hopefully, there's something I can do for him."

"Does Dr. Lux know?" she asked.

"Yeah, I did tell him. And I'll keep him updated with any new information."

"Well, I guess that's all we can do for now," she said. "I sure hope there's some way we can treat poor Watson, or the Clarkes are going to be really *flustrated*." Maggie often used this portmanteau of *frustrated* and *flustered* in situations like these. Over the years, I found that the word actually came in quite handy, and I'd started using it myself. I was *flustrated* about half the time, anyway. I never knew whether this word fusion was purposeful on her part or if she thought it was a real term. I think I was better off not asking.

As she pushed herself forward to stand, the table against which she was leaning suddenly shifted two inches to the right. It made a screeching sound as the metal feet scraped against the tiled floor. A brief look of panic flashed on her face as she started to fall backwards. I reached out and grabbed her right shoulder with my left hand and her waist with my right hand. I caught her just in time to prevent another full-blown fall to the ground. I opened my mouth to remind her for the umpteenth time that those tables shouldn't be leaned on. Before I could get out a word, she held her index finger directly in front of my face. "Don't say a thing," she admonished me as she turned and walked determinedly back towards her office.

And I didn't.

The next morning, I sat down at my desk in the left corner of the doctor's office and looked up the Clarkes' number listed on their electronic record. Mrs. Clarke answered the phone.

"Hi, Judy. It's Dr. Schmidt from Oak View Vet Clinic. I was just calling to check in on Watson."

"Oh, hello, Dr. Schmidt," she said. "Watson actually seems to be feeling quite a bit better. He's moving around a lot more and gobbled up his breakfast this morning. Jerry told me about his visit with you yesterday. It seems like removing all that fluid helped him a lot."

"That's great," I said. "His abdomen was stretched pretty tight. Draining all that fluid just reduced the pressure. He must have been more uncomfortable than we realized."

"He's a pretty stoic dog," said Judy. "Sometimes I think that's not a good thing. He's just so darn good-natured that he'll put up with almost anything before he complains."

"Yeah, I hate dogs like that," I said ironically. "It takes a long time before you realize there's a problem."

"Yep. That's Watson. By the way, do you have any results yet?" she asked.

"Not yet. It's way too early. The lab samples just went out last evening. It usually takes three to four days for the pathologists to examine the samples and issue a report."

"OK," she said. "It doesn't hurt to ask."

"Nope, it doesn't," I said. "I'll call you as soon as the results come in."

It took another three days for the pathology report on Watson to come back. It was Thursday at lunchtime, and I'd just finished a busy morning of appointments. I checked the lab website for new results and Watson's report was at the top of the list. I could feel my blood pressure shoot up when I saw his name. I wanted to know, but I didn't want to know. The contents of this report could spell the end for Watson.

Abdominal fluid: Modified transudate with moderate numbers of inflammatory cells. Eosinophils predominated this population. Large numbers of parasitic tetrathyridia are visualized. These tetrathyridia are most consistent with the cephalic form of Mesocestoides.

Liver cytology: Samples consist of a mixture of degenerative hepatocytes and a mixed inflammatory cell population. Large quantities of fragmented and intact Mesocestoides tetrathyridia predominate.

Holy crap! This was not at all what I was expecting. I read the report again for confirmation. My emotions fluctuated between excitement and fear. Watson did *not* have cancer! This was great news. It might instead be something I could fix. But Mesocestoides? In the realm of pet parasites, this tapeworm was a weird one. It got about ten minutes of lecture time in vet school. Generally considered a benign parasite of wildlife, it would only occasionally infect pet dogs and cats. What the hell was Watson doing with big pockets of it in his liver? It was a disgusting concept to visualize that his liver was pockmarked with large masses of Mesocestoides larvae. I had no idea how to treat this, or even if it could be treated.

I recalled an incident from my time working as an assistant for Dr. Weaver in San Diego. Dr. Weaver was a kindly, gentleman vet, a couple of years away from retirement. He was a friendly white-haired jokester, and his clients adored him. He'd generously hired me on as an untrained helper when I'd decided to pursue vet school. One day I was acting as his surgery tech while he performed a spay on a six-month-old kitten. The kitten was lying on her back on the surgery table. She was breathing an oxygen mixture diluted with halothane gas. When Dr. Weaver made the initial incision with his scalpel, a gush of pale yellow fluid bubbled up from the small hole and spilled over the edges of the incision. Tiny white flakes were visibly floating in the fluid. I was alarmed at this development. Dr. Weaver noticed my reaction but was completely nonchalant.

"It's just another Mesocestoides cat," he said. "We see these every once in a while. It's not a big deal. We'll flush out her belly and give her an ivermectin injection. She'll be fine."

Dr. Weaver had me open a bag of sterile saline. He then spent ten minutes rinsing the abdomen of the little cat with the saline and suctioned out the remainder of the fluid. He then calmly continued on with the spay procedure to sterilize the kitten.

"Jeff. Go draw up 0.1 milliliters of ivermectin and just give it S.Q.," he directed.

I grabbed a syringe and drew up 0.1 ml of the clear viscous deworming medication. I then reached up under the blue sterile drape and injected the contents under the skin in the kitten's scruff.

"What's Mesocestoides?" I asked.

"Oh, it's a type of tapeworm. Sometimes it breaks loose into the abdominal cavity. We see it occasionally in these feral kittens. They probably get it from eating mice and lizards and critters like that. A shot of ivermectin takes care of it."

He was so matter of fact about the whole thing and I got the impression he saw this all the time. But now *I* was the licensed vet, and I hadn't seen a case of Mesocestoides since that kitten in San Diego twenty years ago. And in Watson's case, it was *a really big deal*. His liver was full of these repulsive parasites. It was making him sick. I'd been prepared to euthanize him for it. Could I just treat him with an injection of ivermectin?

I got on the phone to call the Clarkes. Jerry picked up the phone on the third ring.

"Hi, Jerry. This is Dr. Schmidt. I'm calling about the lab results for Watson."

I could hear Mr. Clarke take a deep breath on the other end of the line. He was clearly prepping himself for the bad news he knew was coming. I'd been on the other end of calls like this in the past. It was a terrible feeling. My heart went out to him.

"Hi, Dr. Schmidt. Thanks for the call. So, what did you find out?"

"Well, it's good news, I think," I said. I didn't want to keep him dangling too long. "Watson doesn't have cancer."

"Really? Oh, boy ... what a relief," said Jerry. "Judy and I were worried sick. But what do you mean *you think* it's good news?"

"Well, it turns out that those lesions in his liver are caused by a rare type of tapeworm. It's called Mesocestoides. It's usually considered a benign parasite that comes from wildlife. It can sometimes live in a dog's intestines. But, Watson has massive amounts of this parasite larvae encysted in his liver. That's really weird and I'm not sure how to treat this. I need to do more research on how to properly manage this situation. I've never heard of it causing this type of liver damage before.

"So, do you think we can treat him Dr. Schmidt?"

"Probably so, but I'm honestly not sure. Give me some time to figure this out. I just got the report a few minutes ago."

"OK. Just let us know what you come up with," said Jerry. His voice sounded ten pounds lighter. I didn't know a voice could be lighter, but there it was.

"Yes, I'll certainly do that," I said and hung up the phone.

Thirty minutes later, I was able to pin down Dr. Lux in the surgery suite. It wasn't the ideal location for a consultation, but I needed some help and anxiously wanted his opinion. He was in his sterile cap, gown, and gloves and standing at the end of the table working on a red chow chow dog. The dog had torn the anterior cruciate ligament in his left knee and Dr. Lux was in the process of cleaning out the tattered fragments. His blue OptiVISORs were perched on his head and covered the top part of his eyes. They bobbed up and down as he spoke. I was standing back against the wall so as not to risk contaminating his sterile field.

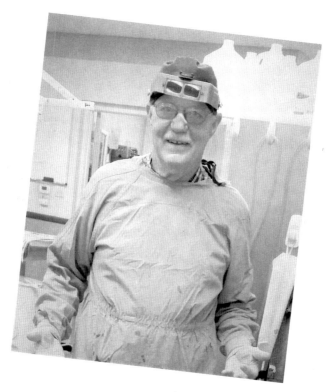

Dr. Frank Lux

"So, all those black spots in his liver are actually nests of tapeworm larvae?" asked Dr. Lux.

"Yep. Have you ever seen anything like that before?"

"Nope," he said shaking his head. "I've occasionally seen young cats with abdominal effusion with those tapeworm fragments. I'd see them sometimes when I opened them up for a spay at the shelter. But they weren't sick. I'd just flush out their belly and give them a dewormer. They did fine. But I've never seen it in a dog, and certainly not like this."

"Yeah. I saw that once at a practice I worked at twenty years ago." I went on to tell him the Dr. Weaver story.

"So do you have any idea on how to treat it in Watson?"

"Not really. It's possible that just giving him praziquantel orally or an injection of ivermectin will kill all the larva, but I'm just guessing. This might be a good case to call the university. They have vets there who specialize in parasite research. Maybe this is something they've seen before."

"Good idea," I said. "I'll give that a try. It's just so difficult to reach anyone over there sometimes. It can take forever to get a consultation."

"Have you looked it up in some of the textbooks?"

"I tried. *Greene's Infectious Diseases* doesn't have a section on Mesocestoides at all and neither does *Ettinger's Internal Medicine.* The *Nelson* book has one sentence about Mesocestoides. It says that it rarely causes abdominal effusion. But nothing about it invading the liver, and it doesn't say anything about treating it. Weird, huh?"

"Yeah," he said. "I think you've got a real oddball there. Give U.C. Davis a call and see if one of the parasitologists can help you."

"I'll get on that now," I said.

I went back to my desk, sat down, and put on my reading glasses. I was now in my mid-forties, and it was getting more difficult to see things up close. I went to the U.C. Davis website. I opened the webpage for the School of Veterinary Medicine and started looking for some information to connect with a parasitologist. I had two parasitology instructors in vet school: Dr. Conners and Dr. Boyd. They'd both been excellent, and I'd found their lectures fascinating. Parasitology is a creepy but captivating topic. It takes an interesting individual to pursue this as their specialty. According to the website, Dr. Conners had left the university, but Dr. Boyd was still there. It listed his office phone number, so I picked up the receiver and dialed.

"You've reached the office voicemail for Dr. Christopher Boyd. My office hours are Monday, Wednesday, and Thursday from 9 a.m. to 12 p.m. Please leave a message and I'll return your call as soon as possible." The message was in Dr. Boyd's own voice. That was encouraging and made me feel better. Maybe there was a real live person to talk to over there.

"Hi Dr. Boyd. My name is Jeff Schmidt. I was a vet student of yours about fifteen years ago. I have an adult golden retriever patient with a severe case of Mesocestoides. He has parasitic cysts in his liver and a lot of abdominal effusion. I'd really appreciate it if you could give me a call and guide me on how to treat this." I left my office phone number, paused, then reluctantly hung up. I guess there was nothing left to say on the message, but I was uncomfortable leaving this problem in the hands of the voice mail gods. I hoped I'd hear back from him soon. I wasn't comfortable with Watson's current medical status, and I didn't want to let down the Clarkes. But Dr. Boyd was a very busy man. Was he even in town? In addition to teaching vet students, graduate students, and undergrad students, he was deeply involved in wildlife parasite research. Back when I knew him, he was out of town a lot in the field. He reminded me of the main character in the movie *Never Cry Wolf*. Not only did he travel all over the world doing research, but he looked like the actor in the movie.

The next morning, I found myself in the middle of another uncomfortable conversation in exam room one. "Valerie, the reason Smoochie-Cat keeps getting these bladder infections is that she can't clean herself back there. I'm happy to treat her infection and help her feel better. But unless we get her to lose weight, this is going to just keep happening over and over again."

"Oh, I know, Dr. Schmidt. And I've been very careful about the amount of food I've been giving her. Didn't she lose any weight since last time?"

"She gained half a pound," I replied.

Poor Smoochie. She was a white cat with some calico patches on her face and weighed in at twenty-four pounds. A healthy weight for her was around eight pounds. She looked like someone had trapped a kitten inside an old Garfield costume if Garfield had unkempt greasy fur, significant breathing problems, and got a new bladder infection every three months. In the four years I'd been Smoochie's vet, I'd made this same speech to Ms. Miller at least ten times. Still, I always felt uncomfortable doing it. By the looks of it, Ms. Miller had a similar issue and I'm sure her personal physician was treading over this same ground. I didn't want to rub salt in the wound, but she returned on a regular basis to get my professional opinion. It would be disingenuous to not give her my honest assessment.

"Cats are normally very fastidious creatures. They spend hours each day grooming themselves. As gross as it may seem, part of this grooming is their genital region. Smoochie-Cat just can't reach back there because she's way too heavy. So, she gets urine and feces stuck to her and she can't clean it off. It's like a diaper rash in babies. The skin gets moist, raw, and painful. It *really* hurts them." I added the last part for emphasis. Most clients could identify with pain.

"But I don't understand why she keeps gaining weight," she said. "I'm only giving her a half a cup of food twice a day."

"What about the other cats?" I asked. "How are they getting fed?" I knew Ms. Miller had at least three other cats. *But were there only three others?*

"Well, I only put out a half cup of food for each of them twice a day," she said defensively. "I'm very careful about measuring the amount. They each have their own bowls. Except for the kitten. I have him on kitten food, and I leave that out all day. I know kittens need to eat more frequently because they're growing."

She had a new kitten? This was news to me. I decided to ignore this new nugget of information in order to stay on topic.

"So, what's keeping Smoochie from eating the other cat's food?"

"Well . . . her dish is the pink one," replied Mrs. Miller innocently. "And it's the only one in the pantry. All the other dishes are in the laundry room."

"So, she can't get to any of the other food dishes?"

"Well . . . she can . . . I guess," she said, possibly just now realizing the error in her system. "They all have free rein of the house. But she *really* does like her pink dish the best. She also likes to have her privacy when she eats."

I barely resisted the temptation to bang my head against the steel exam table. I'd been trying to get this cat to lose weight *for years*. I felt like I spent fifty percent of my appointment time counseling pet owners about obesity. It was a frustrating co-dependency where many folks overfed their pets as a misdirected form of love. I'd bet a million dollars that dainty little Smoochie was not just politely eating out of her own pink food dish. But it wouldn't help me to lose my patience with Ms. Miller. Even though I'd covered this ground umpteen times now, I would patiently give it another go. I took a deep, calming breath and forged ahead.

"First of all, a half cup of food twice a day is still too much for her. Even if that were *all* she was getting, she would still gain weight on that. She should only be getting one-half cup of diet food *once* a day to really start losing some weight."

Ms. Miller looked horrified at this suggestion, like she'd never heard of this before. (Well, unless we counted three months ago in this same room.) "Only one-half cup a day? Won't she starve on that amount?"

"Nope," I replied. "She'd be fine. Furthermore, I'd bet dollars to donuts she's also eating the other cat's food. She didn't get to twenty-four pounds just by eating a cup a day. And now you have a kitten? I didn't know about that. Kitten food has about fifty percent more calories than adult cat food. If you're leaving the kitten food out all day, she's likely scarfing down some of that as well."

"OK, OK, Dr. Schmidt. I get it," she said. "So, what do we need to do to help her feel better today?"

"We really need to clean up her rear end. It's stinky and painful. We should also get a urine sample to make sure the bacteria in the urine is susceptible to the antibiotic I'm going to prescribe."

At this point there was a knock on the exam room door. Receptionist Robi poked her head inside. "Hey, Dr. Schmidt. Sorry to interrupt, but I have a Dr. Boyd from U.C. Davis on the phone asking for you. I guess he's returning your call from yesterday?"

My pulse quickened. I was elated he was getting back to me so fast. "Thanks, Robi. Please tell him I'll be there in just a minute."

Robi pulled back from the doorway and quietly closed the door.

"Sorry for the interruption," I said to Valerie. "What I was getting at is that her rear end is really raw. It'll hurt her if we do this all awake. She'll hate it. So, I'd recommend we give her some sedation drugs to get this all done. We can shave and clean her sore butt area, give her an antibiotic injection, and get a urine sample all while she's asleep. Would that be OK?"

"Yes, that's fine with me. How long will this take?"

"Probably about thirty minutes," I said. "If you don't mind, you can just wait in here. We'll bring her back to you as soon as she's done."

"OK," said Valerie. "That's fine. I brought a book."

As she extracted a blue paperback from her purse, I scooped up the cat and left the room. It was definitely a two-handed lift. I made sure to bend at the knees to save my back.

Shannon was waiting for me in the hallway.

"Let me guess," she said. "Another Smoochie-Cat butt treatment special?"

"Yes. How'd you guess? We need a urine culture as well."

"OK. Hand her over," she said resignedly. She'd cleaned up Smoochie's fecal-matted perineum at least five times before. I'm sure it wasn't the highlight of her day.

I rushed over to my desk, grabbed the phone, and hurriedly sat down. Eagerly, I pushed the blinking button for line number three.

"Hello, this is Dr. Schmidt," I said.

"Hey, Dr. Schmidt, this is Chris Boyd. I got your message about that Mesocestoides case. That sounds fascinating. Tell me about it."

"Thanks for returning my call, Dr. Boyd. I really appreciate you getting back to me so quickly. I don't know if you remember me, but I was one of your parasitology students in vet school about fifteen years ago. I figured you might be my best hope to help me on a case like this."

"Yeah, Jeff. I remember you well. You were always so curious. You asked some great questions."

I was flattered. Out of the thousands of students in all his classes, did Dr. Boyd really remember me? I couldn't be sure, but this wasn't the time to reminisce with him. I proceeded to explain to him the exam findings, the ultrasound results, and the lab tests on Watson. He listened patiently and only interrupted on two occasions to ask some clarifying questions. I breathlessly finished my five-minute presentation and paused.

"So, is this something you've seen before?" I asked him.

"I get calls like this a couple times a year," said Dr. Boyd. "Almost all the calls are from vets in this general area. I'm not sure if it's because I'm known around here, or if this is a hotbed for the disease. But I travel all over the world, and I've almost never heard of this anywhere else. However, your dog sounds like one of the worst cases I've heard of. You're saying his *entire liver* is filled up with these parasite cysts?"

"Yes," I replied. "It's terrible. I really thought it was cancer. I was prepared to put him to sleep."

"Please send me a copy of those ultrasound images and the cytology report," he said. "And, if possible, some of his abdominal fluid. This is something I've been studying. I'm trying to figure out if the Mesocestoides that gets into the abdomen is a different subspecies from the common type we all know. I'm in the process of developing a PCR test to help with that."

"OK. I'm happy to do that. But is there anything we can do to treat him?"

"I can't say for sure, Jeff. This is a pretty rare scenario, and it's hardly been studied at all. That's why you couldn't find anything about this in the textbooks. Like I said, I only get a few calls a year, but the folks in my lab are working on it. We don't even know for sure how they get it. There's some speculation that the dogs pick it up by eating wetlands creatures like snails or salamanders . . . maybe frogs. But no one's been able to prove it. Does this dog live in an environment like that?"

"The Clarkes just live in a suburban neighborhood," I said. "But Mr. Clarke takes Watson down to the American River two to three days a week. He lets him run around loose for exercise. God knows what he gets into down there."

"Yeah, that makes sense," he said. "Maybe you can check with the Clarkes. See if it would be OK for me to call them. It might help me map out where these infections are coming from."

But, how do we fix him? I thought impatiently.

"Sure," I said. "I can do that. The Clarkes are very nice folks. I'm sure they would be glad to help."

"Anyways, you were asking about treatment," said Dr. Boyd. "There's no proven treatment currently because it's so rare. However, we've had a few dogs get good results by giving them fenbendazole."

"Just plain old fenbendazole?" I said. Fenbendazole is a common dewormer for livestock and chickens. It comes in a one-pound tub of concentrated white powder. The trade name for fenbendazole was *Panacur*.

"How much do you give?"

"The very high end of the dose-range for the dog's size," he said.

"And how many doses do you administer?" I asked. Usually, Fenbendazole is given in just one oral dose, or sometimes, depending on the parasite, for three or four consecutive days.

"You give it every single day for months," he said. "You keep giving it until there is no sign of the parasite at all."

"Wow. Are there any problems giving that drug at those dosages for months on end?"

"Nobody's studied the effects of giving this much for this long in a dog," he said. "But so far it seems OK. We've had a couple dogs completely recover."

"OK. Great. That gives me some hope, then. I'm glad I talked to you. Thanks, Dr. Boyd. I'll email those ultrasound photos and overnight ship some of the abdominal fluid we saved from Watson. Thanks again."

"You're welcome, Jeff. Happy to help," he said. "Please give me updates and let me know how he's doing. There aren't many of these cases out there, so I'm trying to gather all the information I can. Also, remember to check with the Clarkes to see if they're OK talking with me. I'd like to get more detailed information about where this dog may have picked this up. Maybe I can go down there to collect some samples."

"OK. Will do," I said. "Thanks again for the consultation. I'm going to start Watson on fenbendazole right away."

Man, I thought to myself as I hung up the phone. *I got really lucky. One of the only parasitologists in the world who's studying this disease is in my own backyard. And . . . he called me right back the next day. Sometimes it's better to be lucky than good. Dr. Boyd may have just saved Watson's life.*

I found Shannon in pharmacy restocking the shelves. We'd just received a large order of supplies and she was meticulously checking to make sure the shipment matched her order. Boxes and plastic packaging were strewn all over the floor around her. Standing precariously on a rickety rolling stool, she clung on to a cabinet shelf with her left hand. The risk of breaking her neck was evidently worth the thirty seconds of time it saved her to grab a step stool. Between her and Maggie and Sabrina, I should really call my insurance agent about an increase in coverage.

"Shannon. What the hell are you doing?" I said. "You're going to kill yourself using that as a ladder."

"I know, I know," she said. "I just needed it for a second."

We'd been over this particular safety issue about a hundred times. She was just plain stubborn about it. She and Maggie had a lot in common.

While she stood two feet above me, I noticed her right hand was holding a brand new one pound jar of Fenbendazole. Huh? What a coincidence!

"Well, before you break your neck for that jar of Panacur, you might as well come down and give it to me. I'm going to need it for Watson Clarke."

"Really? Is that the treatment to kill off the tapeworms?" she asked.

"Yeah. Evidently it is. I just got off the phone with one of the parasitology professors at U.C. Davis. He says that Panacur's the best option for treatment."

"There's already an open jar on the shelf by your shoulder," she said. "I was just restocking."

"Yeah, I know," I replied, "But I need the whole jar."

"You're going to send home the *whole* jar?"

Normally a one-pound jar of Panacur lasts six to nine months at the clinic. It was dispensed out in tiny little plastic bags. An average-size dog would get about half of a teaspoon a day.

"Yessiree," I said. "Watson is going to be on it every day for several months."

"Holy crap." She leaned over unsteadily and handed me the brand-new jar. "Is that safe?"

"I sure hope so. Dr. Boyd says it's OK."

Shannon slowly lowered her hands to the countertop and then carefully eased her feet back to the floor. I was relieved she'd made it back to earth without falling. She wasn't exactly known for her grace and coordination. "Well, I guess now I need to go order another bottle."

I was seated back at my desk in the doctors' office. I had Mr. Clarke on the phone.

"Hello, Jerry. It's Dr. Schmidt again.

"Hi, Dr. Schmidt. How's it going?" said Jerry.

"Good. I have some encouraging news about Watson. I just got off the phone with Dr. Boyd at U.C. Davis. He's a specialist in parasitology. He informed me that dogs suffering from Mesocestoides in their abdomen is rare and not that well understood. But there is a possible treatment. He's had some success putting dogs on a cattle dewormer for extended periods of time. The medication is called fenbendazole. I'm getting some ready for you to pick up right now."

"That's great news, Dr. Schmidt. Judy will be ecstatic. How do you give the medication?"

"It comes in a tub of white powder. I'll include a plastic measuring scoop with the medication. Just give one full scoop every day mixed in with his food. You'll probably have to give it for several months. We have to make sure every last parasite is dead before we stop the medication."

"OK, got it," said Mr. Clarke. "When can I come pick it up? I want to start right away."

"Give us an hour to get it ready," I said. "Oh, and one more thing. Dr. Boyd would like to call you and speak to you directly. He's trying to study this organism and figure out the life cycle. There's hardly anything about this in the textbooks. His lab is trying to develop a new test for it. They're also trying to figure out how dogs get it. Is it OK to share your phone number with him?"

"Yes, certainly," he said. "I don't want another dog to ever get this again."

"He's trying," I said. "I'll see you in an hour."

At 1 p.m., I looked up from the desk in the doctor's office. The office windows looked directly out onto the parking area and I saw Mr. Clarke's Lincoln Town Car pull into the parking lot. I watched as he found an open space directly on the north side of the building. I could see him get out of the car and open his back door for Watson, who hopped right out like a puppy. I got up from my desk and went to get his jar of Panacur from the pharmacy and met him in the lobby just as he came in.

"Hello, Jerry," I said as I reached out to shake his hand. Watson's leash was tangled around his wrist. He had to detach it before he could return the handshake.

"Good afternoon, sir," Mr. Clarke said in return. "Is that Watson's new medication you've got there?"

"Yes, this is it," I said, handing it to him. "Say, Watson's looking pretty good. He must be feeling better without all that fluid weighing him down."

I bent down to say hello to Watson. He grinned up at me, wagged his whole butt, and gave me a dainty lick on the nose.

"I'm going to start this as soon as we get home," said Jerry enthusiastically. "Thanks a lot for getting a hold of Dr. Boyd. Judy wanted me to thank you as well."

"I was happy to do it. He called me back pretty quick and was very helpful on the phone. By the way, I'm going to need to recheck Watson every week or two to monitor how he's doing. I'll need to recheck his ultrasound each time. Would a week from today work for you?"

"I'm making Watson my number one priority, Dr. Schmidt. You just tell me when I need to be here, and I'll make it happen."

Robi was standing attentively at the reception desk and heard the whole conversation. She looked at the computerized appointment schedule. "Dr. Schmidt, you have an opening at three next Friday. Can I put Watson in there?" she asked.

"Yeah, perfect," I said. "Thanks. Alright, Jerry. Robi will make that appointment for you and check you out. I'll see ya next Friday at three o'clock."

"Great," said Jerry, "I'll see you then."

The following Friday it was 3:15 p.m. before I was able to get into exam room four. Mr. Clarke and Watson were waiting for me. Today Mrs. Clarke had joined the party.

"Hey, Jerry. Hi, Judy. Sorry I'm late," I said. "It's been a hectic day and I've been unable to keep up."

"No problem, Dr. Schmidt. We don't mind waiting," said Judy. "We're just glad Watson is still feeling good."

"That's great," I said. "I hate to rush, but can I borrow Watson for his ultrasound? I don't want to run out of time."

"He's all yours," said Jerry as he handed over the pup's leash.

My technician of the day was Amy. She was already waiting for me in the ultrasound room with the machine turned on, the lights dimmed, and the table cleaned.

"He looks fairly happy," she said. She knew Watson pretty well. "But his belly is a little saggy."

"Yeah, I noticed that too," I said. "Probably the fluid is starting to come back. That's not good. It's only been a week."

Amy and I hefted Watson up on his back in the middle of the padded ultrasound trough. I squirted a generous amount of gel on his belly and grabbed the ultrasound probe.

It didn't take long to see what was going on. "Well, he's got a fair amount of fluid in there, but not nearly as much as before. We might as well drain it while he's here. Otherwise, he'll start to get uncomfortable again. His liver looks about the same. Let me go clear it with the Clarkes. Can you get the pump and needles ready?"

"Sure," said Amy. "You know where to find me."

Judy and Jerry were patiently waiting for me in room four. They were fine with waiting a bit while Watson had his fluid removed. I told them it should be faster than the first time and I didn't think he would have to be sedated.

Just like his owners, Watson was fine for the procedure. I easily drained two liters of fluid from his abdomen on this visit.

I walked Watson back to the exam room. He smiled and wagged the whole way.

"Well," I said as I entered the room. "That wasn't too bad. Watson was super cooperative. He held still on his back while we sucked out the fluid. There was only about half as much as last time."

"How did his liver look?" asked Judy.

"Pretty much the same. But he's only been on the medication for one week. I think it's too soon to see a difference. I'd recommend we recheck him—and re-drain him, if needed—every week from now on. That way I can keep track of how he's doing."

"That sounds like a good plan," said Jerry. "3 p.m. works for you?"

I quickly accessed the electronic scheduler. "Yeah, three is fine," I said. "We'll make Fridays at three our official Watson check-up time from now on."

Judy and Jerry stood up and I shook hands with both of them. "See ya next week," they said in unison.

I smiled, waved, and gave Watson a pat on the head. "See ya next week," I said.

The next Friday, Watson was back with Judy solo. She looked very smart and professional in black trousers and a beige blouse. She'd placed a shiny gold dog-paw pin on the left lapel of her camel-colored blazer.

"Hi, Judy. You sure look nice. You're making the rest of us look scruffy."

"Oh, thanks Dr. Schmidt. I just got off work from the bank an hour ago. I had to rush right home to get Watson and bring him back here. Jerry's in Arizona on a business trip."

"So, how's it going?" I asked. "Any problems getting that powdered medication in him?"

"No problem at all. We just mix it with a little canned food, and he scarfs it down."

"How's he feeling?" I queried.

"For the first few days after you drained his abdomen, he was really good," she said. "He was prancing around like a puppy and stealing our other dog's toys. The last couple of days, he's been OK, but not quite as happy. I think the fluid is coming back."

"Any problems with diarrhea? Vomiting?"

"Nope," she replied. "His GI tract seems fine."

I kneeled down to look at Watson eye-to-eye. He wagged his tail, licked my cheek, and lifted his left paw. It was the Watson handshake I'd come to expect. I took it in my right hand and gave it a gentle up-down. "Good to see you too, buddy," I said to him. While I was down there, I went through a basic physical exam. Overall, he seemed pretty normal. No tummy pooch today.

Me & Watson

"Alright, Judy, is it OK if I take him back for his ultrasound?"

"Sure, Dr. Schmidt. That's fine. Watson likes you," she said.

"Would you like to come with him?"

"Nah, that's OK," she said. "When it comes to medical stuff, I'm a wimp. I might pass out on you. Besides, I've got some calls I need to make."

"OK," I said. "If he's got a lot of fluid, is it OK to drain, or would you like me to check with you first?"

"Dr. Schmidt, Jerry and I completely trust you," she said. "You just do whatever you think is right for my Watson."

"Got it," I said. "Back in a bit."

Watson's ultrasound showed more fluid, but not as much as the week before. Amy was my assistant again this day. With her help, we drained off a liter of abdominal fluid—half as much as before. And . . . his liver lesions were looking *better*. Every single liver cavity was at least twenty percent smaller. I was elated. I felt like Jonas Salk.

I proudly walked Watson back to see his mom.

"Well, we did drain his abdomen," I said. "But there was a lot less fluid today. Only one liter this time. And all his liver lesions are smaller. I think the Panacur is doing the trick. Those parasites are dying."

"Oh, that's fantastic," said Judy. A happy glow came over her. "Dr. Schmidt, you've made my day." She stood up, walked across the room, and gave me a hug. "We'll be here next week."

That evening I'd finished all my appointments for the day, still riding a high from the improvement I'd seen in Watson. I was worn out and bedraggled, but I owed Dr. Boyd an update. I sat down at my computer and opened my Outlook email program. I penned an email of gratitude to Dr. Boyd. It read:

"Dr. Boyd, IT'S WORKING! Jeff"

I attached three images of Watson's liver from his most recent ultrasound.

I could fill him in on the details later. The images told much of the story.

I continued to see Watson each week at 3 p.m. Same routine: Each week I'd give the pup a quick check-up and examine his abdomen with ultrasound. Each week I'd drain off some fluid and check his liver. On each visit, the amount of fluid was progressively reduced.

By week six, he didn't have enough fluid to bother draining, and his cavernous liver lesions were eighty percent smaller than their original, diseased size. Watson continued to feel better. His increasing energy and a frisky playfulness were a joy to see. The Clarkes were thoroughly pleased with his progress.

"He seems to be doing so well, Dr. Schmidt . . . and you didn't drain any more fluid today. Do you think we're done?" asked Mrs. Clarke.

"That's a good question," I said. "I don't think anyone really knows the answer. This is such a rare condition even the experts are guessing. I spoke to Dr. Boyd last week and he recommends we keep him on fenbendazole for at least another month. He wants us to keep going until he has no abdominal effusion, and his liver is pretty much back to normal. However, I don't think we need to keep having him come in every week. Why don't we start going to every other week for the time being?

"OK, Dr. Schmidt. You're the boss. You've gotten us this far," she said.

My next recheck with Watson broke the pattern. It was two weeks later on a Thursday. It was ten in the morning. The Clarkes were planning on a weekend getaway to Lake Tahoe the next day and they were taking Watson with them. I'd completed his ultrasound and was walking him back to exam room three. Dr. Lux saw me in the hallway. "How's Watson doing?" he asked. He'd been keeping track of Watson's progress the whole time.

"He's doing really good," I said. "We can probably stop his medication pretty soon. There's no fluid and his liver is ninety-nine percent back to normal."

"That's great," he said, "He deserves a vacation."

"Yep," I replied. "Funny you should say that. The Clarkes are actually headed up to Tahoe tomorrow morning."

"Good for them," replied Dr. Lux. "Tell 'em to not to let him eat anything from the lake."

I steered Watson back to the exam room and opened the door. Watson ran over to Judy. He put his front paws on her lap and pushed his head against her torso.

"I think Watson might be done," I said with an uncontrolled grin. "He didn't have any fluid in there and his liver is just about normal."

"That's it!" said Mr. Clarke loudly slapping both hands on his knees. "We're going to Tahoe with him to celebrate. It's going to be one big Poochapalooza!"

I couldn't help smiling at his enthusiasm. "That sounds like a great idea. Let's keep him on fenbendazole for at least another two weeks just to be extra safe. I'll give Dr. Boyd an update to see if he's OK with that plan. By the way, Dr. Lux says don't *let him eat any lake creatures.*"

"Ha! We won't. Thanks a million," said Judy.

"Yeah, thanks a million," said Jerry. "No offense, Dr. Schmidt, but we're getting the heck out of here. We've been seeing just a bit too much of you lately."

"I don't blame you," I said. "Go have some fun with your dog."

Maggie caught up with me in the back hallway forty minutes later.

"I was just talking to Mr. and Mrs. Clarke," she said. "They seemed very happy. They believe Watson may be cured."

"Yeah. He didn't have any fluid in his abdomen today. His liver still isn't one hundred percent normal, but it's a heck of a lot better."

"Let's celebrate," said Maggie. "My treat. Let's head over to your Mexican place for lunch."

"Sounds good to me. I've got three more appointments this morning. I'll come to your office when I'm done."

Maggie and I had a favorite lunch spot called Tejana's. It was a little family-owned Mexican restaurant. Most of the staff knew us there and were very friendly. It was conveniently located in the same shopping complex as the vet clinic. We just had to brave walking across the hazardous parking lot to get there. The lot for Oak View was a bit of a danger zone. We'd had several fender-benders right outside the building. It was on the corner of an intersection and impatient drivers would cut through it rather than wait for the light to change at the intersection.

My last morning appointment was for Chuck the Cat. His owners were a middle-aged couple with a knack for great pet names. Their other cat was *Lumpy,* and their dog was named *Biscuit.* I'm not sure why, but these names always made me chuckle.

At 12:15 with Chuck the Cat's annual appointment complete, I grabbed my jacket and headed over to Maggie's office. She was in the middle of submitting the employee hours for payroll. I waited around for a minute or two until she looked like she was at a good stopping place. "Are you ready to go?" I asked as she shut down her computer.

"Yeah, I am. Let's get going. I'm hungry today."

I smiled to myself. Maggie always claimed she was *starving* but would then eat two tortilla chips and half a taco. I was always ready to help her out with the leftovers.

Maggie grabbed a teal sweater from the back of her chair. She generally wore subdued, earthy colors, so this was a bold departure for her. She hoisted herself up with an elderly grumble and maneuvered her arms through the sweater. I opened the front door for her, and we headed outside to brave the parking lot. I had to watch Maggie carefully here. I'm not sure if her parents ever taught her to look both ways before she crossed the street, or, if she just figured *I'm old and to hell with it.* She had a habit of charging out right in front of oncoming cars. They'd have to slam on their brakes to avoid her and we'd had a few close calls over the years. You could see the drivers get startled and then mad. Many of them wanted to chew out the jaywalker, but then realized they were going to have to confront a doddering old lady. Usually they'd just wait impatiently, tapping their fingers on the wheel until she went by. I'd look at them and give them an apologetic shrug. Today was no different. As she stepped down from the sidewalk and started to walk across the lot, I preemptively reached out my left hand so I could grab her if needed. Sure enough, a white Lexus coupe was trying to cut through the lot at thirty miles per hour. I grabbed her right shoulder with my left hand to halt her long enough for the car to pass. She didn't even seem to notice. After the car went by, we continued on to our lunchtime destination.

We placed our orders at the front counter and found a quiet spot in the corner, settling in at the standard-issue Formica table to wait for our food.

"So," said Maggie. "I thought it would be good to let you know that the Clarkes were very pleased with you. They credit you for saving Watson's life. They came into my office and talked with me for about thirty minutes."

"That's very nice of them," I said. "The fact is, I got lucky. I happened to know one of the few parasitologists who was studying the disease their dog happened to have. I had no idea what to do."

"I knew you would fix him," she said.

"How the heck could you know that?" I asked. "I didn't know what in the hell I was dealing with. I was near ready to put him to sleep."

Maggie leaned forward in her chair and put her elbows on the table. "Dr. Schmidt, you know I've been in the veterinary business for almost forty years," she said. "My husband was a farm animal vet, and I managed his business and did his books until he retired."

"Yeah, I knew that," I said. I'd met her husband Dick on a couple of occasions. He was a nice, dignified older gentleman, about ten years her senior.

"Then I went to work for Dr. Lux," she said. "I was his office manager at Placer Vet Clinic for close to twenty years before he sold and went to work at Pacific Street Vet Hospital."

I nodded my head and dipped a tortilla chip in the hot salsa, not sure where she was going with this.

"When I found out you were opening your own place, I wanted to make sure it was successful. You should know by now that I won't work for anyone I don't respect." As she said this, she reached out and put her left hand on top of my right hand.

"I'm seventy-four years old Dr. Schmidt, and I probably should have retired years ago. I knew you'd take care of the clients Dr. Lux and I cared about. The Clarkes are a perfect example. You treat people with honesty and respect. You're just like a young Dr. Lux. When Mr. Clarke came in that day with Watson, I actually told him he should see *you*, and not Dr. Lux. I changed around the appointment schedule to make that happen. Dr. Lux is good, but he's slowing down a little and he's not as patient as he used to be. I *knew* you'd fix Watson."

I paused my chip-dunking to take this all in. I thought we were just going out for a casual lunch. I was honored and humbled and stunned all at the same time. Maggie could be a harsh critic, but this was the biggest compliment I'd ever received, and made all the more special coming from her. I was thrilled to hear it!

About four months later, Maggie was diagnosed with advanced colon cancer. She went through two surgeries and chemotherapy in an attempt to get rid of all the cancerous cells. The treatments slowed it down, but it was not a cure. She still came into work every single day despite her progressively weakened condition. Finally, she was too tired and too anemic to function. In the end, she could barely stand. One Thursday morning at 6:30, she called me and apologized for not being able to come to work. In her weakened voice I could tell how much guts it took to make that call. The cancer may have been killing her body, but it was letting me down that was killing her spirit. She went into hospice care and passed away at home about a month later.

I never forgot the confidence she bestowed on me. In fact, she may have been my biggest fan. The place was never quite the same without her at the helm.

Dick & Maggie

CHAPTER 11

FLAT

SATURDAY

"Good morning, Cheeto. How are you today?"

"Meep," answered the little orange kitten talking to me from his perch on the exam table.

"Are you having a rough day?"

"Meep, meep."

Cheeto belonged to the Harrison family. In their early forties, Will worked for a computer tech company, and Michelle was in biotech. They were devoted to their sons, John, who was eight, and Austin, who was ten. Both boys were incredibly polite and respectful. They said *please*, and *thank you*, and they always asked if they could ask a question before they asked a question. I'd known them for at least six years and was responsible for caring for their two Labrador retrievers named Molly and Sam. I was thoroughly impressed with the entire family and excited to see their new addition. They were visibly excited about their new kitten and eager to show him off. This was their first family cat.

This was only the second time I'd seen Cheeto. I first met him a couple weeks ago when he was brought in for his first kitten exam. He was an adorable little orange tabby and quite a little character. At only ten weeks old,

Cheeto would look me right in the face with bright blue eyes and consider me thoughtfully. He seemed to understand everything I said to him. He would listen to me speak, then, after a polite pause, he would answer me right back. His vocabulary was limited, however. "*Meep, Nowwp, Yawps* and *Yip*" seemed to be his most common responses. He was amazingly calm and interactive for such a little thing. He had sat patiently while I looked at his teeth and took his temperature. He was even cooperative when I drew a few drops of blood from his hind leg for viral testing. Most kittens *hate* this. Not Cheeto. He seemed to know we were on his side. He didn't offer any resistance when I gave his first kitten vaccines.

Cheeto

When I was all done with the serious part of the exam, I lifted him up with two hands under his front legs and held him about three inches from my face.

"You are a good little boy, Cheeto," I had told him, giving him a little peck on the tip of his tiny pink nose. "It was very nice to meet you."

Cheeto looked me right in the eyes, politely paused for a heartbeat, and said "Yip."

Now Cheeto was back for another reason. The whole crew arrived with him, and it made the exam room a bit crowded.

"So," I said toward the group. "I understand you're worried about Cheeto's hind end. What's concerning you?"

Michelle spoke up first. "Dr. Schmidt, Cheeto had diarrhea ever since we got him. It's yellow and pasty. The last couple of days, after he's gone to his litter box, I've noticed his little butt is red and swollen. It seems to bother him, and he keeps licking at it."

Michelle was blonde, fit, and kept her entire family, including the pets, in ship shape. She was a very intelligent and competent lady. She sold medical equipment for a living, and we'd had more than one crisis treating her dogs over the years.

"Does he seem to feel OK otherwise?" I asked. "Is he eating and drinking, OK? Is he playful?"

"He seems fine to me," replied Michelle. "He eats like crazy, and he runs around the house like a Tasmanian Devil."

"He attacks my feet and bites my socks!" John chimed in. "He goes 'crazy cat' sometimes."

"Well, that's all good to hear," I said. "Healthy kittens are frisky little devils. So, he must not be feeling too sick. Let me look at his furry little bottom."

I gently flipped Cheeto around and lifted his butt end so I could get a good look. Mr. Harrison helped to hold him in place for me. I could see the problem at once: Cheeto's anal region looked like a little red sausage.

"I see what you mean. Cheeto's starting to get a rectal prolapse. The area is so inflamed that his rectum is starting to turn inside out. It must be pretty uncomfortable for him. This sometimes happens when kittens have bad diarrhea."

"Can I ask a question?" said Austin.

"Sure," I said.

"Will he die?" he asked.

Poor guy. I felt terrible that he was so worried. I needed to reassure him that this little gem of a cat would be OK.

"No," I said. "We can fix this. However, sometimes it does take time and it can be a hassle."

"So, what do we need to do to fix him?" asked Michelle.

"Just give me a minute and I'll be right back," I said.

I left the exam room and went to find my tech, Shannon. I found her just as she was coming out of exam room number two. She'd just checked in my next appointment and was getting ready to draw up a couple vaccines.

"Shannon. I need a quick hand with the little orange kitten in room one. He's starting to get a rectal prolapse and I need to show the owners how to treat it."

"OK. Be right there," she said.

I fished around on our medication shelf and found a tube of Panalog ointment. Shannon and I marched back into room number one where Cheeto was snuggled up against Austin's neck.

"OK," I said. "Shannon's going to help me show you how to treat Cheeto's problem." Shannon lifted Cheeto from Austin's grasp and held the kitty with his butt towards me and his tail gently pulled back.

"OK," I said. "Now watch what I do. I'm going to need you to do this four to five times a day whenever you see his butt start to pooch out like this."

On cue the whole Harrison family looked over my shoulder to see what I was doing. I took a cotton-tipped applicator out of the jar sitting near the treatment sink and applied a liberal amount of ointment to one end, completely saturating the cotton. With Shannon keeping Cheeto from wiggling, I coated the protruding portion of the kitten's rectum with the ointment. Then I gently pushed the protruding portion back inside. Cheeto made one tiny "peep" and that was it. Everything stayed in place and his rear end instantly looked happier.

"That's it," I said. "He's a pretty good little kitten and he'll probably let you do this at home. Whenever you see that area starting to pooch out, just use this method to push it back in. That ointment will reduce the swelling and increase the chance it will stay in place. It's most likely to prolapse again after he uses the litter box." I added, "As you can see, it's a two-person project. One person to hold and the other one to do the procedure."

"I can help," Austin piped in.

"Perfect. Shannon will get you a packet of these swabs and a fresh tube of ointment to use on him. If it's not better in a few days, let me know."

"OK, Dr. Schmidt. Thank you," said Will. "I think we can do that."

"Oh, one more thing," I said. "I'm going to send you home with a little plastic container for a stool sample. The next time he poops, please bring in a sample and we'll check him for parasites."

The next morning, when I was checking on lab reports, I saw that there were already results available for Cheeto Harrison. The family was obviously worried and had brought in a stool sample right after the exam. They were certainly on the ball. I clicked on Cheeto's name to see that, sure enough, he had parasites in his fecal sample, specifically coccidia. Now I had an explanation for his severe diarrhea problem.

I called Michelle on her cell phone to give her the news. It was a workday, so I didn't expect anyone to answer the home phone. But Michelle was the glue that held the family together and I knew she monitored her cell phone closely. "Hello, Dr. Schmidt," she said.

"Hi, Michelle. Thanks for bringing in that stool sample for Cheeto. It was helpful. It looks like he has a parasite called coccidia. This is a single-celled organism that's fairly common in kittens. It infects the lining of the intestine and interferes with its ability to absorb nutrients and water. This is the reason for the diarrhea. It's also the reason his bowels are cramping and causing that prolapse problem. I'll get a medication called Albon ready for you to pick up later today. You just give it once a day. It will clear up the coccidia over the next couple of weeks. We'll still need to watch his rectal prolapse problem, though. Just killing the parasite doesn't necessarily mean that it will go away too."

"Sounds good, Dr. Schmidt," she said. "I'll pick up that medication as soon as it's ready. By the way, his rectal problem has come back three times since yesterday, but each time, we were able to put it back in. It's incredible how cooperative he is for this. He doesn't like it, but he still lets us do it. He's a *really* good little kitten."

"He sure is," I said. "He seems like a real sweetheart. Try not to worry too much. We'll get him through this."

TUESDAY

On Tuesday morning, my stomach dropped when I saw that Cheeto was my 11 a.m. appointment. *Uh-oh,* I thought.

At 11:05 Shannon, my technician, found me at my desk. The look on her face told me there was a problem.

"I have Cheeto ready to see you in room number two," she said. "His rectal prolapse looks worse. About twice as much is hanging out as before."

My heart sank. I'd hoped that I fixed this problem. *Is nothing ever simple?* This was a sweet little cat with a very nice family. I just wanted him to heal up, grow up, and have a great life. *Here we go again*, I thought as I entered the exam room.

"Hi, Michelle," I said as I entered. She came solo this time.

Michelle was dressed smartly in a charcoal skirt and matching blazer. Cheeto's unplanned vet appointment was clearly interfering with her work commitments.

"Hello, Dr. Schmidt," she said. "I think Cheeto's rear end is getting worse. We keep pushing it back in, but it keeps popping back out. Today it's out more than ever."

Michelle was resilient and practical. She had two young boys that were getting scraped and bruised every day. She understood that getting emotional wouldn't help the situation, but I could tell she was struggling to keep her worry in check.

I hoisted little Cheeto out of his cat carrier.

"Good morning, Cheeto," I said looking him right in the face.

"Meeeaap," said Cheeto. He didn't sound as perky as he had on Saturday.

I turned him around to look at his furry little orange rear. As I feared, today there was twice as much rectum prolapsed as three days earlier. It looked red, swollen, and angry. There were scattered bits of jagged cat litter stuck to the swollen tissue. *Ouch!* I'm sure the bits of debris added even further to his discomfort.

"Yeah, you're right, Michelle. This is definitely not what I was hoping for. The tissue is so swollen, he just keeps pushing it out. We're going to have to find a way to keep it in there. Can you leave him with me for a few hours? I will sedate him for a minor procedure. I'll reduce that prolapse again and put in a row of sutures called a "purse string," which will partially close his anal opening to keep him from prolapsing. We can't leave the purse string in too long or his bowels will get backed up. But if we leave it in for a few days, it should allow some time for the swelling to go down. Hopefully, when we take out the purse string, everything will stay in place."

Sitting across from me, I could see some of the tension leave Michelle. As a woman of action, she felt better just knowing there was a plan in place.

"Sure, Dr. Schmidt," said Michelle. "What a relief. I trust you. Just do what you need to do and call me when it's time to pick him up."

I finished up my morning appointments (a poodle with a skin infection and a Great Dane with a sore eye) and headed back to the treatment room. Shannon had already prepared a treatment area and an anesthesia machine for Cheeto's mini surgery. I gave the little three-pound cat an intramuscular injection of a sedative. The sedative took effect quickly because he was so small. Shannon anesthetized him by carefully holding a mask over his tiny mouth and nose. The mask connected to an anesthesia machine that delivered oxygen and diluted anesthetic gas. On each breath, the rubber reservoir bag would slightly rise and fall. The amount was almost imperceptible due to the hamster-sized volume of his lungs. Cheeto was too small to safely place an endotracheal tube into his airway so he would have to get his anesthesia just by mask. They didn't make tubes in his size. This method was not ideal, as it somewhat compromised safety, but for a critter this dainty, it was unavoidable. I was hoping the entire procedure would only last a few minutes.

I drew up two milliliters of Mannitol, a hypertonic sugar solution, which would reduce the swelling of the tissue and coated the prolapsed portion of Cheeto's bum. After letting this sit for a couple of minutes, I coated the area with KY Jelly for lubrication. I then used my gloved finger and forceps to coax the prolapsed tissue back in past the anal sphincter. The mannitol had helped; the tissue was definitely less swollen than before. Shannon held the prolapse in place with one hand and Cheeto's anesthesia mask with the other hand. With a pair of needle holders, I pulled a length of fine suture from its sterile pack. I then carefully placed a row of sutures around the edge of Cheeto's anal opening. I didn't want to completely close off the opening. This would be bad because he wouldn't be able to poop at all, but I did want to restrict the opening so that it was too small for the prolapse to recur. To accomplish this, I used a one-milliliter plastic syringe as a guide. When I had three quarters of the anal opening surrounded by sutures, I inserted the syringe into the opening. I then snugged down the suture loop to the level of the syringe circumference and finished tying off the loose ends of the suture.

This created a 360-degree restriction and only left about four millimeters of opening.

Shannon turned off the anesthetic gas but left the oxygen flowing for another few minutes while Cheeto gradually returned to consciousness. Just before he was fully awake, she placed a plastic e-collar on his head so he couldn't reach his rear end and chew out the purse string suture. As soon as he woke up, he turned to inspect his rear end. Poor little Cheeto, I'm sure it didn't feel good. With the collar in place, he was unable to undo our work. "Yawp, Yawp, Yawp," said Cheeto. *Why did you do this to me?*

"Sorry, little guy," I said. "I can't have you walking around with your bottom hanging out. It's just for a few days."

I called the Harrisons at home to let them know Cheeto was out of surgery. This time it was Mr. Harrison that answered the phone.

"Hello, Will. This is Dr. Schmidt."

"Hi, Dr. Schmidt. How's it goin'? Michelle told me about the situation with Cheeto. How is he doing?"

"He's doing fine. We just finished his procedure a couple of minutes ago. He was only asleep for about five minutes. He should be OK to go home in a couple of hours."

"OK, good. Do you think this will fix the problem?"

"I sure hope so. We can't leave that purse string suture in there too long or it will cause him serious problems. So, if we remove it in a few days and he prolapses again we may have to consider amputating that portion of his colon."

"How does that work?"

"Well, I only do that as a last resort. A prolapse is a proximal piece of the colon pushing out through a distal piece. So, amputating a half-inch pro-trusion would mean losing a full inch of his colon, and that's not good. The colon is responsible for reabsorbing a lot of water. By shortening his colon, he could have loose stools for the rest of his life. Also, whenever you do a surgery like this, there's a risk of infection and of dehiscence. That's where the sutures don't hold, or the tissue falls apart. That can be really serious."

"Have you done that surgery before?"

"Yeah, but only two or three times."

"Did it work?"

"Yes, it's worked fine on the cats I've done before."

"All right. Let's hope it doesn't come to that."

"Yeah, let's hope so. I'll see you in a couple of hours."

Cheeto went home without incident. He had a follow-up appointment in three days to recheck and remove the purse string.

FRIDAY

Cheeto's next appointment was scheduled for Friday afternoon. The whole Harrison family was with him to make sure everything went OK. We were all hoping that this was his last vet visit for a while.

"How's he doing?" I asked the whole family.

"He hates that cone on his head," John blurted out. "It makes him sad."

"Yeah, I don't blame him," I said. "Hopefully, he won't need that any-more. Is he doing OK otherwise?"

"He's doing OK," said Michelle. "He's eating and drinking all right. He doesn't play around as much, but I think it's just because the cone cramps his style."

"Those e-collars are a hassle," I said. "I hate using them, but if he got to his hind end and took the suture out, we would be back to square one. So, it's a necessary evil, I'm afraid."

"Can I ask a question?" said John.

"Certainly," I said.

"Can we take that cone off his head today?" said John.

"Yep," I said, "I think we'll give that a try and see how he does."

"Let me borrow Cheeto for a minute," I said. "I'll take him into the treatment room, take out that suture, and make sure everything looks OK."

"OK, Dr. Schmidt," said Austin.

I scooped up the three-pound ball of fluff, tucked him under my arm, and walked back into the treatment room. Cheeto was in a bad mood. He was normally more talkative and would look me right in the face. Today he avoided any eye contact and didn't make a peep. He was giving me the silent treatment. He was almost cuter when he was grumpy. "Loren, can you help me with this little guy?" I asked one of the vet assistants.

"I don't know," said Loren. "He looks pretty vicious to me."

"You can get one of the Hannibal Lector muzzles for him if you want," I joked.

Loren wasn't very intimidated by Cheeto's bad attitude. She scooped him from me and tucked him under her armpit, butt outward.

I reached up and turned on the overhead treatment light, then donned a pair of magnification visors so I could find the tiny piece of black suture near his butt. I grabbed the loose end of the suture with a small pair of medical graspers called hemostats and gave a gentle tug. Using a small suture removal scissor, I passed one end under the suture loop and *snip*, cut it loose and pulled out the entire purse string suture. There was a tiny amount of bleeding from the suture holes, but generally his little rear end looked pretty good. Everything seemed to be staying in the right place so far.

I toted Cheeto back into the exam room where his family was expectantly waiting for him.

"OK," I said. "That went fine. He was a good little boy. We'll just need to watch him closely for the next few days to make sure his rear end stays in the correct place. Make sure you still give him his coccidia medication."

"OK, Dr. Schmidt. We will." The whole family chimed in.

Cheeto added a hearty "Meep, Meep." He was obviously much happier with the cone off his head and the suture out of his butt.

SATURDAY

There were four vets working at the clinic that day, but I was the only one who really knew what was going on with Cheeto. I wasn't at work, but I decided to call the Harrisons from home to make sure Cheeto was doing OK.

I held my breath and dialed Mrs. Harrison's cell phone number. She was the one I most consistently got ahold of. She answered on the second ring.

"Hi, Dr. Schmidt. Thanks for calling. I didn't know you were working today."

"Hi, Michelle. I'm not actually working in the office today. I'm at home catching up on my records. But I thought I'd call and make sure Cheeto is doing OK."

"That's so nice of you to call on your day off from work," she said. "I'm happy to report he is doing fine. He's eating like a pig and running around chasing our two dogs. His prolapse issue seems fixed."

I performed a mini fist-pump . . . *Yes!* I was so relieved at hearing this good news. I could feel the muscles in my neck and face relax as some of the tension left me. Cheeto had wiggled his way into my heart, and evidently, I was more worried than I'd let myself believe. This was a super nice family and an adorable little cat. I just wanted things to go smoothly, for once.

"That's great to hear. I'm back in the office on Monday so just give me a call if there's any problems." *Please, please, please let's not have any problems,* I thought to myself.

"I will, Dr. Schmidt. Thanks, and have a good weekend," she said.

"You too. Goodbye," I said.

MONDAY

Mondays were my surgery days. I looked forward to this day of the week because there was less paperwork and fewer phone calls. Just me and a technician in our private little surgery sanctuary. Shannon was my surgery technician and we'd been working together for many years. She knew my likes and dislikes and was dedicated to making our procedures flow seamlessly. I was in the surgery room dressed in a blue sterile surgery gown, mask, cap, and sterile gloves spaying a golden retriever puppy. Robi, the receptionist, paged the surgery room from the front desk.

"Shannon," she said. "Are you there?"

"Yes, I'm here," Shannon replied.

"I have Mrs. Harrison on the other line," said Robi. "She says Cheeto's rectal prolapse has come back. What do you want me to tell her?"

Ughhhh . . ., my heart sank. Even though I was across the room, I could hear the whole conversation.

I had to shout to be heard through my surgery mask over the intercom. "Please tell her I'm in surgery most of the day, so I can't really give her a specific appointment time. But if she can drop Cheeto off, I will look at him as soon as I can."

"Alrighty. Will do," Robi replied.

"Oh my God, Shannon," I said to her. "That kitten is going to give me a stroke. I'm running out of tricks to fix that little guy."

"You should talk to Dr. Lux about Cheeto," she replied. "He's good with fixing those rectal prolapse problems on kittens. I've seen him do it a bunch of times."

"Really?" I said. "I will. I didn't know he was a rectal prolapse expert."

Dr. Lux had started practice in an era when there was no specialization in veterinary medicine. A general practice veterinarian in those days had to fix (or try to fix) *everything*. It was sink or swim back then, and a lot of leeway was given for medical ingenuity. Shannon had been working with Dr. Lux for at least six years before I knew her. I met them both working at my previous vet clinic several years before. I was desperate to come up with some new idea that might save this situation.

The minute I finished my surgery, I tracked down Dr. Lux. He was seeing outpatient appointments that day and I cornered him in his office sitting at his desk. Today he wore an unzipped maroon doctor's coat with a black stethoscope dangling out of one pocket. His wire-framed glasses were so smudged that I'm not sure how he could see anything.

"Frank, I really need some help," I told him. "Shannon said you are an expert in rectal prolapse cases and I have a little kitten that's becoming a royal pain in the butt."

I proceeded to tell Dr. Lux about the two-week saga of Cheeto's coccidia, diarrhea, and recurring rectal prolapse adding, "On a few occasions, I've just amputated the prolapsed section and anastomosed the cut ends together. But I don't love doing it that way. Sometimes they lose a pretty significant chunk of their intestine. Cheeto's only a three-pound kitten. And if that reattachment point leaks, he might die from peritonitis. Shannon told me you have a better way of treating these."

"Didn't you ever learn about the FLAT technique?" he said, smoothing out his moustache.

"Huh?" I said. "The *FLAT* technique? I've never heard of it. What the hell is the FLAT technique?"

"Well," he said. "This is what you do . . . all you need is some needle holders and some nonabsorbable suture. Something like 3-0 Nylon works fine. You anesthetize the cat and lay them down on their left side. You shave and do a surgical prep on the right side of their lateral abdomen. Get the prolapse reduced just like you did before. Then you lube up the pinky finger of your left hand and insert it into their rectum as far as you can. No glove though . . . you can't use a glove on your hand."

"Wait, wait. . . . You perform a rectal probe with your pinky finger with no glove? Gross . . . why can't you use a glove?"

"You can't use a glove because you will lose some sensation. You need to carefully feel what you're doing to make this work. Once you have your finger in there, you'll use it to press the wall of the colon against the right inside of the kitten's body wall. Kittens are so tiny that you can easily see and feel your finger pressing outward through their abdominal wall. Then you get your needle holders with the Nylon. From the outside, pass a single suture that goes through the body wall into the outside wall of the colon. You don't want to fully penetrate the colon with your suture as this could cause contamination, so you must *feel* where you're at. That's why *no glove*."

"You do this all blind?" I asked. "Just by feel?"

"Yep," he said. "Once you have a single good stitch that goes through the body wall and catches the outer wall of the colon, you finish off by passing the needle back out through the abdominal wall. You then just tie a solid square knot. This stitch forms a permanent pexy site between the colon and the inner body wall. This prevents another prolapse."

I stood there for a moment with a puzzled look on my face. If this worked, it was a simple and ingenious solution. But why hadn't I ever heard of it before?

"So, you've done this before, and it works?" I asked.

"Many times," he said. "At the S.P.C.A., it was a common kitten problem. You had to be able to fix these without many resources. Just make sure you scrub your hands well before you go eat a sandwich."

"Huh . . .," I said. "I've never heard of that. But why is it called the FLAT technique?"

"It stands for Frank Lux Ass Tack," he replied with a grin.

I was in the middle of a luxating patella surgery on a white toy poodle named Bruno when Cheeto arrived. Bruno's kneecap tended to pop out of place whenever he jumped on the sofa. I had a rounded bone file in my right hand. I was in the process of deepening his trochlear groove so the patella would stay in the proper place. It had been about an hour since my FLAT lesson. Shannon hurried out to the lobby to get Cheeto from Michelle. She took a quick peek at his hind quarters then came right back to give me a report.

"Yeah, it's happened again," she stated. "Worse than before. About twice as much is hanging out . . . at least an inch."

"Damn," I said. "Give him a sedative injection, an antibiotic injection, and make sure he has an e-collar on. I'll look at him as soon as I'm done here."

It was hard to focus on the rest of the patella surgery. I still needed to replace the patella and suture Bruno's knee back together. My mind was buzzing about all the awful possibilities with Cheeto. Dr. Lux sounded confident. Maybe the FLAT method was the way to go. It might be better than amputating two inches of rectum. We had to do something *today* or that entire piece of prolapsed rectum would necrose. Then he would be in worse trouble.

As soon as I finished up my surgery, I went over to check out little Cheeto. He didn't look happy sporting the dreaded collar strapped to his head. As Shannon had described, one inch of angry swollen rectum was hanging out of his rear end. *Poor guy*, I thought. He must be miserable. I walked over to the office, sat at my desk, and picked up the phone to call Michelle Harrison. I took a deep breath before punching in her number. This was not a conversation I wanted to have.

"Hi, Michelle," I said. "It's Dr. Schmidt. I'm sorry to see Cheeto has prolapsed again. I was so hopeful after our conversation on Saturday."

"Hi, Dr. Schmidt," she said. "I know. I feel the same way. We were doing so well for the past couple of days, but this morning I looked at him and could tell something was wrong. He was dragging his butt and had a worried look on his face. When I turned him around to look, it almost made me cry."

"Well, I consulted with Dr. Lux on Cheeto. He's been a vet much longer than me and has seen quite a few of these cases. He has a technique for fixing these that I hadn't heard of before (I left the *FLAT* acronym out of this conversation). It's a surgical method that keeps the colon in place without having to amputate it."

I briefly described the procedure to her.

"If it's OK with you, we'll do this on Cheeto as soon as possible. His prolapse is pretty bad this time and I don't want to leave it that way for any longer than necessary."

"Sure. That sounds good to me," she said. "Anything we can do to fix him. He's a great little cat and my boys love him to death."

"OK," I said. "We'll get this done in the next couple hours and I'll call you when we're finished. It should be fine for him to go home today."

I found Dr. Lux as he was coming out of exam room number two.

"Frank. I talked to Cheeto's owner, and we have the green light to go ahead with the FLAT procedure. Can you do it over your lunch break?" I asked.

"Sure," he said. "I just have one more appointment to finish up. Are you sure you don't want to do it?"

"No thanks," I said. "I've never done it before, so I'd rather watch one first. And my luck with this cat hasn't been great so far."

"No problem. Have the little guy anesthetized and ready to go at 12:30," he said.

By 12:30 Shannon and I had little Cheeto under anesthesia with an I.V. drip and the right side of his abdomen shaved. He was in the surgery room with a surgical pack and some 3-0 Nylon on hand. The sterile pack and surgical room were probably overkill—this wasn't exactly going to be a sterile, germ-free procedure. But the lighting was better there, and I wanted to maximize our chance of success.

Dr. Lux came in still wearing his light blue doctor's coat with the OptiVISORs resting on his head. No need for him to do a surgical scrub, considering where his hands were going. Just like he'd explained to me earlier, he applied a generous amount of lubricant to the prolapse and coaxed the swollen appendage back in place. He prepped his black nylon suture with the needle loaded into the needle holders. He put a generous amount of lube on his left pinky finger and gently inserted it into the tiny cat's anal opening. This took some doing; Dr. Lux's fingers were quite large. He turned and adjusted his left hand by rotating his elbow. Now you could see the outline of his pinky finger protruding from the right side of Cheeto's abdomen. Next, he carefully took a deep stitch of tissue with the needle through the skin. His needle went through the thin wall of abdominal muscle and into the wall of the colon, where he was holding it in place with his pinky finger. This was the tricky part and he had to reposition the needle a few times, all by feel. If the retaining stitch perforated the colon, he could get bacteria loose into his abdominal cavity. This is a serious, sometimes fatal condition. Once he had a good hold on the colon wall, he rotated the curved needle tip back out through the body wall and skin. He gently pulled out his left pinky finger and then tied the suture ends together with three square knots. The entire procedure took ten minutes.

"That's it," he said. "I'm pretty sure that sucker's not going to prolapse again."

Cheeto appeared to be doing fine. He was taking even, slow breaths. I wish I could say the same for my breathing. His rectum was staying inside where it belonged. We turned off the anesthesia to start his recovery and I relaxed a little. I really liked this little orange cat and I hoped we'd conquered this problem once and for all. If this drama continued much longer, I was going to have to resupply my liquor cabinet.

Cheeto went home that day around 4:30. I spoke with Michelle on her way out the door.

"He seemed to do well for the whole procedure," I said. "He's a tough little cat. I'm glad Dr. Lux was here today. I've never seen that procedure before, and I've never read about it anywhere. He knows a lot of good tricks."

"Yeah," said Michelle. "We've known Dr. Lux for twenty years and we love him. He was the only vet we ever saw until we met you. Now we feel lucky to have both of you to call on when one of our pets is sick."

"Thanks," I said. "Tell Will I say hello and let me know if you have any more problems with Cheeto over the next few days."

I should've taken a two-week vacation right then and there. Cheeto wasn't done with me yet.

THURSDAY

I was just finishing up my 8:30 appointment. Francine was a dainty little calico cat. She was recovering from a dentistry two weeks ago where I'd removed three rotten teeth. She was healing up nicely, and I was just saying goodbye to Mrs. Borcher. Amy was my vet tech for the day and was waiting for me in the hallway. I'd been working with Amy for five years and she was a model of composure and efficiency. She made it her life's mission to keep the appointments moving and me on schedule. She knew me well. Sometimes I got overly "chatty" with my favorite clients, and I'd lose track of time. When she saw me going down this path, she'd politely knock on the door, stick her head in, and say something like, "Dr. Schmidt, I just wanted you to know that I checked in your nine o'clock appointment." Message received. Time to cut the chit-chat and get down to business.

As Amy approached me, I handed her Francine's chart. I gave her some instructions for a prescription toothpaste and turned to go into the next exam room when she stopped me.

"Dr. Schmidt. While you were in your last appointment, Mrs. Harrison called. She says Cheeto isn't feeling good and wouldn't eat his breakfast this morning." Amy knew the whole Cheeto story. "I just told her to bring him right in. He'll probably be here in the next half an hour."

Ohhh myyy God, I thought to myself. Now what the heck was going on? I'm not sure I could handle any more Cheeto drama.

"OK," I said in an artificially casual tone of voice. "Just let me know when he gets here." I proceeded to exam room two where Frisco the

Chihuahua was waiting to ambush me. His favorite game was *bite-the-vet*. He never got tired of it.

Mrs. Harrison dropped off Cheeto twenty minutes later while I was in the middle of fending off Frisco. Amy checked him in and spoke to her.

"Mrs. Harrison thinks his stomach hurts," she said. "He cries when you touch him around his tummy. His rectal prolapse issue looks fine to me."

The news from Amy made me cringe. The one complication that struck fear in my heart was Cheeto developing peritonitis. It usually manifests as lethargy and a painful abdomen. I had a few minutes before my 9:30 appointment to check on the poor little guy. He looked sad and his eyes were a bit sunken. He was dehydrated and he cried at the slightest touch of his abdomen. *Please don't let this cat have peritonitis*, I prayed. We've come too far with him to have him die at this point.

I gave Cheeto an intramuscular injection of a sedative/pain medication combo and two antibiotic injections. We took his temperature. It was normal. *Whew . . .* this was a good sign. My 9:30 appointment had still not arrived. Cheeto got a little sleepy, so Amy took advantage, quickly placing an I.V. catheter. I wanted to look inside his abdomen to see if I might determine the problem. We placed him on his back, shaved the rest of his belly and carried him into the imaging room. I dimmed the lights and set the ultrasound machine to a higher frequency. This optimized the image for high resolution but didn't allow for deep penetration. He was little, so I didn't need to see in there very far. I fearfully placed the probe on his abdomen directed at the pexy area and scrutinized the monitor. I fully expected to see a belly full of infected fluid. Nope, no fluid. The area around the FLAT looked normal. I was relieved but surprised. *If he didn't have peritonitis, then why did his belly hurt?* I decided to do a methodical scan and look at everything. Starting at his liver in the twelve o'clock position, I slowly moved the probe in a clockwise direction. Gallbladder and liver? Normal. Left kidney? Normal. Small intestine and colon? Normal. Right kidney? *Oh, crap.* Cheeto's right kidney was blown up like a balloon. It was twice as big as normal, and the inner pelvis of the kidney was distended. This condition is called hydronephrosis. It's usually caused by an obstruction of the ureter: the tube that transports urine from the kidney to the bladder. When this tube is clogged, the kidney continues to make urine, but the urine has no place to go, so the kidney gets full and tight. This really hurts. Somehow the pexy suture that Dr. Lux placed had caused an obstruction of the right ureter. This wasn't as immediately life-threatening as bacterial peritonitis, but it sure wasn't good.

Dr. Lux was doing surgery in the suite next door. The two rooms were separated by a sliding pocket door. I slid the door open so I could confer with him.

"Dr. Lux, I've got Cheeto here in ultrasound. He was dropped off today because his belly hurts and he's feeling sick."

I could tell by Frank's face that his grave concern mimicked my own.

"I just did an ultrasound on him. His right kidney has hydronephrosis."

"Damn," he said. "That pexy suture must have damaged his ureter. I'm just finishing this entropion surgery. Let's get him in here right away. We need to explore his abdomen to see if this is something we can fix."

"Yeah. I agree," I said. "Amy, get Cheeto prepped for surgery right away. I'll go call Mrs. Harrison so she knows what's going on."

I hurried to my desk and sat down to make the call. I hated to give this poor woman more bad news, but I had to be honest with her. There wasn't a way to sugar-coat this situation and we didn't have any time to waste. Michelle picked up the phone right away.

"Hi, Dr. Schmidt. Did you figure out what's wrong with Cheeto?"

"Yes. I hate to tell you this, but it looks like he has a *new* problem. The ultrasound shows that his right kidney is obstructed. It's swollen like a balloon, which is causing him pain. I think that somehow the procedure on Monday caused damage to the ureter."

"Can you fix it?" she asked.

"I don't know yet. The only way to find out is to surgically open his abdomen and see what's going on. Dr. Lux is in surgery but is ready to do this right away. I hate to put you on the spot, but I can't waste any time. Is it OK for Dr. Lux to go ahead with the surgery?"

"Yes," she said. "Let's get after it right away. I'm so glad he's available to do this right now."

"Thanks," I said. "I'll call you with an update as soon as I can."

I rushed back to the surgery room. "Go ahead with the surgery on Cheeto. Mrs. Harrison says *thank you.*"

"Got it," Frank said. "We'll have him in here in ten minutes."

Amy said, "Dr. Schmidt. Your 9:30 appointment has been waiting for you for ten minutes."

Arrrggghhh! I wanted to gouge my eyes out.

"OK, Amy. We're turning Cheeto over to Dr. Lux and Coreen. Let's keep going with our appointments."

I went in to see my next appointment: a beagle named Charlie with a left ear infection. He was wiggly and stubborn and didn't want to hold still. He made it impossible to get a good look. I went to get Amy to hold him down. By this point, we were both frantic, stressed, and well behind schedule. She held on to Charlie like a pro wrestler. I prescribed an oral antibiotic and an antibiotic ear ointment. Then I rushed back to the surgery room.

"What's going on Frank?" I poked my head past the door to the surgery suite.

"Well, the good news is the pexy site looks good. There's no bowel leakage and the colon isn't going anywhere. The bad news is my stitch went all the way around the ureter and entrapped it. I'm not going to be able to fix it, so I don't have much of a choice. I'm just going to have to remove his right kidney."

"Crap," I said. "Well, I guess he can live OK with one kidney. What else can we do?"

"Nothing," he said. "It's a shame, but he'll be fine with one kidney. I'm sorry."

"OK. Let me go call Mrs. Harrison to let her know what's going on."

As I left the surgery room and headed for my desk, Amy intercepted me. "Dr. Schmidt. Your next appointment is ready for you," she said.

"OK, but I've got to call Mrs. Harrison right away. I'll be there as soon as I can."

I rushed back to my desk and grabbed the phone to call Michelle. She answered right away. "Hi, Michelle. It's Dr. Schmidt. I need to give you an update on Cheeto."

"Thanks, Dr. Schmidt. I've been worried sick about him."

"I know. Me too. Dr. Lux has him in surgery right now. He found that the suture he placed to pexy the colon entrapped Cheeto's right ureter. Cat ureters are tiny little tubes and I'm afraid his ureter is damaged beyond repair. Dr. Lux thinks we need to remove that kidney. It's hurting him and making him sick. I'm very sorry. It's a real shame for him to lose a kidney. However, his left kidney is normal, and he can do fine on just one kidney."

"So, he can live a normal life with one kidney?"

"Yes. It's certainly not ideal. We'll need to monitor his kidney function especially as he gets older. But he can live a pretty normal happy kitty life."

"OK. I understand. Go ahead and do what you need to do."

"We'll do it immediately."

I rushed back to the surgery room.

"Frank. I talked to Mrs. Harrison. She's OK with taking out that kidney."

"Good," he said. "Because I already took it out. He's all done. We're just turning off the anesthesia right now. Don't worry. I'll take care of him. You go see the rest of your appointments."

I hustled back to the exam rooms. I could hear my heartbeat pounding in my ears. My blood pressure felt like 220 over 180. Little Cheeto was taking years off my life.

Over the next few hours, the pace slowed down, and I was able to get back on schedule. Amy was checking in patients, getting histories, and making up medications like a women possessed. By the time my appointments resumed at 2 p.m., she had us back on track.

I was still seeing the last of my evening appointments when Michelle came to pick up Cheeto, so Dr. Lux spoke with her in my absence.

"How'd that go?" I asked Frank as I plopped down at my desk. I was wrung out after the day's events.

"Good," he said. "Michelle's a sweet lady and kept thanking me for saving her cat. I'm amazed how gracious she was considering how things went down."

"We need that cat to live another twenty years," I told him. "I can't handle another one of those for a while."

"More like twenty-five years," he said. "By then we should both be retired."

I wasn't sure if I would *ever* see the Harrisons again. After what transpired with Cheeto, I certainly wouldn't blame them for being frustrated and angry. I felt bad about how things turned out with him. We managed to fix his original problem, but losing a kidney was a high price to pay and something I never anticipated.

I checked in with the Harrisons by phone the next day and the day after that. By all accounts, Cheeto was doing fine. Two weeks after his surgery, he came in for a tech appointment to get his abdominal sutures removed. I

I WANT TO GO WHERE THEY WENT

wasn't in the office that day, so I missed him, but Shannon did the procedure and reported that he seemed to be doing well.

Three months later I was checking the appointment schedule and saw the Harrisons had a 3 p.m. appointment for a new puppy exam. At 3:05 Shannon came to let me know they were waiting for me.

The whole *fandamily* was packed into the small exam room. John was sitting on Will's lap, and sitting on John's lap was a chubby, wiggly black lab puppy.

"Hello," I said. "It's good to see all of you. And you've got another lab puppy? Three labs and a cat . . . you guys are gluttons for punishment."

"His name is Rocky," John blurted out. "He likes to lick me on the face!"

As soon as John said the pup's name, Rocky erupted in a spasm of uncontrolled tail wags and started licking John's neck.

"Wow. I can see that. It looks like he really loves you."

"He does!" said John.

I did the routine puppy exam and initial vaccine series on Rocky. He seemed like a sweet, happy dog and I didn't notice any problems.

As we were wrapping up the appointment, Michelle spoke up. "Dr. Schmidt. We also brought Cheeto with us. He's in the car. We thought you might like to see him after all you've been through with him. He's doing great."

"Yeah. I'd love to see him," I said. "Can you bring him in?"

"I'll go get him," said Austin. "He's getting really big."

As Austin left to get Cheeto, I realized I had some odd trepidation about seeing him again. I was happy to hear he was doing well, but for a while there, everything I did for him seemed to go wrong. Maybe I was bad luck for that little orange cat? Could I have a case of Cheeto P.T.S.D?

One minute later, Austin staggered back in. He was using both hands and leaning backwards to support the weight of the pet carrier. I helped him hoist the carrier up onto the exam table. Rocky thought this was great fun and erupted in another spasm of tail wagging.

I was now sitting on an exam stool with the table at chest level. I opened the front door to the carrier and found Cheeto and I looking at each other face to face. He couldn't wait to come out. He acted like he owned the place. He strutted right over to me at head level and looked right at my face. My anxiety at seeing him disappeared immediately. I reached over with both hands and gently hoisted him up by his armpits. He was BIG. At only six months, he already weighed at least nine pounds. He still had the same bright blue eyes, but his orange tabby coat was much darker than I remembered.

Recalling our previous conversations, I said, "Cheeto. It's good to see you." I was looking directly into his eyes. "You're looking very handsome today. Are you feeling better?" Cheeto had the best cat vocabulary on the planet.

"Meep, Meep, Yawwp," said Cheeto.

Cheeto went on to live a full and happy cat life. I saw him several times a year for many, many years. He was the most loved cat in the county.

Me & Cheeto

There are two means of refuge from the miseries of life: music and cats.

—Albert Schweitzer

CHAPTER 12

Two Kinds of Crazy

I was already tired of staring into the microscope. I pulled back from the scope and rubbed my dry eyes with the palms of my hands. I'd only examined eight slides so far. I looked at the pile of slides on the counter to my right. I had at least ten more to go. My neck was tight and my back hurt from standing hunched over the scope for the past twenty minutes. This set-up was not built for ergonomics.

"Dr. Schmidt," said Adam. "I'm just about finished in here. Are you going to be much longer? Do you want me to lock up?"

"That's OK, Adam," I replied. "I've still got a ways to go. Just lock up the front doors and I'll take care of the back when I go."

It was seven-fifteen at Oak View Veterinary Clinic. The rest of the staff had already left for the day. I was examining slides on the microscope and Adam was busy wiping away the evidence of another busy day. I used to have his job when I was younger. It was a lot of work. Too much work, really, to ever be *done*. You just had to do the best you could with the time you had. You could never get a pet clinic completely clean.

Adam had been working for me for two years. I liked him. He had a good work ethic and a quirky sense of humor. His passion was playing bass in a local *Speed-Metal* band. Two or three days a week, he'd leave his part-time job as janitor at the vet clinic to go straight over to one of the local clubs to perform. His soft voice and easygoing demeanor somewhat belied his wild side. He was six feet tall, thin, and had a scraggly goatee. His hair was brown and hung just below his shoulders. His favorite t-shirts all had the sleeves cut off to better display the intertwining tattoos covering most of the real estate on both arms. I'm sure at the local night clubs no one had him pegged as a gentle pet-loving type of guy. That vibe didn't market well to most of the speed metal crowd.

"Alright then. I'm going to take off," he said. "I've got a gig tonight at the Onyx Club. I hope our singer shows up tonight. Last week he didn't show, and I had to fill in. It was a disaster."

"Yeah, Adam. Good luck. Have a good night, buddy."

"You too, Dr. Schmidt. I'll see ya tomorrow."

Adam headed for the front lobby. I could hear him finagling with the front doors as he locked them up. The lock on the north side door was a bugger. You had to position it just right to engage the bolt.

What was the name of Adam's band? He'd told me before on multiple occasions. Slasher? Slayer? Serpent? It was something like that. Out of curiosity, I'd listened to a couple of his songs. They were way too harsh for my tastes. I'm just too old, I guess. It sounded like a freight train applying its breaks . . . at four times normal speed . . . but louder. *It's funny how different people are*, I thought to myself. When I was his age, I was loading battle tanks on railcars in Bad Kissingen, West Germany. I was twenty-five years older than him, yet we got a long fine. If I wasn't his boss, we'd probably be buddies.

I caught myself mind-wandering. I realized that my musings were just my procrastinating brain preventing me from looking at the rest of the damn slides. I removed slide number eight from the microscope stage and slid number nine in its place. Back to work.

I scanned three more slides. It took me two minutes to thoroughly examine each one. I didn't see anything unusual. This was getting ridiculous. It was my fault. A fool's errand. I'm the one who agreed to review all these samples for Mr. Bradley. Everyone else at the clinic just thought he was crazy. I was beginning to see their point.

I straightened up from my hunched position and stretched. I had to take a break from examining the samples Mr. Bradley brought in. I'd been at the clinic since seven in the morning and had last had something to eat at one in the afternoon. I'd been on my feet almost all day. I felt tired, hungry, sticky, and gross. Working as a vet at an animal clinic was a dirty job. Now that Adam had left the hospital, it was spookily quiet. It was an eerie contrast when a place normally so full of activity goes dead after hours. I felt like an intruder sneaking in under the cover of darkness, but I owned this place, so I guess it was OK.

I reached to my right and carefully lifted another microscope slide from the array arranged neatly on a white trifold paper towel. Next to the slides was a pile of small zip-lock plastic bags. Each bag contained a little sample that Mr. Bradley had brought me to examine. A couple of the bags had a clump of fibers that looked like they were from his couch or carpet. Some of them had a small clump of fur and flakes of dead skin from his dog, Clarence. A few of the baggies appeared to be small piles of dirt or dust. Then there were the ones from Joe. Evidently, Mr. Bradley had somewhat of a skin condition himself. Psoriasis or eczema, or something like that. As a special bonus, he'd brought in several samples of his own dried skin. Some had small bits of hair attached. Mr. Bradley was convinced that his dog suffered from some type of skin parasite. He believed the dog's parasite had caused his own skin issues as well. Last week I'd agreed that if he brought in some samples from his house (carpet fibers, dust, lint, whatever), that I'd look at them through the microscope to see if I could find anything. Bless his heart. I really was trying to help him. I'd rather hoped he'd forget about this offer. He didn't. Today he showed up with a brown paper bag in his hand. He handed it off to one of the puzzled receptionists and told her Dr. Schmidt knew why he was bringing it in. I'm sure the receptionist, Jackie, assumed it was my weekly drug delivery. Because of Joe's appearance and demeanor, she made the right decision not to ask any questions. The bag was dutifully dropped off on my desk. I'd have a chance to examine the contents later in between my appointments. There were at least twenty individual baggies in there. Later, when I examined the baggies more carefully, I saw that each one was labeled in black marker. The labels read, *CARPET, SIDEWALK, CLARENCE-SHOULER, CLARENCE-HEAD, BEDDING, LIVING ROOM, DOG BED, JOE LEG, OFFICE, CLARENCE-STOMACH, JOE-ELBOW,* etc. etc. This was disturbing. He'd brought me samples from his *own body*. I'm his vet, not his doctor. He was pushing the limits of my patience.

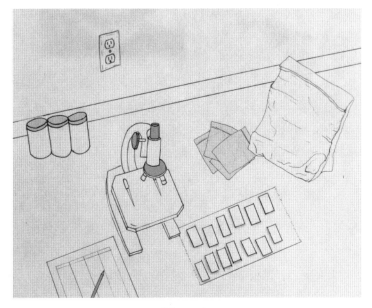

Microscope

I meant what I said, and I said what I meant. An elephant's faithful one hundred percent. The old Dr. Seuss rhyme went through my head. It's funny the things that push their way into your brain when you're tired. It was silly, but I'd made this my professional mantra and it had served me well. Oak View Vet Clinic had been voted the best veterinary hospital for the past five years. I tried hard to always follow through and overdeliver. Joe was one of my clients and his dog was one of my patients. I told him I would do this for him, so I'd stick to my promise. This was especially important in Joe's case. I got the impression he came from a background of a lot of broken promises.

I finally finished looking at the last slide in the pile. Thank goodness! I was done. None of the slides had anything resembling a parasite. No mites, no lice, no microscopic eggs, no fungal spores, no anything. Just dog hair, human hair, some debris, and dead skin. I took the last slide off the microscope and tossed it in the red *sharps* container on the countertop. I then bent over to finish off the chart I'd started two hours ago. The last entry read, #20-Clarence-Tail-NEG. There. I was done. Twenty slides examined. I'd stayed late after work for ninety minutes to get this done. *An elephant's faithful. . . .* As I suspected, it was a big waste of time. I didn't find anything that would indicate there was a parasite problem. I'll wait until tomorrow to call Joe with the results. I was plumb out of patience for one evening.

I first met Joe three months ago. He was my 3:30 appointment on a Tuesday afternoon. He was a new client at the clinic. I found him seated on one of the black padded chairs in exam room one. He was dressed in baggy, old, faded jeans and a loose, threadbare grey hoodie sweatshirt. He was a burly guy with shoulder length scraggly hair, a broad face, and a five o'clock shadow. He looked tired and grumpy. I was immediately on guard.

"Good afternoon, sir," I said as I reached out my hand to shake. "I'm Dr. Schmidt."

Mr. Bradley didn't get up from his chair. He slowly reached out his right arm with a bent elbow for a half-hearted handshake. This seemed to take him a lot of effort. He didn't offer his own name in return.

"Nice to meet you," I said. "Are you Joe?"

"Yep, that's me."

"Well, thanks for coming in today, Joe. That's a cute little dog you've got there. What's his name?"

"That's Clarence," he replied. "He's seven."

"Hi, Clarence. Nice to meet you too," I said.

I reached over to pet Clarence on the head. He was sitting by Joe's left knee. He was a cute little guy. He was a medium size male dog of about thirty pounds. Something about the droopy look on his face and his sad brown eyes made me think, *Beagle*, but there were obviously some other breeds in there. He had a crazy mixture of dark brown, light brown, and grey spots over a white base coat. His ears were droopy. His legs were certainly longer than a normal beagle. He seemed like a nice little dog, but slightly worried.

I was rapidly getting the impression that Joe wasn't much of a talker. He must have come to see me for a reason, but he wasn't very forthcoming. Evidently, I was going to have to drag it out of him. On my previous appointment, I couldn't get the woman to *stop* talking. This was a completely different challenge.

"I like that name, Clarence," I said. "It's like the angel in *It's a Wonderful Life*. It seems to fit him."

Joe just looked at me with a puzzled expression on his face. Maybe he'd never seen that movie.

"Anyway," I said. "What's got you in here with Clarence today?"

"I think he has a skin problem," Joe said. "He has these scabs and crusts, and they seem to make him itchy."

"Oh, really? How long has this been going on?"

"Months," said Joe. "My last vet never did figure it out."

Alarm bells went off in my head. So, this wasn't just a casual visit. It was more like a second opinion. I got the impression that Mr. Bradley wasn't very happy with his previous vet. I was his backup plan. In these situations, you're only getting one side of the story. Often, the other side is a doozey. I sensed hazardous waters ahead.

"Hmm . . . how bad is the itching? Does it keep him up at night? Does he have any raw spots on his skin?"

"It's medium," said Joe. "He'll sometimes chew or scratch himself at night before he goes to sleep, but it doesn't seem to keep him up. He sleeps with me, so in the morning, I'll see some hair and crusts of skin in the bed. He does have a few raw spots. Here, let me show you."

Without warning, Joe pulled Clarence's legs from underneath him. Clarence flopped over on his back. It was a little rough. No wonder Clarence had that worried expression on his face.

I sat down next to Clarence to get a closer look. I was at the age where my close-up vision was deteriorating. I wore a pair of *Click-It* reading glasses around my neck and I put these in place. I bent over Clarence and began to examine his skin. Clarence amicably flopped his tail a few times and held still. I started at his neck and worked my way down to his belly. Then I took a careful look at his tail. Everything looked normal to me.

"Where are the raw spots you're seeing?" I asked.

"See those areas near his elbows," he said. "There's almost no fur there at all. And see how crusty they are?"

"Yep, I see those," I said. "Anything else?"

"Yeah," he replied. "Look at how much hair he has on his chest and his sides. But his belly is almost completely bald. I think that's one of the worst spots for him."

The areas Mr. Bradly pointed out were normal hairless regions for a dog. Once dogs get to a certain age, they almost all lose the fur on their elbows from chronic wear. Often dogs will get thick, crusted callouses in this region, especially if they spend a lot of time lying on concrete. Many dogs have little or no hair on their tummies. It's a common pattern. From what I could see Clarence's skin was normal. I observed some little flakes of dandruff, but certainly nothing alarming.

I took a few moments to explain this to Joe.

"So, all dogs have that?" he asked.

"Yeah, pretty much," I said. "Especially once they reach a certain age. Overall, his skin looks fairly normal."

"Well, what about all the itching? Do you think he might have any parasites?"

"It's possible," I replied. Is he on any medication to kill fleas and ticks?"

"Not anymore," he said. My last vet put him on something like that, but it didn't seem to do anything."

"Have you been *seeing* any fleas or ticks?" I asked.

"Not really," said Joe. "Sometimes I see little black flecks and white crusts. I can't tell if they're moving. My near vision is bad. Are those parasites?"

"Probably not," I said. "Fleas and ticks are small, but you can see them with the naked eye. There are some skin parasites that are microscopic and live in the layers of the skin. Some mites are like this. But most of the prescription flea/tick medications prevent these. If he's not on any prevention, then mites are still a possibility, I guess."

"How do we check for those?" asked Joe. He was still holding Clarence down on his back.

"I can do a procedure called a skin scraping. I use a scalpel blade as a scraper. I take three to four regions of his skin and scrape off some of the layers onto a slide. I can then look at the slides on the microscope."

"Doesn't that hurt him?" he asked.

"A little," I said. "I'd need to scrape the skin down to where it just starts to bleed. It's not fun for him, but it's not horrible either."

"Let's go ahead and do that Dr. Schmidt. I'm really concerned he has a parasite."

"OK. Keep him right there. I'll need to get some slides and scalpel blades. I'll be right back."

Ten minutes later I'd completed the skin scrapings. Clarence was cooperative. With Joe holding, I collected a skin sample from four different regions. I'd scraped on the underside of his chin, his ventral chest, his ventral abdomen and at the base of his tail. Each spot was now raw and oozing a bit. I dabbed some Panalog ointment on each location to ease the discomfort.

"All done, Joe. Just give me five minutes and I'll check these out under the microscope."

"Do you need Clarence anymore?" he asked. "I might take him out for a pee break and put him back in the car."

"That's fine. I think we're all done with him. At least for now."

I carefully grabbed the doorknob with my left hand while balancing the tray of slides in my right hand. As I left the room, Correen was waiting for me.

"Watcha doing, Dr. Schmidt?" she asked with a cheerful expression on her face.

"I told Mr. Bradley I'd look at these skin slides for him."

"That guy's a bit intense, don't you think?"

"Yeah. I guess he is," I replied. "It turns out he wasn't happy with his last vet. He feels the main problem never got resolved. So, I'm trying to be extra conscientious."

"His last vet is probably glad to be rid of him. By the way, your next appointment just checked in. It's Dan Brewer. He wants you to check out his dog's testicles."

"On Smokey? Didn't I just do that last week?"

"Yeah, but evidently, he thinks you missed something. I'll put him in room five. Don't take too long with Mr. Bradley. You're already ten minutes behind schedule."

"*Oh my God.* I'm not sure I can handle another testicle exam on that dog. It's getting ridiculous," I said. "This is at least the third time."

"He takes Smokey's balls very seriously," she replied with a grin. "Don't keep them waiting too long."

I *hated* being rushed. It really added to my daily stress. There didn't seem to be a good way around it. We scheduled thirty-minute appointments. This was more generous than most vet clinics, but it still didn't leave me enough time for the more intense clients and complex cases. My techs were always giving me grief for spending too much time with them. But these were the folks that paid our bills and paid their wages. It never felt right to me to rush people through. Neither Joe Bradley nor Dan Brewer were clients you could hurry. It just didn't work. *Here we go again,* I thought. My conversation with Maggie from two weeks ago echoed in my head.

"Dr. Schmidt, have you ever noticed that all the crazies come to see you?" she commented.

"Really? The other docs don't see the same number of kooks that I do?"

"Nope, not even close. You're a kook magnet," she said. "I think it's because you spend so much time with them. They love you."

"I can't help it, Maggie. Some of these people need more help than just fixing their pets."

"I know, Dr. Schmidt. That's why I love you."

I didn't know what to do about this problem. I'd always spend more time with my clients than most of my colleagues. Sometimes the pet owner requires more care than the pet. This could be extremely time-consuming, but it was also one of the secrets of my success. Oak View was considered one of the best vet clinics in the city. I was proud of that. I decided I wasn't going to do anything about this *problem*. It was a double-edge sword. I probably couldn't change my ways even if I wanted to.

Seven minutes later, I was back in room one with Mr. Bradley.

"Well, Joe, I looked at those slides, and I didn't see mites on any of them. Maybe it's not a parasite and more of an allergy. Why don't we treat him for that to start off and see how he does?"

"Does that skin scraping identify *every* type of parasite he could have?" he asked.

"Well, no. Not really," I said. "It's mainly just looking for bugs that live in the layers of the skin. There's no one test that rules out everything."

"So, what do you think we should do?" Joe asked.

"I'd recommend we put him on a broad-spectrum parasiticide called Revolution, just to cover our bases," I said. "It's a good idea for all dogs to be on something like this, even if just as a preventative. I'd also start him on an anti-itch shampoo. Use this to bathe him twice a week. Additionally, I'd recommend a tablet called Temaril-P. This is a pill that has two medications in it. It has a small amount of a steroid and it's combined with an antihistamine. Let's try this for two weeks and see how he feels."

"Steroids, Doc? Like you're going to make a bodybuilder outta him?"

I'd heard this joke a hundred times before, but I gave Joe a cursory chuckle and shook my head.

"No. It's a different type of steroid. It's good at reducing inflammation. It won't turn him into Arnold Schwarzenegger."

"OK, doc. I'll give that a try," he said.

"Great. I'll ask Correen to get those meds ready," I said. "She'll meet you in the lobby in a few minutes."

Joe stood up to leave. "Oh, one more thing, Doc."

Uh-Oh. I was already running late. Now he was going to add something else? I consciously pushed down my frustration and donned my magical hat of patience.

"Yes?"

"Do you think he could have *internal* parasites?"

Man, this guy was sure obsessed by parasites, I thought.

"Yeah, he could, Joe. But internal parasites don't usually cause skin issues."

"How do we check for those?"

"I'd need you to bring in a stool sample. We'd send that out to the lab to look for parasites that could be living in his GI tract."

"OK. Let's do that too," he said.

"Alright, Joe. It was nice to meet you," I said. I reached out my right hand to shake.

Joe stared down at my hand for a moment. He seemed to hesitate, then he reached out to give me a firm calloused handshake. Joe had big sausage fingers and a strong grip. He was a formidable guy.

"Hi, Dan. How's it going?"

I'd relocated to room number five. I was twenty minutes late for my appointment with Mr. Brewer. I plopped down on an exam stool. It'd been a long day. I was running out of gas.

"I'm sorry I'm late. Sorry to keep you waiting."

"Aww . . . that's alright, Dr. Schmidt. I just hung out in the lobby flirting with the new blonde girl you've got up there." Dan gave me a sly wink. "What's her name?"

Dan was a master at making people uncomfortable. He did it purposefully to see how they'd react. I'd known him for a long time and knew it was an act. He had a heart of gold, but a weird sense of humor. The problem is most other people didn't know this.

"Dan, she's only been working here for two weeks. Don't scare her away. You've got to give her a little time to get used to you."

"Doc, if I knew you were hiring chicks like that, I would've come in a half hour early."

"If you don't behave yourself, I'm going to go get Maggie," I said. "You don't want her coming in here to give you another *talk*."

"Oh, shit no," he said. "That woman doesn't like me. I'll behave."

"OK, good."

"Anyways," he said. "I was just messin' with you. I was really just chatting with Robi. She told me I had to shut up and go sit in the exam room to wait for you. That lady doesn't take any crap."

"She's on to you," I said. "And you're right. She doesn't take any crap."

Robi had known Dan for at least four years. She knew exactly how to handle him. When Dan gave her a hard time, she just returned the serve with even more force. Dan enjoyed the verbal tennis match.

"So, are you really having another problem with Smokey's testicles?"

Smokey was a white boxer. He was a rock-hard ball of muscle. He wore a permanent goofy look of wonderment on his face. When I said his name, he popped up, ran over, and put his front legs on my lap. I really liked this dog.

"Yeah. I know last time you didn't find anything wrong, but I found a new spot I'm worried about. I want to make sure it's not skin cancer."

I sighed. "OK. Let me take a look."

Dan grabbed Smokey by the mid-section. He lifted Smokey's hind end and placed his belly over his left knee to give me the maximum face-to-testicle view. He did have some impressive testicles. They were big, round, pink, and almost completely hairless. I think Dan was rather proud.

"See right here, Dr. Schmidt. He's got this dark patch right between the two balls. That's not melanoma, is it?"

Dan was a registered nurse. Sometimes he knew too much. He loved this dog to death and obsessed over every pimple.

I took a careful look at the area in question. There was a five-by-five-millimeter region of discoloration. I'm pretty sure it was there the other couple of times I'd looked. I carefully felt the area and ran the skin between my thumb and forefinger. Smokey wagged his nub of a tail. There wasn't any mass effect to this darkened region of skin. It was just pigment.

"I'm pretty sure this is just pigment, Dan. Like a freckle. A real tumor would usually have some thickness to it. This is just skin. Keep an eye on it (I knew he would) to make sure it's not getting bigger. But I'm ninety-nine percent sure it's not a tumor."

"Alrighty, Schmitty," he said. "I feel better. I just wanted you to look at it."

He put Smokey back on all fours.

"Anything else?" I asked. "Is he doing fine otherwise?"

"Oh, yeah. He's doing great. He ran five miles with me yesterday."

"Really? You ran with him for five miles?" I was skeptical. Smokey was a magnificent physical specimen. He could probably run all day. But Dan didn't have the body of a runner. He was built like a tank. I couldn't visualize him running five miles.

Dan & Smokey

"Well, actually I was riding my bike," he said. "Smokey ran along beside me. He's a stud."

"Yeah, I think we agree on that one," I said. "Have a good night, buddy. Don't scare away my new receptionist on your way out. Her name's Kelley, by the way."

Three days later, I was on the phone with Joe Bradley. He'd dropped off a stool sample the day before, and I'd received the lab report that morning. It was negative.

"Hello, Joe. This is Dr. Schmidt." I was sitting at my desk with the phone trapped between my right shoulder and my head. I was trying to type records, check lab work, and have a phone conversation at the same time.

"Yeah. What did you find on that poop sample?" he asked.

Joe didn't waste any words with a greeting. No "Hello, Dr. Schmidt." No "good to hear from you." No "nice weather we're having." Nope. Nothing like that. Just "what's in the poop?" I found myself trying to match his level of brevity.

"Nothing," I said.

"Huh? Nothing? What da ya mean by that?"

"Pretty much just that, Joe. They didn't find any parasite eggs at all in Clarence's feces."

"Well, how good is that test?" he asked. "Does it catch everything?"

"Well, no test is perfect. The test is called a fecal floatation. The sample you brought in is mixed with a liquid called a floatation medium. The specific gravity of the medium is such that any parasite eggs will float. The top layer of the sample is skimmed off and it's examined under a microscope for any eggs. Some species of worms only shed their eggs intermittently, so this could result in a false negative. It's also possible that he has a parasite but at such low numbers that the eggs were just missed. It's got a reliability of about eighty-five percent."

"So, there's a fifteen percent chance he does have parasites, even though the test is negative?"

"Yeah, I guess it's fair to say that," I said.

"So, what are we going to do about that?"

"Uhm . . . what do you mean?"

"Well, you just said there's a fifteen percent chance he has intestinal parasites, right?"

Joe sure wanted this dog to have a parasite. He wasn't giving up easily. *He's like a dog with a bone*, I thought.

"If he doesn't have any GI symptoms and since the test is negative, we don't need to do anything." I paused. I could tell from the long silence that Joe wasn't happy with this answer. "However, if you'd like to be extra cautious, we could always treat him for parasites anyway, just to cover our bases. The medication wouldn't hurt anything."

"Yeah. Let's do that. Please give him something extra strong," he said.

"OK, I will."

I may have gone overboard with the deworming prescription. I wanted to make sure there wasn't any way Joe would come back later and accuse me of not being proactive. I put Clarence on a course of fenbendazole. This is a potent broad spectrum dewormer. For most parasites, a single dose is enough. For some of the more resilient parasites, a three-day course is needed. I made up *ten* doses for Clarence. In my defense, the dosage range for this drug is quite high. The instructions read *Give the contents of one packet mixed in with canned dog food, once a day, for five consecutive days. Wait two weeks, then repeat.*

The next week at lunchtime, Dr. Lux and I were sitting at our small built-in desks in the doctor's office. We were having a working lunch, trying to check lab work and make phone calls between bites of a sandwich. This was our standard modus operandi. I'd just hung up the phone and taken a sip of diet Coke.

"Hey, Schmitty," said Dr. Lux. "Before you get back on the phone, I have something to tell you."

"Yeah, what is it?" I spun around in my chair. Dr. Lux's desk was directly behind mine on the opposite side of the room.

"I saw Mr. Brewer this morning with his dog Smokey. He wanted me to examine his testicles."

"You're kidding," I said. "I just saw him last week for the same thing."

"Yeah," said Dr. Lux. "I saw that in the record. "He has a little pigment spot he's worried about. He thinks maybe you missed something."

"Did I miss something?"

"Nope. Pretty normal dog testicles. Maybe a bit bigger than normal. Quite impressive really. I think Dan's very proud," he smirked.

"He sure has a weird thing for that dog's testicles," I said. "That's the third time I've seen him for that."

"Ha! That's nothing. I betcha I've examined that dog's testicles seven or eight times by now. I've even suggested just cutting them off since he's so worried about them all the time. He wasn't having any of that."

"Have you ever examined them and found anything wrong?

"Nope. Not really. Maybe a little rash a couple of times. I think it's a bit of a fetish. He just boosts Smokey's rear end up on the table so I can get a good look. A couple of times his wife was there with him. She just sits there and rolls her eyes. My tech would be rolling her eyes too. But it's easy money I guess."

"Maybe for Christmas the whole clinic can chip in and buy Smokey a scrotum sweater," I suggested. "Something festive for the holidays."

"That's a great idea," he said. "Although I'm pretty sure Karen could just knit him one for free." Karen was Frank's wife. She was a good sport. She'd probably do it.

"Well, I'm glad you see him more than me," I said. "Maggie says that I get all the kooks."

"Oh, I get my fair share," said Frank. He turned around and went back to munching on his sandwich.

Two weeks went by before I saw Joe again. I saw his name on the appointment schedule at 5:30 in the evening. I inwardly groaned. He wasn't the easiest guy to get along with. He was grumpy and suspicious. I was hoping he was over the whole skin parasite thing. Maybe Clarence just had a sore tooth or a torn toenail. Of course, I wasn't that lucky.

"Good evening, Joe. How's it goin'?" I greeted him in exam room number two.

"Hi," he said as he lumbered to the nearest chair. He didn't look at me and certainly didn't offer a handshake. Clarence moped alongside him like the dog in *The Grinch that Stole Christmas*.

"What can I help ya with today?" I asked. I was forcing myself to be cheery. I'm not one hundred percent sure why. Maybe my subconscious decided this was the antidote to the gloom that seemed to follow Joe.

"Well, none of that stuff you did last time is working," he said.

I did a quick review of his record from our last visit. I was trying to remember all the *stuff* he was referring to.

"So, you gave him all ten courses of the powdered dewormer?"

"Yes."

"Did you see him pass any worms in his stool?"

"No."

"You've been giving him those medicated baths twice a week?"

"Yes."

"And you've been giving him those anti-itch pills that I prescribed?"

"Yes."

"And he's still itchy?" I asked.

"Maybe a little," Joe said. "But it's not so much the itchiness, it's those goddamn parasites that are the problem."

"So, your actually seeing parasites on him, now?"

"Yeah, I'm pretty sure I'm seeing them," he said.

I bent over Clarence and ran my fingers through his fur. I spent some time rolling him over and looking at the skin on his armpits and belly. Honestly, he looked normal to me. I didn't see any skin lesions. I certainly couldn't find any fleas or ticks. *How should I handle this with Joe?*

"You did start that topical Revolution I sent home, right? You have to put that on once a month."

"Yeah, I did it," he said. "I just gave him his second dose yesterday."

"Huh, that's weird. What do these parasites look like?"

"Kinda like little hairs. Maybe tiny worms. They're pretty small. I have to put on my reading glasses to see 'em."

"Where do you see them? On Clarence?"

"Sometimes I see them on him, but sometimes they're on his bed where he's been sleeping. I've seen them a few times in the dustpan after I've swept up the floor."

I went on a ten-minute Q and A with Joe. I was trying to get to the bottom of his concerns. It was a difficult and confusing line of query. We'd pursue one line of questioning to the point where I thought I understood his complaint, then he'd contradict himself and completely throw me off track. Veterinarians have a mental check list of five or six skin parasites they deal with on a daily basis. There's another six to seven gastrointestinal parasites that we commonly treat. Ninety-five percent of these parasites would already be dead with the protocol I'd prescribed. In addition to lab tests, the symptoms and description from the pet owner can often point to the diagnosis. But Joe kept leading me in circles.

"So, you see these little worms. Sometimes on him and sometimes in his environment. What color are they? Do they move?"

"Usually they're white," he said. "But sometimes they're kinda grey."

OK, I thought. *Maybe we're getting somewhere.* Flea larvae look like little white worms. They're very small but can be seen by the naked eye with good eyesight. Sometimes, in a bad flea infestation, you can see the larvae on the dog or on the floor. If you look closely, the larvae do wiggle around a bit. The topical flea treatment I sent home should have killed any fleas, but in a severe infestation it can take a couple of months to eliminate all the life-stages in the environment.

"I do see them move, sometimes," he said. "They can hop around from place to place."

"Wait. You see them *hop*?"

"I think so," replied Joe. "I'll see one on the floor, and it'll suddenly disappear and then reappear a few inches away. I think it's jumping from one place to another."

What the heck was he talking about? Adult fleas can jump like crazy, but not flea larvae. They don't have any legs. Is there a small white worm that jumps? It certainly wasn't in my mental database. Joe had admitted his vision wasn't very good and he needed reading glasses. Maybe he was just misjudging the situation.

"Whenever I see those little hairworms, I notice that I get more red spots on my skin and start to itch."

Fleas and ticks can bite people and cause some discomfort. So, this wasn't outside the realm of possibility, but humans are not a flea's preferred host. When fleas get on people it's the parasite equivalent of mistaken identity. Also, fleas were easy to identify, and they don't look like worms. I couldn't wrap my mind around his description.

Suddenly, I had an idea. Did Joe have any other pets? I'd only seen Clarence, and he hadn't mentioned any other animals, but I had encountered this scenario before. Sometimes pet owners would bring in their dog for treatment but not tell me about the four other cats they had at home . . . or rats . . . or ferrets . . . or reptiles.

"Joe, is Clarence the only pet you have?"

"Yeah, it's just him."

Oops. So much for that theory. "What about outside? Do you have a big yard? Do you have any squirrels or rabbits or skunks? What about stray cats?"

"Yeah, I have a nice big yard with oak trees and grass. There are a lot of squirrels, but that's about it. I've seen a neighborhood cat a couple of times, but he doesn't stick around. Clarence barks at him and scares him off."

"And your yard is all fenced in?"

"Yeah, it's completely fenced in," he said. "Clarence can't get out. He only goes out when I take him for walks."

"Speaking of his walks, when I'm walking him around the neighborhood, I have to pick up his poop. Sometimes when I pick it up, I see little flakes of yellow and black on the sidewalk next to his crap. Sometimes I see these in the house, too. Do you think that could be something?"

Now, I appreciate that Mr. Bradly was trying to supply all the information he could to help me solve this mystery. But the problem was that *none* of it made much sense. A parasite that looked like a tiny worm that hopped from place to place. One that affected dogs and people. And now what were these flakes he was talking about? Maybe I was just being dense. It'd been a long day and I needed to wrap this up at some point.

"I'm honestly not sure what that is. I can't tell if what you're seeing is really a parasite or not. I'll tell you what, could you collect some samples and bring them in for me to examine? Maybe some of the flakes you see on the floor, or the little worm things you're observing? Anything you're seeing that seems weird to you. I can look at these under the microscope and try to identify what it is you're dealing with."

"I guess I can do that," replied Joe. "What do you want me to put them in?"

"I'll give you some small plastic sample bags," I said. "Whatever you collect just put in there and I'll look at them. Label each one with a marker so I know where they came from."

I reached into one of the exam room drawers and pulled out a handful of small clear plastic baggies. We'd sometimes use these to send home treats or individual doses of medications. I handed them to Joe.

"Here ya go," I said. "When you get the samples, you can just drop them off at the front desk and I'll look at them as soon as I get a chance."

Joe looked down at the baggies in his hands skeptically. "Alright," he said. "I guess I can do that. He picked up Clarence's leash and shuffled toward the door that would take him back to the lobby.

It was two weeks later, a Tuesday morning. The previous night I'd spent an hour and a half examining the samples Joe had brought me. I could still see the Sharpie-labeled baggies marked in Joe's block-style printing, all capital letters. *CARPET, SIDEWALK, CLARENCE-SHOULER, LIVING ROOM, DOG BED, JOE-L LEG, CLARENCE-STOMACH, JOE-ELBOW, CARPET, CLARENCE-HEAD. Ugh.* Looking at the debris in twenty small plastic baggies was a lot more work than I'd anticipated, and I hadn't mentioned a fee. I decided it wasn't fair to charge him anything. I didn't quote a fee and I didn't find anything worth reporting. I remembered that at the time, I just wanted to bring the appointment to a close. Of course, I didn't say anything about bringing in samples of his own skin. That was more than I bargained for and struck me as a little creepy.

I sat down at my desk and resolved to call Joe right away. I didn't know how he'd take this information and I wasn't looking forward to this conversation.

"Hi, Joe. It's Dr. Schmidt from Oak View Vet Clinic."

"Hi, Dr. Schmidt. Did you look at all those samples I brought you?"

"Yeah, I looked at them all last night, Joe. I hate to tell you, but I didn't find anything abnormal. Nothing that looked like a parasite, parasite larva, or parasite egg."

"Huh," he said. "That's pretty weird. What about all those wormy things I was seeing? You didn't see any of those?"

"Nope. Nothing."

"Did you see things moving in there?"

"No. Not really."

"What do you mean *not really*?" said Joe.

I felt like I was being interrogated.

"Did you see some stuff moving or not?"

"Not," I replied.

"Well, what the hell are you going to do about all the parasites I'm seeing? Are there some other tests you can run?"

The early thrumming of a headache was forming behind eyes.

"Uhm, well. Let me think about that. You think Clarence is still a bit itchy," I said.

"Oh, yes. Very itchy all the time," replied Joe.

This wasn't what he'd previously told me.

"And you really think you see these little hair-worms coming out of his skin?"

"Yeah, I'm pretty sure they are. They seem to freeze and stop moving when I shine a light on them, so I have to be quick to spot 'em."

"Well, I guess we could biopsy his skin."

"What's that all about?" asked Joe.

"Sometimes there are problems *inside* the layers of a dog's skin that you can't see from the surface. Deep fungal infections, autoimmune disorders, even Demodex mites, are a few examples. I can use a small, round cookie-cutter type instrument to take a *plug* out of his skin and send it to a pathologist to examine."

"How come you never mentioned that *Demon-X* mite before?" he asked.

I smiled, despite myself, at his mispronunciation of *Demodex*. I think *Demon-X* was a much better name.

"Because Demodex is microscopic. You can't see it with the naked eye. You've been telling me you can *see* these parasites."

"Huh, well maybe that's what he's got."

"Maybe . . . I guess," I said. "I usually would have seen them on the skin scraping, but it's possible they could have been missed."

"So how much would it cost to do that cookie-cutter thing?"

I had to think about this. For most conditions that require a skin biopsy, two to three samples are plenty. But this hinged on being able to hone in on a particular lesion. In Clarence's case, there weren't any visible skin abnormalities. I'd have to get multiple biopsies from all over his body to ensure I had a representative sample. I explained this to Joe.

"So normally, if I send out two to three samples, the lab fee is around two hundred bucks. If I take eight to ten samples, you're likely going to be close to a thousand dollars just for the lab fee. Additionally, you'll get charged for the procedure time, which would be another couple hundred."

"Why so expensive?" he asked.

"It's a lot of work to prep and examine all those samples," I replied. I flashed back to all the time I'd spent last night looking at the slides. "And you're paying a board-certified pathologist to do it. Those guys are highly trained experts, and they don't work for free."

"OK. I'll have to think about that," said Joe. He didn't sound too happy. He abruptly hung up the phone. I thought this might be the last I heard from him. I was wrong.

"Dr. Lux, I don't know what I should do with this guy," I said.

Dr. Lux was twenty years my senior and he'd seen some wild stuff. He was a veterinarian in the Vietnam War, if that gives you any idea. It was lunch time again and we were seated at our respective desks. This was when I'd ambush him with weird questions. He was a good sport about it. I think he enjoyed having an eager listener for his war stories.

I went on to explain to him my frustrations with Mr. Bradley.

"That guy sounds a little bit unstable," he said. "He sees hairy worms coming out of his dog?"

"Hair-worms," I replied. "He says they're really small and he can barely see them, but he thinks they jump. Except for when he shines a light on them. Then they stop moving. You ever heard of anything like that?"

"Yeah, I have," he said.

"Really? You've heard of those hair-worm things before?"

"No, but I've had crazy-ass clients before. Have you heard of *Delusions of Parasitism*?"

"I don't think so," I said. "Some type of psychological condition?"

"Yeah, It's a real thing. You can look it up. Pretty interesting actually. About twenty years ago I had a client with it. She was strange all the way around. She was skinny as a rail and pale as a ghost. I'm pretty sure she was on some type of drugs. She got it through her addled head that she had some type of GI parasite she got from her dog. We tested the dog's stool for parasites at least three times and finally put him on an aggressive course of dewormer despite the fact that all the tests were negative."

"Yeah, that's pretty much what I did with Joe's dog," I said.

"She also went to her own doctor to get checked and he didn't find anything either. Anyways, after all that, she still wasn't convinced. She started digging through her own feces with chopsticks to look for parasites. Believe it or not, she was convinced she saw them in there. At some point she came in to see me and brought some of her own shit for me to look at. She wanted to point out all the parasites that I (and her doctor) had missed."

"You're kidding me," I said. "She brought in her own crap for you to look at? *Oh my God*. What did you do?"

"I told her I couldn't help her anymore," he said. "I wanted to help her, but I'm only a vet, not a psychiatrist. I didn't see her anymore after that. I don't know what happened to her."

"Can't you reason with them?" I asked. "I mean if you prove to them scientifically that there's nothing there, don't they come to some sort of realization?"

"I don't know," he said. "It's hard to prove a negative and I don't think that usually works. At least not with this lady."

That evening I thought about my discussion with Frank regarding Mr. Bradley. I did some research on Delusions of Parasitism. From what I could glean, it was considered a very rare psychological condition. Sometimes it was secondary to long-term drug use, especially methamphetamines, but in other cases, it was the primary psychosis with no other symptoms. Most patients were resistant to treatment because of the stigma associated with mental illness, combined with the steadfast belief that they have a real parasite infestation. This certainly fit with what I'd seen with Joe. On the surface Joe seemed like a reasonably rational guy. He was coherent in our conversations, except when it came to the topic of parasites. I didn't see any obvious evidence of drug use, but I didn't know him well and this was certainly not my area of expertise. He wasn't the easiest person to like, and I'll bet he didn't have a lot of friends. I was trying to be supportive, but he didn't make it easy. Additionally, as a veterinarian, I certainly didn't know *every* parasite on the face of the earth. I'd never asked him about traveling to exotic vacation spots. There are some bizarre parasites in tropical areas. It was possible I was missing something. Was I confident enough in my knowledge to just declare him as being crazy?

It was three weeks later that I had my next encounter with Joe. He showed up at eleven in the morning without an appointment. Maggie caught up to me in the treatment room and announced his arrival.

"Dr. Schmidt, that weird parasite guy is waiting for you in the lobby. He came in without an appointment and says he just has to speak with you. Something about doing a skin biopsy. Anyways, I think that guy may be off his rocker. He's in the lobby telling everyone how you're helping him identify an undiscovered type of parasite. Do you know what he's talking about?"

"Yeah, kind of. I've been dealing with him for a couple of months now."

"Do you want me to tell him to go away and come back when he has an appointment?"

"No, that'll probably just make him more agitated," I replied. I glanced at my watch. "Tell him that if he doesn't mind waiting, I'll be free to talk to him in an hour. Maybe he can take his dog for a walk in the meantime. Did he bring his dog?"

"Yeah, he has a little beaglish dog with him. OK, I'll tell him." Maggie pushed herself away from the treatment table she'd been leaning against and unsteadily headed up front to talk to Joe. She'd only gone a few steps when she stopped herself and turned around. She'd forgotten something.

"Oh, speaking of crazy, I also got a call this morning from Dan Brewer. I guess Smokey's got a testicle problem and he wants to see if you can ultrasound him. You had a four o'clock cancellation, so I put him in there, seeing as nutjobs are your specialty."

"Great," I said. "It's been at least two weeks since I've seen Smokey's testicles. Anything else?"

"Nope, that's it. I'll go talk to Mr. Parasite."

At 12:15 I was finishing up the last of my morning appointments. It was Ms. Jarvis with her cat Mango. Ms. Jarvis was one of my favorites. She was a middle-aged single lady with three cats. She was soft spoken, funny, exceedingly polite, and appreciative. Unfortunately, Mango was in the early stages of kidney insufficiency, so I was monitoring his lab work closely. Ms. Jarvis was extremely diligent and followed all my instructions to the letter. She made my job easy. I escorted Ms. Jarvis to the check-out area. In my left hand was Mango's clipboard and a printout of his recent lab work. In my right hand was Mango's pet carrier. Robi was waiting for us. The rest of the office staff had left for lunch.

"Hi, Robi. We're just checking out Mango for Ms. Jarvis. Mango had some lab work and a refill of Sub-Q fluids."

"Alright, Dr. Schmidt. No problem. I can take care of that."

Robi's voice was cheery and professional, but her demeanor was off. She was clearly uncomfortable about something. As she spoke, she performed a quick flick of her head to the left and rotated her eyes in the direction behind her. She was trying to alert me to something. When I glanced in the direction she'd indicated, I immediately knew what had her concerned. Joe was seated at the far end of the lobby glowering with Clarence at his feet. His eyes were lasered in my direction.

I nodded at Robi to let her know I was aware of the situation. I said my goodbyes to Ms. Jarvis and made my way across the lobby to stand in front of Mr. Bradley.

"Hi, Joe. Maggie told me you were waiting for me," I said. I extended my right hand for a friendly handshake. Joe didn't return the gesture. He just looked at me and didn't say anything for several uncomfortable seconds.

"I've been thinking about that biopsy," he said.

"I thought that might be what you wanted to talk about," I said. "Are you still having that same problem with Clarence?"

"It's worse."

"Really? I'm sorry to hear about that. Let's go into one of the exam rooms and I'll look him over and we can talk for a bit."

I gestured with my right hand towards the door of exam room one. It was just three feet to his left. He looked at the door suspiciously and looked down at my hand. After a second, he seemed to make a momentous decision. He slowly pushed himself off the bench and shuffled towards the door which I held open for him. Clarence dutifully padded along beside him. Once inside, Joe plopped down on a chair, and I pulled up a stool facing him. He had a frown on his face and appeared to be struggling with some inner turmoil.

I spent the next twenty minutes calmly speaking with Joe. I attempted to address his concerns and answer his questions. It was difficult communicating with him. His default perspective was one of mistrust and suspicion. He acted tired and sometimes confused. Joe stated he was now seeing thread-like worms regularly on both himself and Clarence. He would occasionally see them as they emerged from the surface of his skin. I remembered to ask him about travel history. Had he been on any trips to tropical locations? He claimed he hadn't. I did my best to be patient and open-minded, but I couldn't think of any parasite that fit his descriptions. When I told him this, he became defensive.

"Just because it's not a parasite known to you doesn't mean it doesn't exist," he said.

"That's true," I said. "There are weird parasites all over the world and I can't claim to know them all. Although, I would think the treatments we gave him should take care of almost everything."

"If those parasites were living inside the skin, would you see them in the cookie?"

I was beginning to regret using the "cookie-cutter" analogy. Cookies were starting to lose their appeal for me, but I knew what he meant.

"The pathologist should be able to make them out," I said. "But we'd have to do a bunch of biopsies from different locations in order to be thorough. It's a long shot. Are you sure you want to spend that kind of money on something like this?"

"Well, we've tried just about everything else, right?"

"I could refer you to a vet dermatologist for another opinion," I said.

"What would they do?"

"To be honest, they'd probably start by repeating a lot of the tests that I've already done."

"I don't want to do that," said Joe. "Before we do that biopsy thing, could we give it one more try on the scalpel scraping? And this time I want to look."

Joe's requests were becoming increasingly more unreasonable, but to appease him, I agreed to give it one more try. Normally I wouldn't have this much time to devote to one client, but it was the lunch break, and I had another ninety minutes until my next appointment.

I left the room and gathered the necessary supplies to perform the skin scraping. With Joe holding Clarence, I scraped three skin spots all chosen by Joe. The treatment room was quiet as most of the staff were away for lunch.

Attempting to earn his trust, I took Joe with me to the microscope station as I prepped the slides for viewing. Clarence remained behind in the exam room to resume his nap. With Joe watching, I added a drop of mineral oil to the samples on each slide, mixed the samples with the oil, and carefully applied a coverslip over the slide. I was meticulous on each step so Joe could clearly see what I was doing. I put the first slide on the microscope stage and started scanning the sample at one hundred power. Under this magnification, a nest of thick hair fibers leapt into view. Some of the hairs had been uprooted by the scraping and the hair root was clearly visible. Scattered among the hair bulbs was a smattering of squamous skin cells, red blood cells, hair fragments, and some tiny air bubbles trapped between the two pieces of glass. I scanned the entire slide from top to bottom and didn't see anything resembling a parasite or parasite egg. I then stepped back to make room for Joe.

"I don't see anything that looks like a parasite, Joe. Feel free to take a look." I stepped back to make room for Joe. He was unfamiliar with the operations of the microscope, and it took him a minute to get it adjusted for his eyes. I showed him how to use the knobs on the right side of the scope to move the slide across the stage. His meaty fingers looked at odds with the delicate controls of the scope.

Joe hunched over the microscope, his eyes glued to the binocular lenses in rapt attention. He carefully moved the slide around for several seconds.

"What's that?" he asked.

I was behind him and to his left. I had to take his place at the scope to see what peaked his interest.

"You mean right there in the middle?" I asked.

"Yeah, that thing."

"That's just the root bulb of a hair. Some of the hairs were torn out by the roots when we did the scraping."

"Oh, OK." Joe resumed his review of the slide. It was difficult for him. He'd obviously had no experience in the manipulation of the scope, or experience in what he was seeing at such a high magnification.

"There it is! I just saw something move!" he exclaimed excitedly.

"Really, you saw something move?" Not surprisingly, I was a bit skeptical.

"Yeah, it flicked from left to right."

"OK," I said. "Let me take a look." I bent over the scope. I didn't see anything moving. Or to be more precise, I did not observe any *purposeful* movement. We were looking at a sample of skin and hair in a pond of mineral oil, trapped between two slides. Occasionally an air bubble would shift. Sometimes a strand of hair coiled between the two panes of glass would spring back from its compressed position and cause a shift under the scope. Joe just hadn't done this before. He didn't really know what he was looking at. I tried to patiently explain this to him.

"Hmm," I said. "Some of the hair and bubbles will shift a bit because they are sandwiched between two pieces of glass. That's probably what you're seeing. Let's go to the next one."

Ten minutes later, Joe and I had thoroughly scanned all three slides. I didn't identify anything remarkable. On a couple of occasions, Joe would see something and ask questions. A few more times he reported that he saw something move. I'd quickly check the slide and explain to him what he saw and why it didn't represent a parasite. I wanted to support him and know he could trust me to be straight with him.

"That's the last one Joe. I didn't really find anything remarkable. Are you OK with what we saw?"

"We didn't find any of those parasites in there, did we?"

"Nope," I replied. "Sorry."

"Then I want to go ahead with the biopsy. Can we do it today?"

Jeez-Louise. This guy would just not give up, I thought.

"I think I could get that done later this afternoon," I said. "Are you sure you want to go through with this?"

"One hundred percent," replied Joe.

"Alrighty," I said. "I'll get Clarence from the exam room and give him a little sedative. As soon as I have a time-window I'll get that done for you. I'll call you when he's finished."

I escorted Joe back to the exam room where Clarence was waiting for us. He looked up sleepily from where he'd been passed out on the floor. Joe headed towards the front lobby, and I headed in the opposite direction, Clarence in tow.

The afternoon passed quickly, one appointment after another, and before I knew it, it was time for my weekly Smokey Brewer testicular consultation.

Smokey greeted me at the door of the exam room. His tail nub twitched back and forth furiously, and he jumped up with his front legs on my chest to give my face a big slurp. He was incurably happy and always made me smile.

"Dan, you're killing me. Do you really think Smokey has another problem with his testicles?"

"Yeah, I know, Dr. Schmidt," Dan replied. "But I really think there may be something going on this time. I had him out running by the lake yesterday and as I was watching him, I noticed his left is bigger than the right one. When I felt them, I noticed the left one seemed harder, and it may hurt him a bit. By the way, he came running up behind a lady jogger wearing headphones and scared the crap out of her. She just about jumped out of her skin. It was hilarious."

"OK," I said. "Let me take a look. Have him assume the position."

Dan wrapped his arms around Smokey's mid-section. He hoisted up his butt and placed his belly on his left knee so I could easily see both testicles. They looked normal to me. Were they a different size? Not obviously so. I gently palpated them. Smokey turned his head around to look at me. His expression said, *What the hell do you think you're doing back there?*

"You see what I mean?" said Dan "He doesn't like it when you touch that left one."

I went back and forth palpating both testicles. Right . . . left . . . right . . . left. I couldn't really tell an appreciable difference in their texture, but Smokey did seem to shift around more when I touched the left one. Was this because it was uncomfortable? Hard to say . . . he certainly wasn't yipping in pain.

"Don't you think the left one seems bigger?" said Dan.

"I dunno, maybe a little," I replied dubiously.

"Is there a way to look inside and maybe get a measurement? What about an ultrasound?" His nursing background certainly did give him some medical insight (and paranoia).

"I guess we could put the ultrasound probe on there and have a look around if you want?" I said. Stupid question, I realized. Of course, he'd want to do this.

"Yeah, let's do that," said Dan. "I'm just worried he has a tumor in there or something."

I inwardly sighed. "OK, buddy. Let's get it done. Follow me."

I escorted Dan and Smokey to the ultrasound room. I was lucky. No one else happened to be using it. I turned on the machine and adjusted the settings for low penetration and high frequency. This would give the best resolution of the image for something small like his testicles. (No offense, Smokey.)

I got Dan seated on a rolling stool and again he boosted Smokey's rear into the air. I applied a generous blob of ultrasound gel to each testicle. Smokey again turned to look at me skeptically. This time his expression said, really? *That goop is cold. Enough with the testicle inspections already . . .*

"Sorry, Smokey," I said. "That was probably a little chilly."

With Dan looking over my shoulder, I proceeded to thoroughly examine each testicle with the probe. The internal architecture of a testicle on ultrasound is not very interesting. Normal testicular tissue has a uniform, fine speckled appearance. When the image is frozen on the screen, each testicle can be measured to the tenth of a millimeter. I took multiple images and multiple measurements of each one. At the conclusion of the exam, I printed out the images for Dan and took a moment to compare the dimensions. Smokey's right testicular cross-section was 22.1 millimeters by 32.2 millimeters. His left testicle was 23.2 by 33.0 millimeters. Dan was right, sort of. The left testicle was bigger, but by a miniscule amount. The difference was insignificant. The internal architecture of each testicle was completely normal.

"Well, Dan. The left testicle is bigger than the right. So, you were right about that. But the difference is small. Less than a millimeter. And the tissue inside the testicle looks nice and normal. So, I think you're OK. I don't see any signs of cancer."

"All right, Doc. Thanks for checking this for me. Sorry to keep bothering you with this. He just had me really worried this time."

"No problem, buddy. That's why I'm here. Smokey and I are getting to know one another on an intimate basis."

"You said it Doc. I think he really likes you." Dan smiled, gave me a wink, and shook my hand. I walked with him out to the lobby.

"Until next time, Dan, have a good evening," I gave him a quick wave as I headed back to the treatment area.

"You too, Doc. Thanks again."

I didn't have another appointment until 5:30. I glanced at my watch. 4:35 p.m. That should give me just enough time to get those biopsies on Clarence. Amy held Clarence while I gave him a second sedative injection. While he was getting sleepy, we gathered the equipment we'd need for his biopsy. Ten small biopsies were obtained, and ten small incisions were sutured. We were done in thirty minutes. Poor Clarence. He was shaved up like a patchwork quilt. With his ten little sutured wounds, he looked like he'd been attacked by hungry piranhas. He was up and wagging his tail by 6 p.m. I called Joe to let him know the situation.

"Hey, Joe. It's Dr. Schmidt. I took ten skin biopsies on Clarence. It went fine. He's already awake. He can go home anytime now."

"Huh? What about Clarence? What did you do to him?"

I was puzzled. Surely Joe didn't forget about our conversation from six hours ago.

"Uh, remember you left Clarence here earlier today. You decided you wanted to go ahead with those skin biopsies on him?"

Jeez. I hoped he hadn't forgotten the whole thing. I'd already done the procedure. It was a little late to go back.

"Oh, yeah, yeah, yeah," he said. "The skin biopsy thing. I remember. OK, OK. I'll be over there to pick him up in a bit."

I breathed a small sigh of relief. He did remember. I thought this might've been heading in an uncomfortable direction.

"Alright Joe. It'll take about a week to get the results. I'll call you as soon as they come in."

"OK." And he hung up. No "thank you." No "see ya soon." No "have a good night." Just "OK." Click. Joe took some getting used to.

Dr. Jay Perdoy was the pathologist I chose to review the tissue samples from Clarence. I picked him in particular because of the special circumstances in this case. I knew Dr. Perdoy from my vet school days at UC Davis. He was a pathology resident when I was a student and I'd spent long weeks with him on the necropsy floor. He was smart, honest, and very approachable. He'd opened his own pathology lab in the region ten years after finishing his residency. Some cases just needed special attention. If so, Jay was your guy.

I called him at his office the next day. He was always very accommodating in coming to the phone.

"Hi, Jeff. How's it going?"

"It's going good, Jay. Thanks for coming to the phone," I said.

"No problem at all. You got something for me?"

"Yeah. It's kind of a weird one, so I thought I should talk to you first to fill you in on what's going on."

I went on to tell the story of Mr. Bradley and Clarence. I felt I needed to explain why he would be receiving ten skin biopsies that, in all likelihood, would be perfectly normal.

"So, it's possible you have a parasite delusion situation going on here?" said Jay.

"Yeah, it's certainly possible," I said. "But to be fair, it's also possible I'm just missing something. But his description of the parasite just doesn't make sense to me. He says Clarence has only lived in the Sacramento Valley. No history of exotic travel."

"What does the skin look like on exam?" he asked.

"Ninety-five percent normal," I replied. "I've seen a couple little inflamed spots on occasion, but nothing that seems significant. And I've never seen the dog scratch once in the three to four times he's been here."

"Where did you biopsy?" he asked.

"Uh, let's see. . . . Two from the bottom of his feet. One from the top of his head and one from his face. One from his neck. One from his back. Two from his abdomen. One from his right elbow and one from his tail."

"That should do it, Jeff. If we don't find anything in those samples, you can feel confident there's nothing *to* find."

"OK, good. I just wanted you to have some background on this case when you reviewed the samples. I know it's sort of an unusual request."

"Yeah, I'm glad you called," he said. "I've had a few situations like this before. If anything, I try to be more thorough in my analysis and in my report. These cases are tough. The people involved are often one hundred percent sure there's something there. Sometimes there's legal ramifications. I had one case where the lady ended up getting committed."

"Oh Jesus," I said. "I hope it won't come to that."

"By the way, you said you're sending in ten samples?

"Yeah."

"The price for ten samples would be exorbitant. I'll tell you what. I'll charge full price for the first five samples and just half price for the other five. That'll give the guy a little bit of a break."

"OK. Thanks," I said. "That's very nice of you. I don't get the impression he has a lot of money so I'm sure he'll appreciate it."

"No problem, Jeff. Glad to help you out. I'll be looking for those samples. I should be able to get you a report in about a week."

A week later, I received an email from Dr. Perdoy. Attached was a three-page document with the biopsy findings on Clarence. I printed it out to make it easier for me to read.

I quickly scanned through the report to look for any surprises, then took a deep breath and read it again in detail. Dr. Perdoy had put some work into this one. I could tell he wrote the report knowing it would be read by a skeptic. Each biopsy sample had a number and a note identifying the location it came from. There was a paragraph dedicated to each sample. *None* of the samples had any evidence of a parasite. The text was devoted to describing the type of cells found, their number, and their position within the layers of the skin. There was a lot of repetition because most of the samples were completely normal, but there were a few tissues with minor abnormalities. Both biopsies from Clarence's feet had an increased amount of neutrophils. This was not much of a surprise since dogs don't wear shoes. Their feet are dirty and in constant contact with their environment. The biopsy from his muzzle had a moderately increased number of eosinophils. These cells are often present in allergic responses. Clarence was likely just rubbing his face on the grass or bushes. I had a feeling Joe wasn't going to like this report.

"Hello, Joe. It's Dr. Schmidt from the vet clinic. How are you?"

"Did you get the report back yet?" Joe never wasted any time with small talk.

"Uh, yeah. That's what I was calling you about," I said.

"Dr. Perdoy was the pathologist that examined the biopsies. He's got a good reputation, and it looks like he was very thorough in his report. I'll email you a copy shortly. However, he didn't find any parasites in any of the samples. A few of the samples showed some indication of mild inflammation, his feet and face, but nothing real significant."

"What's that mean?" he asked.

"Basically, his skin is normal. No parasites."

"What's this guy's name again?"

"Dr. Perdoy."

"Do you know him?"

"Yes. He was a pathology resident when I was in vet school. He's been reading most of my pathology samples for the past five years. He's very good."

"So, you think he knows what he's doing? No funny business?"

I wasn't entirely sure what Joe meant by this. Was he implying that somehow Dr. Perdoy would falsify the report?

"No funny business," I replied. "Dr. Perdoy is just about as smart and educated and honest as they come."

"He didn't see any parasites, huh? Hmm . . . I'll have to think about this." Joe hung up the phone.

Now what was Joe going to do with this information, I thought. He'd spend a lot of time, energy, and money on his parasite obsession. At every step, his theory had been shot down. I'd hoped he'd have a moment of self-analysis and that rationality would win the day. But instead, he went straight to questioning the morals of Dr. Perdoy. This was ridiculous. What possible motivation would Dr. Perdoy have for falsifying a biopsy report? He didn't know Joe at all. Joe was all my problem. And boy, was he a problem.

The red blinking message light on my phone was goading me relentlessly. I hated that goddamn light. It was one week later, and I was sitting at my desk writing records and returning phone calls. It never failed, just when I'd finished my last appointment and was ready to leave, I'd stop at my desk and realize I'd received five new voice mails. Clients always wanted to talk right at the end of the day. I checked my watch. 6:50 p.m. I gave myself a hard deadline. I'd return calls until 7:30 and then stop. Any stragglers would have to wait till tomorrow. I had to leave at some point. It was just me and Adam alone in the building again. The rest of the staff had left for the evening. I could hear him running the vacuum on the other side of the clinic. I glanced out the floor-to-ceiling windows to the parking lot. The wind, rain, and darkness pressed in against them. I took a deep breath to calm myself and deliberately punched in the number for Dolly Thornton. This would be a long one; I might as well get started.

Ten minutes later, Adam was rapping on the door to the doctor's office. I wondered why he was knocking; the door was open. I was still on the phone with Dolly. She was concerned that her dog made funny noises and twitched while she was sleeping. I was trying to alleviate her fears when I noticed Adam trying to get my attention.

"Hold on for just a second, Dolly, I've got someone trying to get my attention," I said into the receiver. I put my hand over the phone and looked at Adam standing in the doorway.

"Yeah, Adam. You need me for something?"

"Dr. Schmidt, I was just taking the trash out to the dumpster when some guy came up to me in the parking lot. He said he *really* needs to talk to you. He knows you're here. He saw your car parked out front."

"Doesn't he know we're closed?" I said. "Who the heck is it?"

"I think it's that crazy parasite dude," said Adam.

Oh crap. Somehow even Adam knew about Joe Bradley.

"What do ya want me to do?" asked Adam. "Should I call the cops or something?"

"No, no. It's OK. I guess I can go talk to him. Let me finish up this phone call and I'll go out there in just a minute. Just let him know I'll be out there shortly."

I got back on the phone with Dolly and politely cut the conversation a little short. I didn't feel too guilty about it. We'd been over this same ground many times before.

I stood up from my desk and grabbed my jacket off the back of my chair. I felt better meeting Joe outside rather than unlocking the front door to let him in. I was afraid that once inside, I'd never get rid of him. Hopefully, this wasn't a stupid move. Adam had suggested calling the police. Maybe that wasn't a bad idea. Although, I just didn't want to believe that Joe had slipped so far as to become dangerous. I'd spent a lot of time trying to earn his trust.

I pushed open the heavy metal door that led into the alley behind the clinic. The wind pushed me back and the rain stung my face. The weather out here was worse than I thought. Maybe I should have met Joe inside. I walked ten yards to the end of the alley and turned left. I could see Joe leaning against his car in the parking lot. It was an old black Trans Am. The type of car made famous in *Smokey and the Bandit*. Joe saw me coming and pushed himself away from his car. He was wearing jeans, black boots, a black pea coat, and a black watch cap. He looked rather ominous, especially in the dimness of the parking lot.

"Hey, Joe," I said. "Adam told me you wanted to see me."

"Yeah, Dr. Schmidt. I wanted to talk to you," he said.

"Sure. What can I do for you?"

"I don't know what to do with the parasite problem. I know the skin samples didn't show anything, but I still see them all over. Look at my arms!"

Joe pulled back the sleeves of his jacket. First the left, then the right. The underside of his arms was scratched raw. They were fire-engine red. It was obvious he'd been scratching at them relentlessly.

"Ouch. Joe, those look raw. You really need to stop rubbing at them. You're causing a lot of damage."

"I try," he said. "But those parasites won't leave me alone. Clarence is miserable too."

"Joe, have you seen your doctor for this? I'm a vet. I'm not licensed to treat people."

"Yeah, they all say it's in my head. They won't help me."

Joe was getting closer as he spoke. He was also getting louder. He was getting himself worked up. I could feel the intensity emanating from him. This poor guy. I wouldn't want to be in his head. But I also didn't want to be stuck out in a dark, wet, parking lot with him either.

"Look, buddy, I don't know what to tell you. We've done test after test looking for these parasites and haven't found anything. Maybe your doctors are right."

I was now backed up against the curb of the sidewalk. I'd unconsciously been backing up from Joe. I needed to be aware of that curb, so I didn't trip over backwards in the next few seconds.

Just then Adam appeared around the corner of the building.

"Hey, Dr. Schmidt. I'm finished up here for the night. Are you still able to give me a ride home?"

For a moment, I stood there looking at him. What the hell was he talking about? We'd never discussed him needing a ride. Then it dawned on me. Adam had been watching (and possibly listening) to this parking lot confrontation and was giving me a way out.

"Uh . . . yeah, Adam. Just give me a minute," I said. "I'm just finishing up talking to Mr. Bradley here, then I can give ya a ride."

Adam didn't leave. He had his backpack slung over one shoulder and leaned against the cinder block retaining wall. "OK," he replied. "No hurry."

I turned back to look at Joe. The interruption by Adam had given him pause. His intensity had ratcheted down a couple notches. He took a half step back. I felt badly for the guy. He was soggy wet and straggly strands of black hair protruded from the edge of his cap. His eyes were wild. He had dark circles under them and looked like he hadn't slept in days.

"Look, buddy. I'm sorry, but I don't know what else I can do for you and Clarence. I've tried everything I can think of. I hate to let you down, but I just can't help you anymore."

I turned and walked towards Adam.

"I'll be out to give you a ride in a second," I said. "Just let me grab my keys."

I hurried inside the clinic, grabbed my knapsack and car keys. I didn't want to leave Adam alone out there with Joe for any longer than necessary. When I got back outside, Adam was still leaning against the wall. Joe was still there as well, but he'd retreated to his car and was leaning against it.

Adam followed me to my car and we both got in. I started the ignition and backed out of the parking spot. As we pulled away, Joe was still leaning against his car watching us leave.

"Man, Adam. Thanks for coming out," I said once we were away. "Joe was getting more and more crazy. Maybe I should have called the cops. Do you really need a ride?"

"No, not really," he said. "I rode my bike today. It's still inside the clinic. It only takes me ten minutes to get home. If you just drive around the block a few times we can check to make sure the parasite guy is gone, and I'll grab my bike and ride home."

"Are ya sure?" I said. "I can drop you off, no problem."

"Nah, it's fine. I'll need my bike in the morning, so no big deal."

Adam and I drove around the city, making right turns for ten minutes. When we next passed the clinic, Joe and his car were gone.

"OK," I said. "It looks like the coast is clear. I'll drop you off to get your bike. I'll wait outside to make sure you're on your way before I head home."

"All right. Thanks, Dr. Schmidt."

"No, thank you, Adam. I'm glad I wasn't in the parking lot with Joe by myself tonight."

The next day at the lunch break, I had a chance to talk with Dr. Lux about Joe.

"Hey, Frank. Do you remember that parasite guy we talked about a few weeks back?"

"Yeah. I do," he said. "You're still dealing with that guy?"

"Yeah, I'm afraid so. Although maybe I'm done with him now. I ended up biopsying the dog's skin last week. I was hoping if I could prove there wasn't a parasite, he'd realize he was imagining it and let it go. It didn't work. In fact, he confronted me in the parking lot last night."

I went on to tell Dr. Lux about last night's encounter with Joe.

"Oh man," Frank said. "You were lucky Adam was there. He might've saved your ass."

"Yeah, I know. I owe him a case of beer. Joe was acting erratic. Who knows what was going through his head? The whole thing was scary and frustrating. I really was trying to help that guy."

"There are some people you just can't help, like that chopstick lady," said Frank. "Oh, by the way, this'll cheer you up. Guess who I saw this morning as my eleven o'clock appointment?"

"Who?"

"Dan Brewer."

"*No way.* Please tell me it was just for some vaccines, or an ear infection, or something."

"Nope. I wish. It was the testicle thing again," he said.

"I just saw him last week and did an ultrasound on both testicles. They looked fine."

"I know," said Frank. "I saw the ultrasound images in the record. He just has a weird thing with that dog's testicles."

"Ugh . . . sorry about that," I said. "I thought I'd finally convinced him he didn't need to keep worrying about that."

"No problem," said Frank. "There are two kinds of crazy. Good crazy, and bad crazy. I'll take Dan Brewer any day."

I made it home early that night. It was 6:15 when I pulled into the garage. The house was dark. When I opened the door that connected the garage to the laundry room, I heard the clickety-clack of dog nails on the tile. My buff-colored terrier Sally was coming over to say *Hi*. I noted with some sadness that the pace of her toenail tapping was much slower these days. It used to be frantic with excitement. Now, it was more measured. The tempo of duty and obligation rather than enthusiasm. As I took off my jacket and dropped my knapsack on the dryer, her little otter-face made its first appearance around the corner of the doorway. I bent down to rub the spiky mohawk fur on the top of her head. She pushed against my legs and wagged her tail. She had the most pretty, soulful brown eyes. I liked to believe she understood me when I talked to her. "Sally, where is everybody? You're here all by yourself?" At the sound of my voice, she wagged with more vigor and reared up to give me a quick lick on the chin. I entered the quiet house, turning on lights as I went. My wife, Kim, had left me a note on the white-tiled kitchen counter. Casey, my oldest daughter, was on the junior high volleyball team. She had a game tonight. Kim and Riley (my younger daughter) were on the other side of town watching her play. They wouldn't be home for another couple of hours. Part of me was relieved. Quiet moments were increasingly rare in my life. I'd learned to savor them. I opened the fridge, grabbed a bottle of beer, and made my way to the living room sofa. As I plopped down, Sally jumped up beside me and laid down with her head on my leg. In the quiet sanctuary of my own home, with a dog on my lap, and a beer in my hand I had a chance to reflect.

I remembered my conversation from earlier in the day with Dr. Lux. *There are two kinds of crazy.* . . . I had a feeling there were a lot more than two types, but Dr. Lux had a way of simplifying and clarifying things that was oddly reassuring. But I still didn't feel good about where I'd left things with Joe. I was worried about him as well as Clarence the angel dog. I yearned for some type of resolution to the situation, but this was real life, and it often didn't have a Hollywood ending. As a veterinarian, I often had two patients: the pet and the owner. Treating pets was usually the easy part. I tried to emulate Frank and wash these unfortunate outcomes down the drain of my mind. Then, hopefully, I could face the next day with some degree of enthusiasm and optimism. But it wasn't always that easy. The fact was that I cared about the people that placed their trust in me. I didn't like to give up on them. It was an honor to serve them and important to listen, and not just about their pets. There was another factor to consider. I was the owner of Oak View Vet Clinic. I was the captain of the ship, the leader of the band. The respect and care I showed my clients was an example of how I wanted my entire staff to behave. I set the tone of how our clients were treated and I was proud to operate a business that bettered the lives of people and pets.

As I sat ruminating, I realized I wasn't making a whole lot of sense, even to myself. The beer was only half gone but already a certain amount of fuzziness was creeping in. Sally flipped over on her back and wagged her tail. She wanted me to rub her tummy. The simplicity and trust in the gesture made me smile. This was something I could control. Maybe it was good enough to love your dog, love your family, and just do the best you can. I reached over to rub her in her favorite spot.

Me & Sally

Acknowledgements

In writing this book I've been forced (sometimes unwillingly) to look back on my career as a small animal veterinarian and recognize some of my accomplishments and many of my deficiencies. One of my biggest shortcomings is not giving enough thanks and credit to countless wonderful people (and animals) that gave me their advice, support, mentoring, and friendships. This is my feeble attempt to correct that problem. And, yes, I'm sure I will forget somebody.

To the amazing vet techs and assistants who guided me, assisted me, made me laugh, and saved my ass: Cindy, Sarah, Nicole, Cheryl, Maray, Adam, Amy, Debbie, Correen, Jason, Cindy #2, Shannon, Lorna, Stephanie, Paul, Kaitlyn, Miguel, Sabrina, Loren, Amber, Austin, Marnie, Serafina, and Carrie. You know who you are, and I thank you sincerely.

To the veterinarians who took the time and patience to help me along the way: Dr. Weaver, Dr. Cardeiro, Dr. Feldman, Dr. Nelson, Dr. Ilkiw, Dr. Breznock, Dr. Hossiens, Dr. Coyne, Dr. Smith, Dr. Spann, Dr. Zappas, Dr. Cherrstrom, and Dr. Frye. There are too many to name them all. These are some of the most dedicated and inspirational people I have ever met. The friendship and humor of Dr. Johnson and Dr. Lux are especially noteworthy and will stay with me always.

To Mrs. Maggie Barsaleau. I think chapter ten says it all. I hope to see you again, someday.

My dalliance into authorship has given me the opportunity to reunite with two childhood friends. Brothers Scott and Tom Schinaman. Both have become very successful individuals in their own right and have kindly provided me with valuable feedback on my silly stories. Thanks for your patience with the 1 a.m. emails.

Many thanks to my editor Nancy Cortelyou for taking me on as a new author and putting up with my rookie writing and general pigheadedness. Your cheeriness, timeliness, constructive criticism, and persistence were invaluable. I'm sorry for any hair loss incurred on my account.

The book cover and several of the internal illustrations were created by artist and friend Ann Ranlett of Auburn, California. I met Ann as a client and helped care for her wonderful pets for many years. She did a beautiful scratchboard rendition of my favorite cat, Jack, which hangs in my house to this day. It has a special meaning to me that she helped with this literary endeavor. Thank you, Ann.

Brice Borchers is a budding artist in her own right, and my niece. She penned most of the internal illustrations in the book and displayed infinite patience with my indecisiveness. Great job, Brice, and thank you.

Without a doubt, my biggest debt of gratitude goes to my thousands of pet owners/clients over my veterinary career. I went into this line of work because I loved science and loved the critters, but along the way, I had the distinct privilege of interacting with many, many amazing people. Together we've had some great times and some sad ones. Trusting someone with the life of your pet is no small thing, and I want you all to know I cherish your faith in me and your forgiveness when I failed. Through you, I had the privilege to meet some of the most incredible pets. What a gift.

To noble Gobi, gentle September, petite Annie, and drooly Daisy; to Henry and Rosie, Silly Sally Sue, Samantha, sweet Sophie, and especially handsome Jack. I'll never forget ferocious Sadie, Sam the Man, crazy Lucy, and goofy Chuck. I want to go to where you all went.